TWENTIETH CENTURY VIEWS

The aim of this series is to present the best in contemporary critical opinion on major authors, providing a twentieth century perspective on their changing status in an era of profound revaluation.

Maynard Mack, *Series Editor*
Yale University

DETECTIVE FICTION

A COLLECTION OF CRITICAL ESSAYS

Edited by
Robin W. Winks

Prentice - Hall, Inc. *Englewood Cliffs, N.J.*

A SPECTRUM BOOK

Library of Congress Cataloging in Publication Data

Main entry under title:

Detective fiction, a collection of critical essays.

(Twentieth century views) (A Spectrum Book)
Bibliography: p.
    1.   Detective and mystery stories— History and
criticism—Addresses, essays, lectures. I. Winks,
Robin W.
PN3448.D4D43   1980   809.3'872   80-12744
ISBN 0-13-202689-9
ISBN 0-13-202671-6 (pbk.)

To all those who Disapprove

Editorial/production supervision by Donald Chanfrau
Manufacturing buyer: Barbara A. Frick

10 9 8 7 6 5 4 3 2 1

PRENTICE-HALL INTERNATIONAL, INC., *(London)*
PRENTICE-HALL OF AUSTRALIA PTY. LIMITED, *(Sydney)*
PRENTICE-HALL OF CANADA, LTD., *(Toronto)*
PRENTICE-HALL OF INDIA PRIVATE LIMITED, *(New Delhi)*
PRENTICE-HALL OF JAPAN, INC., *(Tokyo)*
PRENTICE-HALL OF SOUTHEAST ASIA PTE. LTD., *(Singapore)*
WHITEHALL BOOKS LIMITED, *(Wellington, New Zealand)*

CONTENTS

IV.   A Closer Look at Specific Authors

V.   Epilogue: An Eye to the Future

Appendix

Bibliography

A Note on the Essays

All omissions from the essays reprinted here are indicated with an ellipsis (...). Footnotes have not been regularized to a single style; several notes have been eliminated and the remaining notes renumbered — these omissions have not been indicated. Notes appearing in brackets have been supplied by the editor. Full names of individuals mentioned in the texts are, if not central to detective fiction, supplied on the first occasion of mention, but standard authors are left identified as the individual writers introduce them, thus Chandler, Doyle, Sayers, etc., on the assumption that the reader has some familiarity with the major books in the field (or will use the bibliography). In an act of some small arrogance, the volume concludes with syllabuses from two courses on detective fiction taught at Yale University, and with my own personal list of two hundred generally modern favorites.

Robin W. Winks
Yale University

Introduction

by Robin W. Winks

I

"There was a mystery somewhere." The words are relatively trite, the sentiment obvious, and the emotions they engender universal. Everyone, it is said, loves a mystery. In this instance the line is from Rudyard Kipling's *Kim,* perhaps the greatest of all spy novels, but it equally well could be from Shakespeare, Voltaire, or even Homer who, in Book X of the *Iliad,* introduced a simple spy story. The Great Game, as Kipling called it, always has held a deep fascination for those with a high tolerance for ambiguity, a fascination increased in the last century by our assumption of increased rationality arising from the increased impact of science.

But to invoke the names of Shakespeare, Voltaire, Homer, or T.S. Eliot and William Faulkner—both of whom wrote mystery stories—is to cause anxiety and anger among those students of literature who dismiss detective fiction as lacking in literary quality. For every person who argues that detective fiction is the diet of the noblest minds, there is another who finds it wasteful of time and degrading to the intellect. Detection fiction is seldom submitted to the scrutiny of a Leavis (or a Harold Bloom), perhaps because such critics feel it could not withstand such an intense light, perhaps because they would be accused of slumming were they to take it seriously, perhaps because they have simply never thought to do so.

Certainly detective fiction stands central to the variety of debates arising from the concept of "popular culture." Should the noblest minds study popular culture at all? If so, what is popular culture, how is it best made manifest, how might one who would stand outside it in order to examine it best penetrate it? Everyone recognizes that Charles Dickens was popular and Herman Melville was not popular in their time. Having said as much one also has moved subtly from analysis to value judgment. Scholars who seek to recapture the texture as well as the content of what they judge to be a collective mentality in a given country in a specific decade will, popular culture historians say, include the second and third rate in their investigation, while not omitting the first rate. But who is to decide between these

1

categories? And need one always decide? Martin Green, a critic of exceptional perceptions in this field—yet a critic who also is frequently, gro-
tesquely wrong—says that we go to the novels of Dorothy Sayers and John
D. MacDonald because "they give us a detailed scrutiny of its civilization by
a highly moral and highly observant mind caught in that garrulous and
unguarded mood in which we all tell most about ourselves."[1] The scholar
who seeks to judge the long-term imaginative meaning of a period may do
better to study the literature that was *un*popular at the time. *We* do not remember the 1850s and 1860s for Tom Taylor, *we* remember (at least in
America) those decades for Melville and Whitman. Then Tom Taylor was
the author of *Our American Cousin*, a comedy playing at Ford's Theater
when a tired American President sought an evening's relaxation; or creator
of *Ticket-or-Leave Man*, a play first produced in London in 1863 and featuring Hawkshaw the Detective, a figure who always wore a deerstalker hat
and carried a magnifying glass, whose name became part of the common
culture, and whose mannerisms were to be copied by a later, more serious,
creation of "scientific thought."

Obviously the scholar—certainly the historian, if perhaps less the student
of literature—should know both "serious" and "popular" culture; otherwise neither word has meaning. Soon the warfare between "serious" and
"popular" fiction may be as intellectually antiquated, if as emotionally
alive, as the alleged warfare between science and religion. Certainly de-
fenders of detective fiction have spent too much effort trying to establish the
respectable antecedents of such literature, in trying to bring it in from the
cold. It is true that Voltaire, in the tale of "The Dog and the Horse" in
Zadig, has written an early detective story; it is probably true, as several
commentators have maintained, that Zadig's thought processes here inspired Arthur Conan Doyle, since Sherlock Holmes is markedly similar.
But having said this what has one said, other than that Doyle might reasonably, as an intelligent man, have been expected to have read Voltaire, and
that readers of the twentieth century (like those of the eighteenth) enjoyed
encountering men who could appear to be omniscient? Of course Oedipus
is a mystery—a metaphysical and human one; of course it is not a "whodunit." Of course, if one uses such terms as "high" and "low" literature,
then *"King Lear* is in, *Tarzan* is out."[2] Maigret is honored with a statue in
Delfzijl, Holland, and Holmes with a pub on Northumberland Avenue,
London, while I am unaware of any statue of Captain Ahab. This is surely
a comment on cultures and the role literature plays within them, however,
and not a comment on the literature itself.

[1]Green, *Transatlantic Patterns: Cultural Comparisons of England with America* (New York,
1977), p. 130.

[2]Alvin B. Kernan, Peter Brooks, Michael Holquist, eds., *Man and His Fictions: An Introduction to Fiction-Making, Its Forms and Uses* (New York, 1973), p. 1.

Edwin Muir, in *The Structure of the Novel*,[3] has told us that Henry James is an impressionist with a "vocabulary of hints and nods." E.M. Forster said of James that "all that is prearranged is false." Yet his figures have an "unchangeability, [a] completeness from the beginning"; rather, they *become* revealed in the course of the narrative. This is a definition of the dramatic novel, in its affinity with poetic tragedy. Character is not merely to delight in, "It has consequences. It influences events; it creates difficulties and later, in different circumstances, dissolves them." As in the Brontes, there is a balance between necessity and freedom. Neither Forster (here) nor Muir mentions detective fiction, yet these words describe the genre perfectly. So too does Roland Barthes in *The Pleasure of the Text* when he speaks of the "unveiling" that occurs within the style of a writer's prose.[4] David I. Grossvogel prefers to think of detective fiction as a striptease (his word): "...the genre features a hero, the detective, whose existence is a mere function of the mystery he is solving, while that mystery is, in fact, a patent knowledge over which a veil has been drawn at the first page that cannot extend beyond the last."[5] A metaphor for life, in fact.

Recently I read a library copy of Leon Edel's *The Modern Psychological Novel*. It being a library copy and this being the latter part of the twentieth century, the book was laden with scribbled marginalia. At some point shortly after Edel told me that Joyce was the fountainhead of the modern psychological novel, I found myself more interested in the marginalia than in the content, for an individual (whom I had to view as a person of unusual ignorance and limited sensibilities) had written time and again after various quotations remarks such as "God, how awful"; "sounds like a female writer!"; "especially the female mind"; and "the hell she did." I found myself more and more fascinated with a mental effort to recapture the personality, the nature, of the scribbler and less and less interested in what Edel had to tell me. Here, I thought, is the hallmark of detective fiction: an interest in reconstruction through detail as opposed to the larger picture. What actually took place is hidden from the reader; that which the reader is given to read is often not relevant to what happened. This poses the tension so well discussed by Robert Champigny in his "philosophical and technical essay on mystery stories," *What Will Have Happened.*[6] At first glance such a construction is precisely the reverse of the historian's mode of inquiry—of pursuing, as Leopold von Ranke said, "history as it happened." Yet, as I have argued elsewhere, upon closer examination this procedure does parallel the art of the historian during the course of re-

---

[3](London, 1957), pp. 13, 15, 25, 41, 42, 51.

[4]See Hanna Charney's forthcoming work *"This Mortal Coil": The Detective Novel of Manners*, from the Fairleigh Dickinson University Press.

[5]Grossvogel, *Mystery and Its Fictions: From Oedipus to Agatha Christie* (Baltimore, 1979), p. 15.

[6]Subtitled *A Philosophical and Technical Essay on Mystery Stories* (Bloomington, 1977).

search. It is in the finished product that the historian ceases, at long last, to be detective.[7]

As a child of, perhaps, eleven, I can remember being deeply moved and puzzled by Edwin Arlington Robinson's "Richard Cory"; my near-teen-age sentimentalism made me think it a beautiful poem. Now that I "understand" the poem, I like it no less but for different reasons that relate more to cultural roots than to art. As a slightly older child I was gripped by Bunyan's geography: "I come from the Town of Stupidity; it lieth about four degrees beyond the City of Destruction." I read detective fiction today, not exclusively but nonetheless often, because it appeals to whatever it was in me to which these two writers appealed years ago. This does not, I think, suggest that I have failed to grow in literary tastes; rather, it suggests that I am puzzled today by the same questions I was puzzled by as a child, although I puzzle at them differently. *This* may be a lack of growth—to be interested in the same puzzle—but my choice of point of entry into the puzzle relates more to taste than to maturity. There are those who think Vonnegut a good writer ("So it goes") while I think him trivial; there are those who think Eliot inflated ("The last temptation is the greatest treason. To do the right deed for the wrong reason"). I simply think he is a good writer.

Put less allusively, it is not always necessary to demonstrate the importance of a body of literature. If literature, any literature, helps us decode our environment as we wish to relate to it, it is valuable. If it carries us outside ourselves, to return us to ourselves enlarged, surely that is enjoyable. Might the ultimate defense to detective fiction, if it needs one, be not that Faulkner, Hemingway, or Dickens once wrote detective stories, that James Hadley Chase's *No Orchids for Miss Blandish* and *Sanctuary* are "the same" story, but that it allows us to make the answer that Bach is said to have made when asked why he composed: "Why? For the greater glory of God— and because I enjoy it."

II

Assumptions about readership change, of course. Today the eleven-year-old might recognize Vonnegut and not Bunyan. In one of the "classics" of detective fiction, *Trent's Last Case*, published in 1912, E.C. Bentley's quotations from Keats, Wordsworth, and Shakespeare's sonnets, as well as a passing reference to Montaigne, all without comment, tell us something of Bentley's assumptions. When reprinted in 1977, by The Mystery Library (which purports to identify classics for today), the volume was accompanied by earnest footnotes identifying the eighteenth sonnet and telling the reader who Montaigne was. The notes deny the audience, for can anyone really doubt that detective novelists are a bookish lot? Aphorisms, lines from

[7]Robin W. Winks, *The Historian as Detective* (New York, 1969), pp. XIII-XXIV.

Shakespeare, the act of composing a report so that one may order one's thoughts, the letter as clue, all abound; the very Christie title *The ABC Murders* is a literal clue. The pleasures of the text arise from the discrete fact, its relationship to a totality only dimly perceived, and from the fact that is not present, from the dog that did not bark in the night. Such pleasures have not changed from the story of Absalom through Poe to the present, but the writer's entitlement to the facts a reader may have or recognize as absent has changed.

The ideal detective story is one in which the detective hero discovers that he (or she) is the criminal. The implicit psychological assumption here is markedly modern, but it rests upon the oldest of definitions of mystery as "a hidden or inexplicable matter." Oedipus, *The Moonstone,* William Hjorstberg's *Falling Angel* (1978) are a continuing stream by which one penetrates "what is common in human experience throughout time."[8] While detective fiction often is called "sensational," it is, in fact, the opposite of sensational, for though the action may be so, the process is to illuminate a special perspective on rationality. Rather than depend on the sensations alone or even primarily, detective fiction insists that there *must* be some explanation. Freedom and form, crime and punishment, action and will alternate as modes of intelligence and conduct. In the end it is not intentions but results that count.

In detective fiction the divine tension between the exact and the unknown produces the central thrust of the story. Since death is a central puzzle to all major and minor writers, the detective story is seen to be sensational because it focuses on the cause and methods of death rather than on the fact of death itself. Death comes as the end in life, while in detective fiction death is the means to an end. We all know that death may be by accident, yet such fiction tells us that it is for a cause or arises from a cause which may be rationally understood; the theology here differs little from the traditional justifications of death and yet, because the voice, purpose, or intent of the artist is less than cosmic, it appears to trivialize death. Rationalism replaces rationalization, sometimes to the level of parody. Death is thus "taken for granted," critics of detective fiction say, so that in time death seems not to matter.

Of course, this is not so. Good mystery novelists are quite conscious of the quality of parody in their work. When causation is reduced to the level of a simple puzzle, reality has been left behind. The problem is that many Serious Critics seem not to recognize that parody, like laughter, often is the best way to highlight the more fundamental truths. Dorothy L. Sayers's *Gaudy Night* does not fulfill W.H. Auden's definitions of a mystery—printed here as the first essay—for it is a love story, a deeply felt statement about the place of women in modern society circa 1935, and a spirited

[8]John Gardner, *On Moral Fiction* (New York, 1978).

attack on and defense of the task of the historian; that is, it makes its points by excess. When Lord Peter Wimsey declares, in *Busman's Honeymoon,* "If a thing could only have been done one way, and if only one person could have done it that way, then you've got your criminal, motive or no motive," he is not merely parroting a syllogism learned at school, he is satirizing our persistent desire to explain, in order to explain away, all actions. "I do think it looks neater to have a comprehensible motive," Harriet Vane says later in the same book, "Murder for the fun of it breaks all the rules of detective fiction." Could Miss Sayers more directly have parodied those who do not believe in evil as such, who attempt to explain all evil acts in terms of society, childhood, class structure, or indigestion? Hannah Arendt is right in saying that modern man cannot grasp the essential banality of evil. In Michael Crichton's *The Great Train Robbery* Edward Pierce completes the first successful robbery from a moving train. Ultimately apprehended and put to trial, he appeared "to take a degree of delight in his actions which [was] wholly inexplicable." This delight is made explicit in the motion picture version: in the penultimate trial scene Pierce is pressed to explain why he had taken such risks to rob the train. Clearly the prosecutor, and the observers in the gallery, wish him to explain that he did so because of a hard childhood, or to benefit orphans, or even to deprive the British Army in the Crimea (for the year was 1855) of the gold bars destined for their pay, the better perhaps to help Russia. His reply was so shocking to the rationalism of the Victorian age that all who heard it burst out in hysterical laughter. He robbed the train, Pierce said, "because I wanted the money."

III

Perhaps fiction that accounts for motivation so simply (or complexly) cannot expect to be taken seriously. Patricia Highsmith tells us that her first book, *Strangers on a Train* (1950), was written as just "a novel." In it two strangers meet by chance, discover that both would rid themselves of a burden, and realize that since neither would be seen to have a motive for removing by murder the burden of the other, they can enter into a pact from which motive will appear to be absent. Here was a novel about chance, responsibility, crime, and evil; it was not a mystery in the conventional sense of the word. As Miss Highsmith notes, because *Strangers on a Train* was labeled a "suspense novel" (and because Alfred Hitchcock created from it a "suspense film"), she was fated to three-inch reviews in the United States (not so in England and France). The label meant that she would, to the public, go on writing such books: the mask of mediocrity, of superficiality, hovered about her work. Hence, she was financially successful and critically unsuccessful; indeed, unnoticed.[9] Graham Greene would protect himself

[9]Highsmith, *Plotting and Writing Suspense Fiction* (Boston, 1966), p. 141.

by labeling some of his work—some think his best work—"entertainments."

Detective fiction thus becomes a mirror to society. Through it we may see society's fears made most explicit; for some, those fears are exorcised by the fiction. Just as Zane Grey and Owen Wister once reflected America's frontier values, so today has the shoot-out at the O.K. Corral moved into the city, the sod hut is replaced by the condominium and the lone hero riding off into the sunset by the lone man who walks the mean streets of our asphalt jungles. The line from Natty Bumppo to Marlowe and Archer is straight: there must be someone who can protect society against itself, someone who is not bound by the entrammeling bureaucracy of a society too complex to do simple (and quick) justice. The English drawing-room comedy, the novel of manners, the sense of class proprieties, hierarchy, structure in society, which were supported by Agatha Christie, Margery Allingham and others, reflected how the English reader wanted to perceive English society in the Golden Age of detective fiction. Today, Len Deighton, John le Carré, and those who depict a society of cynics, an England bereft of empire, are as reflective of our times as were the mysteries of the blood-stained tea cosies of theirs. It is clear why the historian, at least, should find detective fiction valuable.

As society has changed, so the form of its fiction has changed, even while the old questions remain. If the Bible, or Nathaniel Hawthorne, or Dumas contain detective stories, they do not contain detectives. When Poe's Dupin enters the scene, when Dickens brings on his *deus ex machina,* Inspector Bucket, to resolve matters in *Bleak House,* we are approaching the age of the expert, of the technocrat, of the man (and more recently the woman)[10] who is charged by society with doing its ever more specialized dirty work. The modern detective novel thus moves away from the old "riddle story" to something more rigid, more formulaic, more structured, so that similarities between books begin to define a genre.

The detective novel is created, with clear rhythms, in four movements. First, one defines the problem—or is presented with what appears to be the problem—a murder to solve, a robbery, a crime, a moral offense. Writer and reader then set off on the trail of cause and effect, discarding red herrings, lifting up pavements, laying naked emotions, and generally harrowing each other. This, the second phase, consists of looking for the evidence as it relates to the crime. The question seems almost hermetically sealed by the structure—evidence *as it relates* to the crime—but in time one is led to see that conventional definitions of relevance may be mistaken. It is a matter of some import that one of the cucumbers is missing or that Lady Antimicassar was stung by a wasp. With this one moves on to the third phase, that of assessing the evidence. Here the joys of an infinitely receding horizon beset one, for it appears that the task will never end. Yet it does, as it must, in a

[10]Phyllis White, who writes as P.D. James, nicely satirizes this point in her mystery, *Unsuitable Job for a Woman.*

fourth phase that brings the action back to the beginning, in which judgment is now passed on the meaning of events, and from this judgment arises the revelation of the identity and more obvious motivation of the criminal. The gavotte is complete, the two movements repeated, the individual act made explicable, and—most likely—collective guilt dismissed in favor of the comforting, and perhaps conservative, view that guilt is singular. Someone who has been sailing through life with forged passports stands revealed, personality unraveled, the environment decoded. Punishment follows, as much for having misrepresented oneself in the game of life as for the crime of murder.

Or so it was during the Golden Age, usually associated with the period prior to World War II. The war is blamed for much, not the least for destroying stately rhythms and making the taboo acceptable. Certainly the war did enhance our sense of the evil people do, and in doing so turned the detective novel more toward violence than ratiocination, more toward personality than plot. (Indeed, all novels moved in this direction, except that one dignifies the "higher" type with the catch phrase "the novel of outrage."[11]) Detectives today, at least those in fiction, are less likely to use their little grey cells, as Hercule Poirot said he did, and are more likely to resolve problems of both personality and plot by having a man come through a door with a gun in his hand, as instructed to by Raymond Chandler.[12] The classical puzzle, while not wholly gone, has been displaced in large measure by the novel of police procedure (best seen in the work of Hillary Waugh and Ed McBain in the United States), by a kind of gritty *Waiting for Godot;* by the psychological thriller in which the question is not "whodunit" but "whydunit"; and by the spy thriller. The detective is no longer an amateur, à la Peter Wimsey or Philo Vance, and is no longer wholly of the middle or upper class. He or she may be a Navajo (Tony Hillerman), an Afrikaaner working with a Bantu (James McClure), a central Australian aborigine (Arthur Upfield), a Chicano (Rex Burns), a male homosexual (Joseph Hansen), a lesbian (M.F. Beal), a dwarf, a child, a machine. He (or she) may be evil.

The cloistered pre-war world is gone, nostalgically present in authors of pastiche novels who deliberately seek to parody the past, and all the more gone for that. Murder does not take place very much these days in St. Mary Mead, in snowed-in mountain cabins, on board one's private yacht, or on a private island off the coast of Devon; it takes place in the streets, in massage parlors, in airplane terminals, on buses, in church. Banal social discourse gives way to anal rape. Intricate calculations arising from railway timetables, as in Dorothy Sayers's *Five Red Herrings,* no longer matter, for trains do not run on time. The trend is to embrace the world, to leave the

[11]See Ihab Hassan, "The Novel of Outrage," *The American Scholar,* XXXIV (Spring, 1965), 239-53.

[12]In Chandler's essay, "The Simple Art of Murder."

vicarage and the church fete for an attempt on the life of the Shah, on an entire football stadium, or on the water supply of a sleeping city of millions. Once hero and villain alike played by the rules of the game, once one came to know those rules; now, there are no rules, only the world-weary and the ravagers who betray all from within. Paranoia has replaced the catharsis of placing guilt clearly just *there*, "where it belongs." Privacy is invaded, sex becomes explicit, and the audience changes as the structure of the literature changes, the little old lady in tennis shoes (we are told) being repulsed by the language of the streets. To change the style *is* to change the subject.

In his day Erle Stanley Gardner's books sold 185 million copies in 96 titles; one, *The Case of the Sulky Girl*, sold 3,310,000. He was "the best-selling American author of all time."[13] Never an Anglo-Saxonism escaped his dictating machine. Agatha Christie's books sold over four hundred million copies in 103 languages.[14] Today, with what looks suspiciously like glee, literary journals announce an "All-Incest Issue"[15] and no questions are unthinkable. "Is it too tough for you?" the central figure of *Chinatown* asks, and in the end the question does prove too tough and is asked for that reason. William Gaddis, apparently thinking the thought new, tells us that "believing and shitting are two different things." Garp is thought profound. All along there had been some who felt with Jeremy Bentham that poetry and pushpin *were* the same thing; now it seemed so.

Because detective fiction today is more likely to deal in the language of the street, not to say the gutter, there are those who dismiss it as vulgar. Yet to lump all such fiction together, to see Gavin Lyall and Eric Ambler and Graham Greene, for example, as the same simply because one may react to them in the same way, is to say that all books that are sexually arousing are pornographic. Clearly, this is not so. Books are not the same, despite my or your reaction to them. Those who see an artificial separation, for example, between mystery fiction (which "explains" reality, if through a darkened mirror) and thriller fiction (which does not "explain" but rather "reports actions") are mistaken. Thriller fiction does explain. But "explain" and "account for" do not mean the same thing. One person's vulgarity is another's naturalism, as one person's scholarship is another's pedantry. One suspects that little old ladies in tennis shoes have a more permissive vocabulary today than is conventionally thought.

Detective fiction, then, continues to mirror society, not only in its concern, its moral awareness, and its language. It also helps tell us who and where we are, as individuals. It helps us find laughter in frustration, joy in experience, tolerance in complexity: this is as good a definition of humanity as one might ask. It is moral fiction. For all its excesses, its playing to the

[13]New York *Times Book Review*, December 24, 1978, p. 19.

[14]Nancy Blue Wynne, *An Agatha Christie Chronology* (New York, 1976), p. 1: and H.R.F. Keating, ed., *Agatha Christie, First Lady of Crime* (New York, 1977), pp. 7, 13-24.

[15]*Open Letter*, 3rd ser. no. 9 (Fall, 1978).

gallery, its fairytale childishness, its concern for detail, for order, for all of its ambivalence, it can still be read for pleasure—surely a serious (even "high") endeavor in itself—and for that moment when the author may say in triumph, "fooled you! and fair!" (or when we may say nay). Detective fiction ultimately deals with the individual, with uncluttered landscapes. There is a saying among historians, one will never know precisely why the ship of state sank because there are too many eye witnesses. Detective fiction, in its lonely voice that insists upon individual responsibility, strips the eye witnesses down to two: the author and the reader.

In this sense, then, detective fiction is what some of its disparagers say it is: conservative, almost compulsive in its belief (to which, of course, there are exceptions) that one may in truth trace cause and effect, may place responsibility just *here*, may pass judgment, may even assess blame, and in its determination not to let us forget that there is evil in the world and that men and women, individual men and women, do it. Detective fiction is much like the monument the Hungarian government has erected at Mauthausen, in Austria. Mauthausen, near Hitler's birthplace of Linz, was a German extermination camp. One may visit it today and see the gas oven, preserved by the Austrian government so that succeeding generations should not forget the evil people do. On the lip of the great quarry's cliff, over which many prisoners were pushed to their deaths, governments have placed monuments to their dead. Most of these monuments point to the future, with varying degrees of exhortations to forgive and, perhaps, forget. On the very edge of the cliff stands the monument of Hungary, a great stylized strand of barbed wire. On the plinth are the words, in Hungarian, in German, and in English—"Forget? Forgive? Never!"

IV

The essays in this volume are organized into five parts. The first part looks at the genre in general, while the second part examines the history of the type. Then follow essays on literary analysis. We take a closer look at specific authors, and finally, with an eye to the future, we examine certain needs and emerging types.

Many readers of detective fiction have sought to set out rules for the genre, drawing upon their own complex moral positions with respect to sin, guilt, compassion, retribution, and justice. Most such efforts tend to be both didactic and inflexible, stark and limiting views of how to classify writing. Some authors simply justify the kind of detective fiction they appear to enjoy; others profess to find in the genre an opportunity to examine a professed "love of the neutral truth," to cast an icicle eye. For readers relatively new to, and perhaps critically sceptical about, such fiction, one must begin with some inquiries into the nature of the creature here examined. The first five essays that follow provide just such an introduction.

In the first essay the poet and critic W. H. Auden seeks to throw light on the "magical function" of the detective story. (Auden's clear influence on two particularly fine writers, Ross Macdonald and Amanda Cross, adds to his relevance as our opening selection.) Auden's introduction of Aristotle is then taken up explicitly by Dorothy L. Sayers, who was both a major practitioner of the craft and an Oxford-bred scholar of Dante. This essay consists of a lecture she delivered at her college's Gaudy Night, at Oxford, on March 5, 1935, the same year she finished her fictional masterpiece on precisely that subject, a *Gaudy Night*. Miss Sayers was a remarkable woman who wrote, especially later in life, with learning and sensitivity of evil, sin, forgiveness, hell, and heaven (see especially *A Matter of Eternity*). She is, after Arthur Conan Doyle, the dominant figure in the genre. As her novels clearly show, she also gave much thought to the matters which today we subsume under the heading of "women's lib": of the role of the woman of intellect and sexual candor, of the biological realities of life (here see particularly *Are Women Human?*). One is to understand her remark in the essay printed here, "a female must not be represented as clever," as bitterly addressed to the all-female audience of Somerville College. The third essay then tilts, rather revealingly, at Miss Sayers: it is Edmund Wilson's famous and grumpy declaration-by-question, "Who Cares Who Killed Roger Ackroyd?" Probably no other essay antagonistic to the methods and values of detective fiction is so often quoted today without being read, clear testimony to the great weight once attached to the eminent critic's judgments. The essay, which originally appeared in *The New Yorker*, was preceded by a more general attack, "Why do People Read Detective Stories?" and was followed by the best (but here least applicable) of Wilson's set pieces on detective writing, "'Mr. Holmes, They Were the Footprints of a Gigantic Hound!'" The first of these articles gave rise to Joseph Wood Krutch's response, "'Only a Detective Story.'"

Though Krutch, then professor of English at Columbia, chose to reply to Wilson in the pages of *Nation*, a popular journal, rather than elevate the discussion of detective fiction into the academy of learning, he raised a significant question which has become the focus of much scholarly debate: the role of "dread" in the construction of modern fiction. Auden concluded his essay with a brief aside on Franz Kafka, author of *The Trial*, and in the fifth essay here, drawn from Gavin Lambert's book *The Dangerous Edge* (which is a close examination of the motivations behind the work of such authors as Wilkie Collins, Graham Greene, and Georges Simenon), the theme of dread is examined more directly. At this point the reader should, in the words of R.G. Collingwood, have some notion of the contours of the tiger in the garden which we will then stalk.

Most fiction conventionally designated "popular" lacks both a sound critical and a thorough historical base. Detective fiction in particular has grown so rapidly in recent years—every tenth book published is in this field—that no one has attempted to chart in detail its many courses. One cannot understand the ways in which twentieth-century detective fiction differs (and yet springs) from nineteenth-century fiction without briefly examining the history of the type. The next three essays that follow attempt to provide a quick summary of major developments; other histories are listed in the bibliography.

Up to its date of publication, in 1928, Dorothy Sayers's own short history of crime fiction is still one of the best. Miss Sayers wrote the essay reprinted here as an introduction to an anthology, *Great Short Stories of Detection, Mystery, and Horror,* published a year later in the United States as *Omnibus of Crime.* As a summary of where the genre stood on the eve of its Golden Age, this essay is perceptive though not critically deep. The editor has sought to bring it up to date on certain points by inserting footnotes of his own, indicated by brackets. The post-1929 period is then described by George Grella in terms of formula fiction; Grella (who is Professor of English at the University of Rochester) notes that in the 1930s the detective story took on many of the characteristics of the novel, and especially the novel of manners, to which Dorothy Sayers was herself a major contributor. He also points out that mystery novels were becoming explicit critiques of the societies in which they were set, a development made more intense by American creators of the so-called hard-boiled detective novel. Grella's essay on this last development, therefore, logically follows upon his discussion of the formal detective novel. In this essay he touches upon the relationship between the work of Hammett, Chandler, and Macdonald, and chivalric romance.

The number of scholars and literary critics who have chosen to subject detective fiction to the kind of close analysis customary for more "serious" fiction is very small. Some few essays have appeared in learned journals, some tendentious (or even plain silly) inquiries have been written for psychoanalytic reviews, and on occasion students of Dickens, T. S. Eliot, or Bertolt Brecht have focused momentarily on the element of crime in their work. Aside from a number of German writers, however, there has been very little effort to submit the genre as a whole to literary analysis in depth. The next group of essays will support this judgment, for seldom do they approach the density of inquiry one finds in studies of Eliot, Whitman, or Hemingway, for example. Nonetheless, they do begin the serious critical inquiry, and one—the material drawn from John G. Cawelti's *Adventure, Mystery, and Romance*—intelligently goes to the heart of the problem of "formulaic literature."

Cawelti is interested in particular in the artistic characteristics of formula literature, and he touches upon the Marxist argument as it relates to such literature as a reflection of class values. (This argument is made more explicit by Bertolt Brecht in a little-noted essay, "Über die Popularität des Kriminalromans.") The following essay, on "Detection and the Literary Art," is by a distinguished cultural historian, Jacques Barzun, and while it touches at times on the same points raised by Sayers and Grella in their histories, it is interesting to note the obliquely different angle of approach. Since Barzun maintains—wrongly, I believe—that detective fiction is at its best in the short story, the next essay provides a brief aside on the mutations of the short story as seen by Britain's leading modern critic in the field, Julian Symons. Finally, this section concludes with what may be the most serious case against the detective story that has yet been made, by Erik Routley, a British theologian and mystery reviewer. It should be read in conjunction with a lively yet less well-argued critique, *Snobbery with Violence: Crime Stories and Their Audience* by Colin Watson (London, 1971).

To this point both description and analysis are general. We then turn to a closer look at specific authors. First, Ross Macdonald—widely regarded as the leading North American writer of detective fiction—discusses his own approach to his work in two essays, "The Writer as Detective Hero" and "Down These Streets a Mean Man Must Go." The second title is a commentary both on Raymond Chandler's succinct justification of his figure Marlowe, of whom he wrote that "down these mean streets a man must go," and on Philip Dunham's study of Chandler's work, which bears that title. Thereafter, John G. Cawelti is called upon again, this time to examine the artistic failures and successes of Agatha Christie and Dorothy Sayers.

Having examined three major writers in some depth, we turn to Ronald A. Knox, a religious essayist who also wrote on detective fiction. Monsignor Knox helped to found modern scholarship on Sherlock Holmes, wrote several detective stories himself, and propounded the ten commandments of detective story fiction. This decalogue is placed here, representing as it does the views of 1929, so that the reader may see how far modern detective fiction has departed from the ten commandments: not only has every one of the commandments been broken many times over, but a single writer, Agatha Christie, broke virtually all of them alone, and built a reputation in doing so. In short, efforts to state precisely what detective fiction may and may not do, while interesting cultural statements for their times, have proven quite fruitless.

As we have seen, projecting popular fiction into the future is singularly difficult (and on the whole unrewarding). Yet one may not leave the subject with Ronald Knox, however broken his ten commandments may be. Two relatively slight statements on future directions, therefore, conclude the selections. The first, by George N. Dove, a contributor to *The Armchair Detective*, gently suggests some critical ground that remains to be covered. The second, four short essays I originally wrote for *The New Republic*, briefly describes the work of four major writers in the genre (thrillers included) who, I argue, will have proven to be influential when historians of detective fiction come to look back on the 1970s. These essays may be read in conjunction with another, not printed here, which attempts an overview of the state of the art at the end of the 1970s: John McAleer's "The Game's Afoot: Detective Fiction in the Present Day," *Kansas Quarterly*, X (Fall, 1978), 21-38. All should be read against the superb essay, "Introductory," to *A Catalogue of Crime*, assembled by Jacques Barzun and Wendell Hertig Taylor (New York: Harper & Row, 1971).

The Guilty Vicarage

by W. H. Auden

I had not known sin, but by the law.

ROMANS: VII, 7

A Confession

For me, as for many others, the reading of detective stories is an addiction like tobacco or alcohol. The symptoms of this are: firstly, the intensity of the craving—if I have any work to do, I must be careful not to get hold of a detective story for, once I begin one, I cannot work or sleep till I have finished it. Secondly, its specificity—the story must conform to certain formulas (I find it very difficult, for example, to read one that is not set in rural England). And, thirdly, its immediacy. I forget the story as soon as I have finished it, and have no wish to read it again. If, as sometimes happens, I start reading one and find after a few pages that I have read it before, I cannot go on.

Such reactions convince me that, in my case at least, detective stories have nothing to do with works of art. It is possible, however, that an analysis of the detective story, i.e., of the kind of detective story I enjoy, may throw light, not only on its magical function, but also, by contrast, on the function of art.

Definition

The vulgar definition, "a Whodunit," is correct. The basic formula is this: a murder occurs; many are suspected; all but one suspect, who is the murderer, are eliminated; the murderer is arrested or dies.

This definition excludes:

1) Studies of murderers whose guilt is known, e.g., *Malice Aforethought.*

There are borderline cases in which the murderer is known and there are no false suspects, but the proof is lacking, e.g., many of the stories of Freeman Wills Crofts. Most of these are permissible.

2) Thrillers, spy stories, stories of master crooks, etc., when the identification of the criminal is subordinate to the defeat of his criminal designs.

The interest in the thriller is the ethical and eristic conflict between good and evil, between Us and Them. The interest in the study of a murderer is the observation, by the innocent many, of the sufferings of the guilty one. The interest in the detective story is the dialectic of innocence and guilt.

As in the Aristotelian description of tragedy, there is Concealment (the innocent seem guilty and the guilty seem innocent) and Manifestation (the real guilt is brought to consciousness). There is also peripeteia, in this case not a reversal of fortune but a double reversal from apparent guilt to innocence and from apparent innocence to guilt. The formula may be diagrammed as follows:

Peaceful state before murder	False innocence
|	|
	Revelation of presence of guilt
	|
False clues, secondary murder, etc.	False location of guilt
|	|
Solution	Location of real guilt
|	|
Arrest of murderer	Catharsis
|	|
Peaceful state after arrest	True Innocence

In Greek tragedy the audience knows the truth; the actors do not, but discover or bring to pass the inevitable. In modern, e.g., Elizabethan, tragedy the audience knows neither less nor more than the most knowing of the actors. In the detective story the audience does not know the truth at all; one of the actors—the murderer—does; and the detective, of his own free will, discovers and reveals what the murderer, of his own free will, tries to conceal.

Greek tragedy and the detective story have one characteristic in common in which they both differ from modern tragedy, namely, the characters are not changed in or by their actions: in Greek tragedy because their actions are fated, in the detective story because the decisive event, the murder, has already occurred. Time and space therefore are simply the when and where of revealing either what has to happen or what has actually happened. In consequence, the detective story probably should, and usually does, obey the classical unities, whereas modern tragedy, in which the characters develop with time, can only do so by a technical tour de force; and the thriller, like the picaresque novel, even demands frequent changes of time and place.

Why Murder?

There are three classes of crime: (A) offenses against God and one's neighbor or neighbors; (B) offenses against God and society; (C) offenses against God. (All crimes, of course, are offenses against oneself.)

Murder is a member and the only member of Class B. The character common to all crimes in Class A is that it is possible, at least theoretically, either that restitution can be made to the injured party (e.g., stolen goods can be returned), or that the injured party can forgive the criminal (e.g., in the case of rape). Consequently, society as a whole is only indirectly involved; its representatives (the police, etc.) act in the interests of the injured party.

Murder is unique in that it abolishes the party it injures, so that society has to take the place of the victim and on his behalf demand atonement or grant forgiveness; it is the one crime in which society has a direct interest.

Many detective stories begin with a death that appears to be suicide and is later discovered to have been murder. Suicide is a crime belonging to Class C in which neither the criminal's neighbors nor society has any interest, direct or indirect. As long as a death is believed to be suicide, even private curiosity is improper; as soon as it is proved to be murder, public inquiry becomes a duty.

The detective story has five elements—the milieu, the victim, the murderer, the suspects, the detectives.

The Milieu (Human)

The detective story requires:

1) A closed society so that the possibility of an outside murderer (and hence of the society being totally innocent) is excluded; and a closely related society so that all its members are potentially suspect (*cf.* the thriller, which requires an open society in which any stranger may be a friend or enemy in disguise).

Such conditions are met by: a) the group of blood relatives (the Christmas dinner in the country house); b) the closely knit geographical group (the old world village); c) the occupational group (the theatrical company); d) the group isolated by the neutral place (the Pullman car).

In this last type the concealment-manifestation formula applies not only to the murder but also to the relations between the members of the group who first appear to be strangers to each other, but are later found to be related.

2) It must appear to be an innocent society in a state of grace, i.e., a society where there is no need of the law, no contradiction between the aesthetic individual and the ethical universal, and where murder, therefore, is the unheard-of act which precipitates a crisis (for it reveals that some member has fallen and is no longer in a state of grace). The law becomes a reality and for a time all must live in its shadow, till the fallen one is identified. With his arrest, innocence is restored, and the law retires forever.

The characters in a detective story should, therefore, be eccentric (aesthetically interesting individuals) and good (instinctively ethical)—good, that is, either in appearance, later shown to be false, or in reality, first concealed by an appearance of bad.

It is a sound instinct that has made so many detective story writers choose a college as a setting. The ruling passion of the ideal professor is the pursuit of knowledge for its own sake so that he is related to other human beings only indirectly through their common relation to the truth; and those passions, like lust and avarice and envy, which relate individuals directly and may lead to murder are, in his case, ideally excluded. If a murder occurs in a college, therefore, it is a sign that some colleague is not only a bad man but also a bad professor. Further, as the basic premise of academic life is that truth is universal and to be shared with all, the *gnosis* of a concrete crime and the *gnosis* of abstract ideas nicely parallel and parody each other.

(The even more ideal contradiction of a murder in a monastery is excluded by the fact that monks go regularly to confession and, while the murderer might well not confess his crime, the suspects who are innocent of murder but guilty of lesser sins cannot be supposed to conceal them without making the monastery absurd. Incidentally, is it an accident that the detective story has flourished most in predominantly Protestant countries?)

The detective story writer is also wise to choose a society with an elaborate ritual and to describe this in detail. A ritual is a sign of harmony between the aesthetic and the ethical in which body and mind, individual will and general laws, are not in conflict. The murderer uses his knowledge of the ritual to commit the crime and can be caught only by someone who acquires an equal or superior familiarity with it.

The Milieu (Natural)

In the detective story, as in its mirror image, the Quest for the Grail, maps (the ritual of space) and timetables (the ritual of time) are desirable.

Nature should reflect its human inhabitants, i.e., it should be the Great Good Place; for the more Eden-like it is, the greater the contradiction of murder. The country is preferable to the town, a well-to-do neighborhood (but not too well-to-do — or there will be a suspicion of ill-gotten gains) better than a slum. The corpse must shock not only because it is a corpse but also because, even for a corpse, it is shockingly out of place, as when a dog makes a mess on a drawing room carpet.

Mr. Raymond Chandler has written that he intends to take the body out of the vicarage garden and give the murder back to those who are good at it. If he wishes to write detective stories, i.e., stories where the reader's principal interest is to learn who did it, he could not be more mistaken, for in a society of professional criminals, the only possible motives for desiring to identify the murderer are blackmail or revenge, which both apply to individuals, not to the group as a whole, and can equally well inspire murder. Actually, whatever he may say, I think Mr. Chandler is interested in writing, not detective stories, but serious studies of a criminal milieu, the Great Wrong Place, and his powerful but extremely depressing books should be read and judged, not as escape literature, but as works of art.

The Victim

The victim has to try to satisfy two contradictory requirements. He has to involve everyone in suspicion, which requires that he be a bad character; and he has to make everyone feel guilty, which requires that he be a good character. He cannot be a criminal because he could then be dealt with by the law and murder would be unnecessary. (Blackmail is the only exception.) The more general the temptation to murder he arouses, the better; e.g., the desire for freedom is a better motive than money alone or sex alone. On the whole, the best victim is the negative Father or Mother Image.

If there is more than one murder, the subsequent victims should be more innocent than the initial victim, i.e., the murderer should start with a real grievance and, as a consequence of righting it by illegitimate means, be forced to murder against his will where he has no grievances but his own guilt.

The Murderer

Murder is negative creation, and every murderer is therefore the rebel who claims the right to be omnipotent. His pathos is his refusal to suffer. The problem for the writer is to conceal his demonic pride from the other characters and from the reader, since, if a person has this pride, it tends to appear in everything he says and does. To surprise the reader when the identity of the murderer is revealed, yet at the same time to convince him that everything he has previously been told about the murderer is consistent with his being a murderer, is the test of a good detective story.

As to the murderer's end, of the three alternatives—execution, suicide, and madness—the first is preferable; for if he commits suicide he refuses to repent, and if he goes mad he cannot repent, but if he does not repent society cannot forgive. Execution, on the other hand, is the act of atonement by which the murderer is forgiven by society. In real life I disapprove of capital punishment, but in a detective story the murderer must have no future. . . .

The Suspects

The detective-story society is a society consisting of apparently innocent individuals, i.e., their aesthetic interest as individuals does not conflict with their ethical obligations to the universal. The murder is the act of disruption by which innocence is lost, and the individual and the law become opposed to each other. In the case of the murderer this opposition is completely real (till he is arrested and consents to be punished); in the case of the suspects it is mostly apparent.

But in order for the appearance to exist, there must be some element of reality; e.g., it is unsatisfactory if the suspicion is caused by chance or the murderer's malice alone. The suspects must be guilty of something, because, now that the aesthetic and the ethical are in opposition, if they are completely innocent (obedient to the ethical) they lose their aesthetic interest and the reader will ignore them.

For suspects, the principal causes of guilt are:

1) the wish or even the intention to murder;

2) crimes of Class A or vices of Class C (e.g., illicit amours) which the suspect is afraid or ashamed to reveal;

3) a *hubris* of intellect which tries to solve the crime itself and despises the official police (assertion of the supremacy of the aesthetic over the ethical). If great enough, this *hubris* leads to its subject getting murdered;

4) a *hubris* of innocence which refuses to cooperate with the investigation;

5) a lack of faith in another loved suspect, which leads its subject to hide or confuse clues.

The Detective

Completely satisfactory detectives are extremely rare. Indeed, I only know of three: Sherlock Holmes (Conan Doyle), Inspector French (Freeman Wills Crofts), and Father Brown (Chesterton).

The job of detective is to restore the state of grace in which the aesthetic and the ethical are as one. Since the murderer who caused their disjunction is the aesthetically defiant individual, his opponent, the detective, must be either the official representative of the ethical or the exceptional individual who is himself in a state of grace. If he is the former, he is a professional; if he is the latter, he is an amateur. In either case, the detective must be the total stranger who cannot possibly be involved in the crime; this excludes the local police and should, I think, exclude the detective who is a friend of one of the suspects. The professional detective has the advantage that, since he is not an individual but a representative of the ethical, he does not need a motive for investigating the crime; but for the same reason he has the disadvantage of being unable to overlook the minor ethical violations of the suspects, and therefore it is harder for him to gain their confidence.

Most amateur detectives, on the other hand, are unsatisfactory either because they are priggish supermen, like Lord Peter Wimsey and Philo Vance, who have no motive for being detectives except caprice, or because, like the detectives of the hard-boiled school, they are motivated by avarice or ambition and might just as well be murderers.

The amateur detective genius may have weaknesses to give him aesthetic interest, but they must not be of a kind which outrage ethics. The most satisfactory weaknesses are the solitary oral vices of eating and drinking or childish boasting. In his sexual life, the detective must be either celibate or happily married.

Between the amateur detective and the professional policeman stands the criminal lawyer whose *telos* is, not to discover who is guilty, but to prove that his client is innocent. His ethical justification is that human law is ethically imperfect, i.e., not an absolute manifestation of the universal and divine, and subject to chance aesthetic limitations, e.g., the intelligence or stupidity of individual policemen and juries (in consequence of which an innocent man may sometimes be judged guilty).

To correct this imperfection, the decision is arrived at through an aesthetic combat, i.e., the intellectual gifts of the defense versus those of the prosecution, just as in earlier days doubtful cases were solved by physical combat between the accused and the accuser.

The lawyer-detective (e.g., Joshua Clunk) is never quite satisfactory, therefore, because of his commitment to his client, whom he cannot desert, even if he should really be the guilty party, without ceasing to be a lawyer.

Sherlock Holmes

Holmes is the exceptional individual who is in a state of grace because he is a genius in whom scientific curiosity is raised to the status of a heroic passion. He is erudite but his knowledge is absolutely specialized (e.g., his ignorance of the Copernican system), he is in all matters outside his field as helpless as a child (e.g., his untidiness), and he pays the price for his scientific detachment (his neglect of feeling) by being the victim of melancholia which attacks him whenever he is unoccupied with a case (e.g., his violin playing and cocaine taking).

His motive for being a detective is, positively, a love of the neutral truth (he has no interest in the feelings of the guilty or the innocent), and negatively, a need to escape from his own feelings of melancholy. His attitude towards people and his technique of observation and deduction are those of the chemist or physicist. If he chooses human beings rather than inanimate matter as his material, it is because investigating the inanimate is unheroically easy since it cannot tell lies, which human beings can and do, so that in dealing with them, observation must be twice as sharp and logic twice as rigorous.

Inspector French

His class and culture are those natural to a Scotland Yard inspector. (The old Oxonian Inspector is insufferable.) His motive is love of duty. Holmes detects for his own sake and shows the maximum indifference to all feelings except a negative fear of his own. French detects for the sake of the innocent members of society, and is indifferent only to his own feelings and those of the murderer. (He would much rather stay at home with his wife.) He is exceptional only in his exceptional love of duty which makes him take exceptional pains; he does only what all could do as well if they had the same patient industry (his checking of alibis for tiny flaws which careless hurry had missed). He outwits the murderer, partly because the latter is not quite so painstaking as he, and partly because the murderer must act alone, while he has the help of all the innocent people in the world who are doing their duty, e.g., the postmen, railway clerks, milkmen, etc., who become, accidentally, witnesses to the truth.

Father Brown

Like Holmes, an amateur; yet, like French, not an individual genius. His activities as a detective are an incidental part of his activities as a priest who cares for souls. His prime motive is compassion, of which the guilty are in greater need than the innocent, and he investigates murders, not for his own sake, nor even for the sake of the innocent, but for the sake of the murderer who can save his soul if he will confess and repent. He solves his cases, not by approaching them objectively like a scientist or a policeman, but by subjectively imagining himself to be the murderer, a process which is good not only for the murderer but for Father Brown himself because, as he says, "it gives a man his remorse beforehand."

Holmes and French can only help the murderer as teachers, i.e., they can teach him that murder will out and does not pay. More they cannot do since neither is tempted to murder; Holmes is too gifted, French too well trained in the habit of virtue. Father Brown can go further and help the murderer as an example, i.e., as a man who is also tempted to murder, but is able by faith to resist temptation.

The Reader

The most curious fact about the detective story is that it makes its greatest appeal precisely to those classes of people who are most immune to other forms of daydream literature. The typical detective story addict is a doctor or clergyman or scientist or artist, i.e., a fairly successful professional man with intellectual interests and well-read in his own field, who could never stomach the *Saturday Evening Post* or *True Confessions* or movie magazines or comics. If I ask myself why I cannot enjoy stories about strong silent men and lovely girls who make love in a beautiful landscape and come into millions of dollars, I cannot answer that I have no fantasies of being handsome and loved and rich, because of course I have (though my life is, perhaps, sufficiently fortunate to make me less envious in a naive way than some). No, I can only say that I am too conscious of the absurdity of such wishes to enjoy seeing them reflected in print.

I can, to some degree, resist yielding to these or similar desires which tempt me, but I cannot prevent myself from having them to resist; and it is the fact that I have them which makes me feel guilty, so that instead of dreaming about indulging my desires, I dream about the removal of the guilt which I feel at their existence. This I still do, and must do, because guilt is a subjective feeling where any further step is only a reduplication — feeling guilty about guilt. I suspect that the typical reader of detective stories is, like myself, a person who suffers from a sense of sin. From the point of view of ethics, desires and acts are good and bad, and I must choose the good and reject the bad, but the I which makes this choice is ethically neutral; it only becomes good or bad in its choice. To have a sense of sin means to feel guilty at there being an ethical choice to make, a guilt which, however "good" I may become, remains unchanged. It is sometimes said that detective stories are read by respectable law-abiding citizens in order to gratify in fantasy the violent or murderous wishes they dare not, or are ashamed to, translate into action. This may be true for the reader of thrillers (which I rarely enjoy), but it is quite false for the reader of detective stories.

On the contrary, the magical satisfaction the latter provide (which makes them escape literature, not works of art) is the illusion of being dissociated from the murderer.

The magic formula is an innocence which is discovered to contain guilt; then a suspicion of being the guilty other has been expelled, a cure effected, not by me or my neighbors, but by the miraculous intervention of a genius from outside who removes guilt by giving knowledge of guilt. (The detective story subscribes, in fact, to the Socratic daydream: "Sin is ignorance.")

If one thinks of a work of art which deals with murder, *Crime and Punishment* for example, its effect on the reader is to compel an identification with the murderer which he would prefer not to recognize. The identification of fantasy is always an attempt to avoid one's own suffering: the identification of art is a sharing in the suffering of another. Kafka's *The Trial* is another instructive example of the difference between a work of art and the detective story. In the latter it is certain that a crime has been committed and, temporarily, uncertain to whom the guilt should be attached; as soon as this is known, the innocence of everyone else is certain. (Should it turn out that after all no crime has been committed, then all would be innocent.) In *The Trial*, on the other hand, it is the guilt that is certain and the crime that is uncertain; the aim of the hero's investigation is not to prove his innocence (which would be impossible for he knows he is guilty), but to discover what, if anything, he has done to make himself guilty. K, the hero, is, in fact, a portrait of the kind of person who reads detective stories for escape.

The fantasy, then, which the detective story addict indulges is the fantasy of being restored to the Garden of Eden, to a state of innocence, where he may know love as love and not as the law. The driving force behind this daydream is the feeling of guilt, the cause of which is unknown to the dreamer. The fantasy of escape is the same, whether one explains the guilt in Christian, Freudian, or any other terms. One's way of trying to face the reality, on the other hand, will, of course, depend very much on one's creed.

Aristotle on Detective Fiction[1]

by Dorothy L. Sayers

Some twenty-five years ago, it was rather the fashion among commentators to deplore that Aristotle should have so much inclined to admire a kind of tragedy that was not, in their opinion, "the best." All this stress laid upon the plot, all this hankering after melodrama and surprise — was it not rather unbecoming — rather inartistic? Psychology for its own sake was just then coming to the fore, and it seemed almost blasphemous to assert that "they do not act in order to portray the characters; they include the characters for the sake of the action." Indeed, we are not yet free from the influence of that school of thought for which the best kind of play or story is that in which nothing particular happens from beginning to end.

Now, to anyone who reads the *Poetics*[1] with an unbiased mind, it is evident that Aristotle was not so much a student of his own literature as a prophet of the future. He criticised the contemporary Greek theatre because it was, at that time, the most readily available, widespread and democratic form of popular entertainment presented for his attention. But what, in his heart of hearts, he desired was a good detective story; and it was not his fault, poor man, that he lived some twenty centuries too early to revel in the Peripeties of *Trent's Last Case* or the Discoveries of *The Hound of the Baskervilles*. He had a stout appetite for the gruesome. "Though the objects themselves may be painful," says he, "we delight to view the most realistic representations of them in art, the forms, for example, of the lowest animals and of dead bodies." The crawling horror of *The Speckled Band* would, we infer, have pleased him no less than *The Corpse in the Car, The Corpse in Cold Storage* or *The Body in the Silo*. Yet he was no thriller fan. "Of simple plots and actions," he rightly observes, "the episodic are the worst. I call a plot episodic when there is neither probability nor necessity in the sequence of the episodes." He would not have approved of a certain recent book which includes among its incidents a machine-gun attack

Dorothy L. Sayers, "Aristotle on Detective Fiction." From Sayers, *Unpopular Opinions* (London: Victor Gollancz, 1946), pp. 178-90. Reprinted by permission of the estate of Dorothy L. Sayers and Victor Gallancz, Ltd.

[1]The translation of *The Poetics* used throughout this lecture is that of Professor Ingram Bywater, published by the Clarendon Press.

in Park Lane, an aeroplane dropping bombs on Barnes Common, a gas attack by the C.I.D. on a West-End flat and a pitched battle with assorted artillery on a yacht in the Solent. He maintained that dreadful and alarming events produced their best effect when they occurred, "unexpectedly," indeed, but also "in consequence of one another." In one phrase he sums up the whole essence of the detective story proper. Speaking of the denouement of the work, he says: "It is also possible to discover whether some one has done or not done something." Yes, indeed.

Now, it is well known that a man of transcendent genius, though working under difficulties and with inadequate tools, will do more useful and inspiring work than a man of mediocre intellect with all the resources of the laboratory at his disposal. Thus Aristotle, with no better mysteries for his study than the sordid complications of the Agamemnon family, no more scientific murder-methods than the poisoned arrow of Philoctetes or the somewhat improbable medical properties of Medea's cauldron; above all, with detective heroes so painfully stereotyped and unsympathetic as the inhuman array of gods from the machine, yet contrived to hammer out from these unpromising elements a theory of detective fiction so shrewd, all-embracing and practical that the *Poetics* remains the finest guide to the writing of such fiction that could be put, at this day, into the hands of an aspiring author.

In what, then, does this guidance consist? From the start Aristotle accepts the Detective Story as a worthy subject for serious treatment. "Tragedy," he observes (tragedy being the literary form which the detective story took in his day), "also acquired magnitude"—that is, it became important both in form and substance. "Discarding short stories and a ludicrous diction, it assumed, though only at a late point in its progress, a tone of dignity." I am afraid that "short stories and a ludicrous diction" have characterised some varieties of the genre up to a very late point indeed; it is true, however, that there have recently been great efforts at reform. Aristotle then goes on to define tragedy in terms excellently applicable to our subject; "The imitation" (or presentment, or representation—we will not quarrel over the word) "of an action that is serious"—it will be admitted that murder is an action of a tolerably serious nature—"and also complete in itself"—that is highly important, since a detective story that leaves any loose ends is no proper detective story at all—"with incidents arousing pity and fear, wherewith to accomplish its catharsis of such emotions."

Too much has already been said and written on the vexed subject of the catharsis. Is it true, as magistrates sometimes assert, that little boys go to the bad through reading detective stories? Or is it, as detective writers prefer to think with Aristotle, that in a nerve-ridden age the study of crime stories provides a safety valve for the bloodthirsty passions that might otherwise lead us to murder our spouses? Of all forms of modern fiction, the detective story alone makes virtue *ex hypothesi* more interesting than vice, the detective more beloved than the criminal. But there is a dangerous error going about—namely that "if...detective fiction leads to an increase in crime, then the greater the literary merit, the greater will be the corresponding increase in crime." Now, this is simply not true: few people can have been inspired to murder their uncles by the literary merits of *Hamlet*. On the contrary, where there is no beauty there can be no catharsis; an ill-written book, like an ill-compounded drug, only irritates the system without purging. Let us then see to it that, if we excite evil passions, it is so done as to sublimate them at the same time by the contemplation of emotional or intellectual beauty. Thus far, then, concerning the catharsis.

Aristotle next discusses Plot and Character. "A detective story," we gather, "is impossible without action, but there may be one without character." A few years ago, the tendency was for all detective stories to be of the characterless or "draught-board" variety; to-day, we get many examples exhibiting a rather slender plot and a good deal of morbid psychology. Aristotle's warning, however, still holds good:

> One may string together a series of characteristic speeches of the utmost finish as regards diction and thought, and yet fail to produce the true dramatic effect; but one will have much better success with a story which, however inferior in these respects, has a plot.

And again:

> The first essential, the life and soul, so to speak, of the detective story, is the plot, and the characters come second.

As regards the make-up of the plot, Aristotle is again very helpful. He says firmly that it should have a beginning, a middle and an end. Herein the detective story is sharply distinguished from the kind of modern novel which, beginning at the end, rambles backwards and forwards without particular direction and ends on an indeterminate note, and for no ascertainable reason except the publisher's refusal to provide more printing and paper for seven-and-sixpence. The detective story commonly begins with the murder; the middle is occupied with the detection of the crime and the various peripeties or reversals of fortune arising out of this; the end is the discovery and execution of the murderer—than which nothing can very well be more final. Our critic adds that the work should be of a convenient length. If it is too short, he says, our perception of it becomes indistinct. He objects, still more strongly, to the work that is of vast size or "one thousand miles long." "A story or plot," he reminds us, "must be of some length, but of a length to be taken in by the memory." A man *might* write a detective story of the length of *Ulysses*,[1] but, if he did, the reader would not be able to bear all the scattered clues in mind from the first chapter to the last, and the effect of the final discovery would be lost. In practice, a length of from 80,000 to 120,000 words is desirable, if the book is to sell; and this is enough to allow, in Aristotle's general formula, of "the hero's passing by a series of probable or necessary stages from misfortune to happiness or from happiness to misfortune." Later, however, he conveys a very necessary warning: "A writer often stretches out a plot beyond its capabilities, and is thus obligated to twist the sequence of incident." It is unwise to "write-up" a short-story type of plot to novel length, even to fulfill a publisher's contract.

The next section of the *Poetics* gives advice about the unity of the plot. It is not necessary to tell us everything that ever befel the hero. For example, says Aristotle, "in writing about Sherlock Holmes" (I have slightly adapted the instance he gives)—

> the author does not trouble to say where the hero was born, or whether he was educated at Oxford or Cambridge, nor does he enter into details about incidents which—though we know they occurred—are not relevant to the matter in hand, such as the cases of Vamberry the Wine Merchant, the Aluminium Crutch, Wilson the Notorious Canary-Trainer or Isadora Persano and the Remarkable Worm.

The story, he says —

> must represent one action, a complete whole, with its several incidents so closely connected that the transposal or withdrawal of any one of them will disjoin and dislocate the whole.

In other words, "murder your darlings"—or, if you must write a purple passage, take care to include in it some vital clue to the solution, which cannot be omitted or transposed to any other part of the story....

But now comes the important question: What kind of plot are we to choose? And this raises the great central opposition of the Probable and the Possible. It is *possible* that two Negroes should co-exist, so much alike as not only to deceive the eye, but to possess the same Bertillon measurements; that they should both bear the same Christian and surnames, and that they should both be confined in the same prison at the same time: it is possible, since it actually occurred.[3] But if we are to found a plot upon such a series of coincidences it will have an improbable appearance.

It is open to us to contrive stories based upon such incidents in real life, either giving the characters their real names or otherwise calling upon the witness of history. Thus there have been books founded on the Bravo case, the Crippen murder, the Penge tragedy, the case of W. H. Wallace, and so

[2] I refer, of course, to Mr. James Joyce's novel; not to Homer's poetical treatment of the subject.
[3] The case of the two Will Wests, U.S. Penitentiary, Leavenworth, Kansas, 1903.

on. When the facts are well known, the reader will accept the events as narrated. But it often turns out that the stories so written appear less convincing than those that are wholly invented; and it is frequently necessary to add inventions to the known facts, in order to make these true events appear probable. "So that," says Aristotle, "one must not aim at a rigid adherence to the traditional stories," particularly as "even the known stories are known only to a few." Thus, even where the possibility cannot be challenged, probability should be studied.

But where both names and incidents are invented, then, "a likely impossibility is always preferable to an unconvincing possibility." It may be impossible that the leaden bullet buried in a man's body should be chemically recovered from his ashes after cremation; but, by skillful use of scientific language, Dr. Austin Freeman persuades us that it is probable, and indeed inevitable. Whereas, when an author seeks to persuade us that a pleasant young Cambridge man of gentle birth is affronted by being asked to take his place in a queue behind a taxi-driver or some such person, the incident, though physically possible, offends by its improbability, being contrary to the English character, whose eternal patience in arranging itself in orderly queues is well known to amount to genius. "The story," says Aristotle, "should never be made up of improbable incidents; there should be nothing of the sort in it." Lest this seem too severe, he suggests as a practical compromise that "if such incidents are unavoidable, they should be kept outside the action." ...Similarly, as regards the characters, the impossible-probable is better than the improbable-possible; for (says Aristotle again) "if a detective such as Conan Doyle described be impossible, the answer is that it is better he should be like that, since the artist ought to improve on his model."

In the matter of scientific detail, Aristotle is all for accuracy. If, he says in effect, you cannot attain your artistic end without some impossible device (such as the instantaneously fatal and undiscoverable poison), then, at a pinch, you may be justified in using it:

> If, however, the poetic end might have been as well or better attained without sacrifice of technical correctness in such matters, the impossibility is not to be justified, since the description should be, if it can, entirely free from error. ...

Concerning the three necessary parts of a detective plot—peripety, or reversal of fortune, discovery, and suffering—Aristotle has many very just observations. On suffering, we need not dwell long. Aristotle defines it as "action of a destructive or painful nature, such as murders, tortures, woundings and the like." These are common enough in the detective story, and the only remark to be made is that they ought always to help on the action in some way, and not be put in merely to harrow the feelings, still less to distract attention from a weakness in the plot.

A reversal of fortune may happen to all or any of the characters: the victim—who is frequently a man of vast wealth—may be reduced to the status of a mere dead body; or may, again, turn out not to be dead after all, as we had supposed. The wrongly suspected person, after undergoing great misfortunes, may be saved from the condemned cell and restored to the arms of his betrothed. The detective, after several errors of reasoning, may hit upon the right solution. Such peripeties keep the story moving and arouse alternating emotions of terror, compassion and so forth in the reader. These events are best brought about, not fortuitously, but by some *hamartia* or defect in the sufferer. The defect may be of various kinds. The victim may suffer on account of his unamiable character, or through the error of marrying a wicked person, or through foolishly engaging in dubious finance, or through the mistake of possessing too much money. The innocent suspect may have been fool enough to quarrel with the victim, or to bring suspicion on himself by suppressing evidence with intent to shield somebody. The detective suffers his worries and difficulties through some failure of observation or logic. All these kinds of defect are fruitful in the production of peripety.

Aristotle mentions many varieties of the discovery which forms the denouement. This is usually the discovery, either of the identity of the murderer, or of the means by which the crime was committed.

(1) The worst kind are *discoveries made by the author himself*. These are, indeed, so inartistic as to be scarcely permissible in the true detective story: they belong to the thriller. It is, however, possible, where the villain's identity is known, to make an agreeable story by showing the moves and counter-moves made successively by villain and detective (Wilkie Collins in *No Name;* Austin Freeman in *The Singing Bone*).

(2) The *discovery by material signs and tokens* is very common: in *The Trial of Mary Dugan* the discovery that a person is left-handed leads to his conviction; in *The Eye of Osiris* the identity of the (supposed) Egyptian mummy with the missing corpse is proved by the discovery of identical tooth-stoppings and a Potts fracture in both.

(3) *Discovery through memory* is also used: thus, in *Unnatural Death,* the murder-method—the production of an air-lock in a main artery—is discovered to the detective by his memory of a similar air-lock in the petrol-feed of a motor-cycle.

(4) *Discovery through reasoning* is perhaps most common of all: the murderer was in the house at such a time, he is an electrician, he is tall and smokes Sobranie cigarettes; only X corresponds to all these indications, therefore X is the murderer.

(5) Aristotle's fifth type of discovery is particularly interesting. He calls it *discovery through bad reasoning by the other party*. The instance he adduces is obscure, the text being apparently mutilated and referring to a

play unknown. But I think he really means to describe the *discovery by bluff*. Thus, the detective shows the suspect a weapon saying, "If you are not the murderer, how do you come to be in possession of this weapon?" The suspect replies: "But that is not the weapon with which the crime was committed." "Indeed?" says the detective, *"and how do you know?"*

This brings us to the very remarkable passage in which Aristotle, by one of those blinding flashes of insight which display to the critic of genius the very core and centre of the writer's problem, puts the whole craft of the detective writer into one master-word: *Paralogismos.* That word should be written up in letters of gold on the walls of every mystery-monger's study — at once the guiding star by which he sets his compass and the jack-o-lantern by which he leads his readers into the bog; paralogism — the art of the false syllogism — for which Aristotle himself has a blunter and more candid phrase. Let us examine the whole paragraph, for it is of the utmost importance.

"Homer," says he — if he had lived in our own day he might have chosen some more apposite example, such as Father Knox or Mrs. Agatha Christie, but, thinking no doubt of *Odysseus,* he says Homer — "Homer more than any other has taught the rest of us the art of *framing lies in the right ways.* I mean the use of paralogism. Whenever, if A is or happens, a consequent, B is or happens, men's notion is that, if the B is, the A also is — but that is a false conclusion. Accordingly, if A is untrue, but there is something else, B, that on the assumption of its truth follows as its consequent, then the right thing is to present us with the B. Just because we know the truth of the consequent, we are in our own minds led on to the erroneous inference of the truth of the antecedent."

There you are, then; there is your recipe for detective fiction: the art of framing lies. From beginning to end of your book, it is your whole aim and object to lead the reader up the garden; to induce him to believe a lie. To believe the real murderer to be innocent, to believe some harmless person to be guilty; to believe the detective to be right where he is wrong and mistaken where he is right; to believe the false alibi to be sound, the present absent, the dead alive and the living dead; to believe, in short, anything and everything but the truth.

The art of framing lies — but mark! of framing lies in *the right way....* There is the crux. Any fool can tell a lie, and any fool can believe it; but the right method is to tell the *truth* in such a way that the *intelligent* reader is seduced into telling the lie for himself. That the writer himself should tell a flat lie is contrary to all the canons of detective art. Is it not amazing that Aristotle, twenty centuries ahead of his time, should thus have struck out at a blow the great modern theory of fair-play to the reader? A is falsehood; B is truth. The writer must not give us A upon his own authority, for what he says upon his own authority we must be able to believe. But he may tell us B—which *is* true—and leave us to draw the false conclusion that A is true also.

Thus, at the opening of a story, the servant Jones is heard to say to his master, Lord Smith, "Very good, my lord. I will attend to the matter at once." The inference is that, if Jones was speaking to Smith, Smith was also speaking to Jones; and that, therefore, Smith was alive and present at the time. But that is a false conclusion; the author has made no such assertion. Lord Smith may be absent; he may be already dead; Jones may have been addressing the empty air, or some other person. Nor can we draw any safe conclusion about the attitude of Jones. If Jones is indeed present in the flesh, and not represented merely by his voice in the form of a gramophone record or similar device (as may well be the case), then he may be addressing some other party in the belief that he is addressing Smith; he may have murdered Smith and be establishing his own alibi; or Smith may be the murderer and Jones his accomplice engaged in establishing an alibi for Smith. Nor, on the other hand, is it safe to conclude (as some experienced readers will) that *because* Smith is not heard to reply he is *not* therefore present. For this may very well be the Double Bluff, in which the reader's own cunning is exploited to his downfall. The reader may argue thus:

> Jones spoke to Smith, but Smith did not speak to Jones.
> Many authors employ this device so as to establish the false inference that Smith was alive and present.
> I therefore conclude that Smith is absent or dead.

But this syllogism is as false as the other, "Many authors" is not the same thing as "all authors at all times." It does not exclude the possibility that an author may at some time imply the truth in such a manner that it looks like a lie....

Nothing in a detective story need be held to be true unless the author has vouched for it *in his own person*. Thus, if the author says—

> Jones came home at 10 o'clock

then we are entitled to assume that Jones did indeed come home at that time and no other. But if the author says—

> The grandfather clock was striking ten when Jones reached home

then we can feel no certainty as to the time of Jones's arrival, for nothing compels us to accept the testimony of the clock. Nor need we believe the testimony of any character in the story, unless the author himself vouches for that character's integrity....

Remember, however, that the person telling the story is not necessarily the author. Thus, in *The Murder of Roger Ackroyd*, the story is told by the detective's *fidus Achates* or (to use the modern term) his Watson. Arguing from the particular to the general, we may be seduced into concluding that, because the original Dr. Watson was a good man, all Watsons are good in virtue of their Watsonity. But this is false reasoning, for moral worth and Watsonity are by no means inseparable. Thus, the first man sinned and laid the blame upon his wife; but it would be an error to conclude that all men, when they sin, blame their wives—though in fact they frequently do. There may be found rare men who, having wives, yet refrain from blaming them and are none the less men on that account. So, despite the existence of a first innocent Watson, we may yet admit the possibility of a guilty one; nor, when the Watson in *Roger Ackroyd* turns out to be the murderer, has the reader any right to feel aggrieved against the author— for she has vouched only for the man's Watsonity and not for his moral worth.

This brings us, however, to the consideration of the characters, concerning whom Aristotle takes a very twentieth-century point of view. He says that they must be *good*. This, I suppose, must be taken relatively, to mean that they should, even the meanest and wickedest of them, be not merely monsters and caricatures, like the personages in a low farce, but endued with some sort of human dignity, so that we are enabled to take them seriously. They must also be *appropriate:* a female, he says, must not be represented as clever. This is a delicate point—would he, or would he not, have approved of Miss Gladys Mitchell's diabolically clever Mrs. Bradley? We may take it, however, that the cleverness should only be such as is appropriate to the sex and circumstances of the character—it would be inappropriate that the elderly maiden sister of a country parson should carry out or detect a murder by means of an intricate and clever method knowable only to advanced chemical experts; and so with the other characters. Thirdly, the characters must be *like the reality.* ... Scholars differ about what Aristotle means by this word. Some think it means, "conformable to tradition": that the villain should be easily recognisable as villainous by his green eyes, his moustache and his manner of ejaculating "Ha!" and the detective by his eccentricities, his pipe and his dressinggown, after the more ancient models. But I do not agree with them, and believe that the word means, as we say to-day, "realistic," i.e. with some moderate approximation in speech and behaviour to such men and women as we see about us. For elsewhere, Aristotle takes the modern, realistic view, as when he says, for instance, that the plot ought not to turn on the detection and punishment of a hopelessly bad man who is villainous in all directions at once— forger, murderer, adulterer, thief—like the bad baron in an Adelphi melodrama; but rather on that of an intermediate kind of person—a decent man with a bad kink in him—which is the kind of villain most approved by the best modern writers in this kind. For the more the villain resembles an ordinary man, the more shall we feel pity and horror at his crime and the greater will be our surprise at his detection. So, too, as regards the innocent suspects and the police; in treating all such characters, a certain resemblance to real life is on the whole to be desired. Lastly, and most important and difficult of all, the characters must be *consistent* from first to last. Even though at the end we are to feel surprise on discovering the identity of the criminal, we ought not to feel incredulity; we should rather be able to say to ourselves: "Yes, I can see *now* that from the beginning this man had it in him to commit murder, had I only had the wits to interpret the indications furnished by the author. ..." Inconsistency in the characters destroys the probability of the action, and, indeed, amounts to a breach of the rule of fair play, since we are entitled to believe that a character remains the same person from beginning to end of the story and *nemo repente fuit turpissimus.*

This discourse is already too long. Let me remind myself of Aristotle's own warning: "There are many writers who, after a good complication, fail to bring off the denouement." This is painfully true of detective stories; it has also some application to lectures and speeches upon whatever occasion. But indeed, everything that Aristotle says about writing and composition is pregnant with a fundamental truth, an inner rightness, that makes it applicable to all forms of literary art, from the most trivial to the most exalted. He had, as we say, the root of the matter in him; and any writer who tries to make a detective story a work of art at all will do well if he writes it in such a way that Aristotle could have enjoyed and approved it.

Who Cares Who Killed
Roger Ackroyd?

by Edmund Wilson

Three months ago I wrote an article on some recent detective stories. I had not read any fiction of this kind since the days of Sherlock Holmes, and, since I constantly heard animated discussions of the merits of the mystery writers, I was curious to see what they were like today. The specimens I tried I found disappointing, and I made some rather derogatory remarks in connection with my impressions of the genre in general. To my surprise, this brought me letters of protest in a volume and of a passionate earnestness which had hardly been elicited even by my occasional criticisms of the Soviet Union. Of the thirty-nine letters that have reached me, only seven approve my strictures. The writers of almost all the others seem deeply offended and shocked, and they all say almost exactly the same thing: that I had simply not read the right novels and that I would surely have a different opinion if I would only try this or that author recommended by the correspondent. In many of these letters there was a note of asperity, and one lady went so far as to declare that she would never read my articles again unless I were prepared to reconsider my position. In the meantime, furthermore, a number of other writers have published articles defending the detective story: Jacques Barzun, Joseph Wood Krutch, Raymond Chandler and Somerset Maugham have all had something to say on the subject — nor has the umbrageous Bernard De Voto failed to raise his voice.

Overwhelmed by so much insistence, I at last wrote my correspondents that I would try to correct any injustice by undertaking to read some of the authors that had received the most recommendations and taking the whole matter up again. The preferences of these readers, however, when I had a tabulation of them made, turned out to be extremely divergent. They ranged over fifty-two writers and sixty-seven books, most of which got only one or two votes each. The only writers who got as many as five or over were Dorothy L. Sayers, Margery Allingham, Ngaio Marsh, Michael

Innes, Raymond Chandler and the author who writes under the names of Carter Dickson and John Dickson Carr.

The writer that my correspondents were most nearly unanimous in putting at the top was Miss Dorothy L. Sayers, who was pressed upon me by eighteen people, and the book of hers that eight of them were sure I could not fail to enjoy was a story called *The Nine Tailors*. Well, I set out to read *The Nine Tailors* in the hope of tasting some novel excitement, and I declare that it seems to me one of the dullest books I have ever encountered in any field. The first part of it is all about bell-ringing as it is practised in English churches and contains a lot of information of the kind that you might expect to find in an encyclopedia article on campanology. I skipped a good deal of this, and found myself skipping, also, a large section of the conversations between conventional English village characters: "Oh, here's Hinkins with the aspidistras. People may say what they like about aspidistras, but they do go on all the year round and make a background," etc. There was also a dreadful stock English nobleman of the casual and debonair kind, with the embarrassing name of Lord Peter Wimsey, and, although he was the focal character in the novel, being Miss Dorothy Sayers's version of the inevitable Sherlock Holmes detective, I had to skip a good deal of him, too. In the meantime, I was losing the story, which had not got a firm grip on my attention, but I went back and picked it up and steadfastly pushed through to the end, and there I discovered that the whole point was that if a man was shut up in a belfry while a heavy peal of chimes was being rung, the vibrations of the bells might kill him. Not a bad idea for a murder, and Conan Doyle would have known how to dramatize it in an entertaining tale of thirty pages, but Miss Sayers had not hesitated to pad it out to a book of three hundred and thirty, contriving one of those hackneyed cock-and-bull stories about a woman who commits bigamy without knowing it, and larding the whole thing with details of church architecture, bits of quaint lore from books about bell-ringing and the awful whimsical patter of Lord Peter.

I had often heard people say that Dorothy Sayers wrote well, and I felt that my correspondents had been playing her as their literary ace. But, really, she does not write very well: it is simply that she is more consciously literary than most of the other detective-story writers and that she thus attracts attention in a field which is mostly on a sub-literary level. In any serious department of fiction, her writing would not appear to have any distinction at all. Yet, commonplace in this respect though she is, she gives an impression of brilliant talent if we put her beside Miss Ngaio Marsh, whose *Overture to Death* was also suggested by several correspondents. Mr. De Voto has put himself on record as believing that Miss Marsh, as well as Miss Sayers and Miss Allingham, writes her novels in "excellent prose," and this throws for me a good deal of light on Mr. De Voto's opinions as a critic. I hadn't quite realized before, though I had noted his own rather messy style, to what degree he was insensitive to writing. I do not see how it is possible for anyone with a feeling for words to describe the unappetizing sawdust which Miss Marsh has poured into her pages as "excellent prose" or as prose at all except in the sense that distinguishes prose from verse. And here again the book is mostly padding. There is the notion that you could commit a murder by rigging up a gun in a piano in such a way that the victim will shoot himself when he presses down the pedal, but this is embedded in the dialogue and doings of a lot of faked-up English county people who are even more tedious than those of *The Nine Tailors.*

The enthusiastic reader of detective stories will indignantly object at this point that I am reading for the wrong things: that I ought not to be expecting good writing, characterization, human interest or even atmosphere. He is right, of course, though I was not fully aware of it till I attempted *Flowers for the Judge,* considered by connoisseurs one of the best books of one of the masters of this school, Miss Margery Allingham. This tale I found completely unreadable. The story and the writing both showed a surface so wooden and dead that I could not keep my mind on the page. How can you care who committed a murder which has never really been made to take place, because the writer hasn't any ability of even the most ordinary kind to persuade you to see it or feel it? How can you probe the possibilities of guilt among characters who all seem alike, because they are all simply names on the page? It was then than I understood that a true connoisseur of this fiction must be able to suspend the demands of his imagination and literary taste and take the thing as an intellectual problem. But how you arrive at that state of mind is what I do not understand.

In the light of this revelation, I feel that it is probably irrelevant to mention that I enjoyed *The Burning Court,* by John Dickson Carr, more than the novels of any of these ladies. There is a tinge of black magic that gives it a little of the interest of a horror story, and the author has a virtuosity at playing with alternative hypotheses that makes this trick of detective fiction more amusing than it usually is.

I want, however, to take up certain points made by the writer of the above-mentioned articles.

Mr. Barzun informs the non-expert that the detective novel is a kind of game in which the reader of a given story, in order to play properly his hand, should be familiar with all the devices that have already been used in other stories. These devices, it seems, are now barred: the reader must challenge the writer to solve his problem in some novel way, and the writer puts it up to the reader to guess the new solution. This may be true, but I

shall never qualify. I would rather play Twenty Questions, which at least
does not involve the consumption of hundreds of ill-written books.

A point made by three of these writers, Mr. Maugham, Mr. De Voto and
Mr. Krutch, is that the novel has become so philosophical, so psychological
and so symbolic that the public have had to take to the detective story as
the only department of fiction where pure story-telling survives.

This seems to me to involve two fallacies. On the one hand, it is surely
not true that "the serious novelists of today"—to quote Mr. Maugham's
assertion—"have often," in contrast to the novelists of the past, "little or no
story to tell," that "they have allowed themselves to be persuaded that to
tell a story is a negligible form of art." It is true, of course, that Joyce and
Proust—who, I suppose, must be accounted the heaviest going—have their
various modern ways of boring and playing tricks on the reader. But how
about the dreadful bogs and obstacles that one has to get over in Scott? the
interpolated essays in Hugo? the leaking tap of Thackeray's reflections on
life, in which the story is always trickling away? Is there anything in first-
rate modern fiction quite so gratuitous as these *longueurs?* Even Proust
and Joyce and Virginia Woolf do certainly have stories to tell, and they
have organized their books with an intensity which has been relatively
rare in the novel and which, to my mind, more than makes up for the occasional viscosity of their narrative.

On the other hand, it seems to me—for reasons suggested above—a
fantastic misrepresentation to say that the average detective novel is an
example of good story-telling. The gift for telling stories is uncommon,
like other artistic gifts, and the only one of this group of writers—the writers
my correspondents have praised—who seems to me to possess it to any degree is Mr. Raymond Chandler. His *Farewell, My Lovely* is the only one
of these books that I have read all of and read with enjoyment. But Chandler, though in his recent article he seems to claim Hammett as his master,
does not really belong to this school of the old-fashioned detective novel.
What he writes is a novel of adventure which has less in common with
Hammett than with Alfred Hitchcock and Graham Greene—the modern
spy story which has substituted the jitters of the Gestapo and the G.P.U.
for the luxury world of E. Phillips Oppenheim. It is not simply a question
here of a puzzle which has been put together but of a malaise conveyed to
the reader, the horror of a hidden conspiracy that is continually turning
up in the most varied and unlikely forms. To write such a novel successfully you must be able to invent character and incident and to generate
atmosphere, and all this Mr. Chandler can do, though he is a long way below Graham Greene. It was only when I got to the end that I felt my old
crime-story depression descending upon me again—because here again,
as is so often the case, the explanation of the mysteries, when it comes, is
neither interesting nor plausible enough. It fails to justify the excitement

produced by the elaborate build-up of picturesque and sinister happenings, and one cannot help feeling cheated.

My experience with this second batch of novels has, therefore, been even more disillusioning than my experience with the first, and my final conclusion is that the reading of detective stories is simply a kind of vice that, for silliness and minor harmfulness, ranks somewhere between smoking and crossword puzzles. This conclusion seems borne out by the violence of the letters I have been receiving. Detective-story readers feel guilty, they are habitually on the defensive, and all their talk about "well-written" mysteries is simply an excuse for their vice, like the reasons that the alcoholic can always produce for a drink. One of the letters I have had shows the addict in his frankest and most shameless phase. This lady begins by pretending, like the others, to guide me in my choice, but she breaks down and tells the whole dreadful truth. Though she has read, she says, hundreds of detective stories, "it is surprising," she finally confesses, "how few I would recommend to another. However, a poor detective story is better than none at all. Try again. With a little better luck, you'll find one you admire and enjoy. Then you, too, may be

A MYSTERY FIEND."

This letter has made my blood run cold: so the opium smoker tells the novice not to mind if the first pipe makes him sick; and I fall back for reassurance on the valiant little band of my readers who sympathize with my views on the subject. One of these tells me that I have underestimated both the badness of detective stories themselves and the lax mental habits of those who enjoy them. The worst of it is, he says, that the true addict, half the time, never even finds out who has committed the murder. The addict reads not to find anything out but merely to get the mild stimulation of the succession of unexpected incidents and of the suspense itself of *looking forward* to learning a sensational secret. That this secret is nothing at all and does not really account for the incidents does not matter to such a reader. He has learned from his long indulgence how to connive with the author in the swindle: he does not pay any real attention when the disappointing denouement occurs, he does not think back and check the events, he simply shuts the book and starts another.

To detective-story addicts, then, I say: Please do not write me any more letters telling me that I have not read the right books. And to the seven correspondents who are with me and who in some cases have thanked me for helping them to liberate themselves from a habit which they recognized as wasteful of time and degrading to the intellect but into which they had been bullied by convention and the portentously involved examples of Woodrow Wilson and Andre Gide—to these staunch and pure spirits I say: Friends, we represent a minority, but Literature is on our side. With so many fine books to be read, so much to be studied and known, there is no need to bore ourselves with this rubbish. And with the paper shortage pressing on all publication and many first-rate writers forced out of print, we shall do well to discourage the squandering of this paper that might be put to better use.

"Only a Detective Story"

by Joseph Wood Krutch

The detective story, so I once assumed, was read only by weary statesmen on the one hand and by the barely literate on the other. Discreet inquiry among friends and acquaintances soon revealed, however, a very different state of affairs. It is read either aggressively or shamefacedly by nearly everyone, and it must be, at the present moment, the most popular of all literary forms. "Only a detective story" is now an apologetic and depreciatory phrase which has taken the place of that "only a novel" which once moved Jane Austen to unaccustomed indignation.

My own experience with the genre began with Nick Carter and the once almost equally famous, though now almost totally forgotten, Old King Brady. It continued through Sherlock Holmes and, I believe, the very first of the Mary Roberts Rinehart *opera*. But it stopped there. Philo Vance and Ellery Queen were only dimly familiar names, while Nero Wolfe was known chiefly because he was the creation of a friend and neighbor. Dorothy Sayers and Agatha Christie attained their eminence quite unbeknownst to me, and, so far as I was concerned, Erle Stanley Gardner wrote in vain (under two different names) his five or six novels per annum. During the past twelve months, however, I have read perhaps 150 volumes, among which were included most of the accepted classics as well as a reasonable number of the run-of-the-mill tales.

Even this, I realize, leaves me still a novice, and I dare speak only because so little, relatively, has been said about so astounding a phenomenon. Even those magazines and newspapers which review this sort of writing usually do so in a special department and thus emphasize the fact that detective stories constitute some realm entirely apart. Would it not, for a change, be interesting to encourage some discussion of the "detective story" in relation to something else, to treat it as a branch of fiction or as a department of literature, while maintaining some recognition of the fact that branches and departments are not wholly unconnected?

Many a best-selling novel of the sort commonly regarded as respectable is read from mixed motives. No small proportion of the recent readers of,

Joseph Wood Krutch, "'Only a Detective Story'." From *The Nation,* November 25, 1944. Reprinted with permission of the estate of Joseph Wood Krutch and *The Nation.*

say, *A Tree Grows in Brooklyn* and *Strange Fruit* read those books, in part at least, because they felt some compulsion to do so, some sense that it was a social obligation to be able to discuss what others were discussing. But no one feels any compulsion to read a detective story. Few discuss what they have read with their neighbors. These books are read for pure pleasure, and there is certainly some significance in that fact. Pleasure is, many would maintain, the only legitimate reason for reading any sort of belles-lettres, and it is, I would agree, at least a sounder motive than either the desire for "self-improvement" or an inability to resist social pressure.

Two arguments are sometimes advanced to prove that the detective story must be sub-literary: its authors are sometimes very prolific; and the stories themselves "follow a formula." But neither of these arguments will hold water. Copious productivity has often been one of the most striking characteristics of the great writers of fiction, and comparatively few of the outstanding detective-story writers can have written more than Balzac, Dickens, or Anthony Trollope. As for "following a formula," it would be more accurate to say that certain conventions tend to be followed, and it would certainly be pertinent to ask whether this fact is as damning as it is sometimes assumed to be. No inconsiderable part of the great literature of the world has been written within the limitations of an established tradition, and so written not because the authors lacked originality but because the acceptance of a tradition and with it of certain fixed themes and methods seems to release rather than stifle the effective working of the imagination. Perhaps instead of saying that the detective story follows a formula we should say that it has *form,* and perhaps we should go on .from that to wonder whether this very fact may not be one of the reasons for its popularity at a time when the novel, always rather loose, so frequently has no shape at all.

Great popularity is not, to be sure, proof of literary excellence, but excellence does often attract great popularity. Moreover, works of art which are not good as a whole often owe their temporary vogue to some quality good in itself, and it is surely not impossible that the millions who read detective stories read them because of certain virtues more evident there than in most of the conventionally respectable novels. And it is for those virtues that I should like to see critics look, because I think it might be not only interesting but instructive to have them identified. They might even turn out to be virtues which the conventional novelist has failed to cultivate and for the lack of which his work has suffered.

To the sort of inquiry which I am proposing, the question of the extent to which detective-story writers do or do not exhibit certain of the virtues characteristic of the good novelist is quite irrelevant. No one could deny the broad statement that, in some general sense of the term, Dorothy Sayers writes very well indeed; but neither can anyone deny that certain of her almost equally popular rivals, write, in this sense, very badly. The fact that

Miss Sayers is obviously a woman of cultivation and taste and that in her best work she draws character and creates atmosphere more successfully than do some quite respectable conventional novelists is of course all to Miss Sayers's credit. But since other popular detective-story writers get along very successfully without attempting anything of the sort, it is clear enough that the unique virtues of the genre are not these. Obviously the detective story has some characteristic appeal of its own.

The simple statement that men evidently love puzzles and violence has been repeated so often that it has come to seem almost meaningless, and the fact remains that if this supposedly "natural" taste is to be posited, one still wonders why one particular way of satisfying it should have developed at this particular time. Despite all that one can say about Poe and Wilkie Collins or even Conan Doyle, who is, of course, the true begetter of the modern manner, the contemporary detective story is rather different from anything written before. There are some hundreds of volumes every one of which is immediately recognizable as having been written within a very definite period, beginning, I should guess, about 1925, when the contemporary genre first defined itself.

A few months ago Louise Bogan, introducing the subject in the pages of the *Nation* for what may have been the first time in history, suggested the ingenious theory that the essential element was an element of dread which corresponds to a nameless sense of apprehension characteristic of men living in our insecure civilization. She suggested that this element might gradually detach itself and by so doing give rise to a new and terrible sort of fiction. She implied, if I understand her aright, that Mr. Queen, to take an example, is really an unconscious Kafka or Kierkegaard *manqué*. But in actual fact apprehension is not by any means evoked in all detective stories. It is characteristic of some and serves to mark a sub-species, but the story in which the reader identifies himself with the detective rather than with either the criminal or his victim is at least equally common, and in such stories dread may often be entirely absent as one follows the sleuth in what is to him simply a matter of practicing his profession. If, for example, Mrs. Eberhart, Mr. Hammett, and Mr. Chandler frighten their readers, and if Mr. Gardner manages usually to combine two formulas by personally involving his lawyer-detective in dangerous adventures, many other of the most successful writers—S. S. Van Dine, Mr. Queen, Miss Sayers, Mrs. Christie, and Miss Allingham, for example—usually either employ dread as a very minor element in their effect or, by avoiding it completely, make the detective story one of the most detached and soothing of narratives.

Miss Bogan's suggestion remains interesting and provocative, but I doubt that her explanation is all-inclusive. There are, I suspect, simpler, less subtle reasons why thousands go to the detective story for some sort of satisfaction and relaxation which they find less often in more pretentious novels, and I am wondering if it does not commonly exhibit certain of the very elementary virtues of prose fiction which the serious novelist began utterly to despise just about the time that the detective-story writer stepped in to steal a large section of the reading public away from him. When Shakespeare wrote *Hamlet,* it was "only a play." When Jane Austen wrote *Emma* it was "only a novel." And while I am very far from suggesting that any of the detective stories which I have read are *Hamlets* or *Emmas,* I am suggesting that the fiction writer is in some ways better off and more successful when his public regards the reading of his works as a dubious self-indulgence than when the reading is regarded as a cultural duty.

Perhaps the "serious" novelist has tended to become, in some bad sense, too serious; perhaps, that is to say, he has tended to cultivate certain virtues and to pursue certain ends which, while laudable in themselves, are incompatible with the primary virtues of fiction or, if not quite that, have at least led him to be careless of, if not actually hostile to, these same primary virtues. We have grown accustomed to having reviewers say first of all that a novel is "important" or that it isn't, and to relegate, perhaps to the last paragraph, an expression of mild regret that some "important" novel or other is also structurally formless, stylistically inchoate, and pretty confusing as to intention. Even when such criticism is not made, the terms of praise are terms which do not necessarily imply excellence as fiction. Important novels are commonly described as "dealing with a serious problem," and as being, with rather monotonous regularity, "disturbing," "bitter," "uncompromising," "stark." But a novel can easily be—in fact it very often is—all these things without being readable and without furnishing any of the satisfactions which fiction, from the time of Homer through at least the great Victorians, was generally supposed to furnish.

The distinction is often made between what one "ought" to read and what one will enjoy reading. In connection with works of instruction and information, the distinction is one which is perfectly legitimate. But when it is employed also in connection with works of belles-lettres, it is preposterous in itself and an outward sign that those who permit themselves to employ it are also assuming some real distinction between what is important and what is interesting. But to the artist no such distinction ought to be possible. In art whatever is interesting is, artistically, important; and anything which seems important but not interesting is, artistically, not really important so far as that work of art is concerned. If it is important for some other artist, that artist will make it interesting, and it might be argued that a hopeless decline in the art of writing fiction began *when the novelist willingly acquiesced in a distinction between the important and the interesting.* I doubt that Homer or Chaucer or Shakespeare or Fielding or Balzac or Dickens ever permitted himself such an error.

Certainly it is one of which the detective-story writer is never guilty. He may often fail to be interesting, but he at least acknowledges that when he does so he is failing utterly and unredeemedly. And by acknowledging that fact he is driven to seek the elementary virtues of fiction as surely as the serious novelist who is concerned only to be "important" is led to neglect and despise them.

Two millenniums and a half ago Aristotle pointed out, first, that the "fable" is the most important element in a work of fiction, and, second, that the best fables are "unified," by which, as he explains, is meant that all the parts are inter-related in such a way that no part could be changed without changing all the others. And surely the popularity of the detective story is not unconnected with the fact that, whereas many serious novels are so far from exhibiting any such unity that they sometimes can hardly be said to have any fable at all, the detective story accepts the perfectly concatenated series of events as the *sine qua non* of a usable fable. Moreover, and partly as a consequence, the form of the detective story—that is, progress from the discovery of the corpse to the arrest of the criminal—insures that it shall have that self-determining beginning and that definite conclusion upon which also Aristotle insisted. In other words, the detective story is the one clearly defined modern genre of prose fiction impeccably classical in form.

Happy endings have of course come to seem to most people not only incompatible with "serious" fiction but also vulgar *per se*. But to those who hold this prejudice—in itself one of the most vulgar—it should be pointed out that detective stories commonly provide that particular sort of happy ending which is the most perfect of all and which may be described as "justice triumphant." Indeed, the detective story, alone of all the current forms of fiction—except, perhaps, the "Western"—generally tends to distribute what used to be called poetic justice even to minor characters, including those whose just deserts destine them to some middle state between success and failure. And if any attempt to insist that poetic justice must be administered in all fiction is to impose an almost intolerable burden, the fact remains that one source of the popularity of the detective story may be that in it poetic justice may be achieved without obvious artificiality or improbability. Dr. Johnson once observed as follows in commenting upon those who insisted on incorporating a demand for poetic justice among the "rules" of tragedy: "A play in which the wicked prosper, and the virtuous miscarry, may doubtless be good, because it is a just representation of the common events of human life, but since all reasonable beings naturally love justice, I cannot be easily persuaded that the observation of justice makes a play worse; or that, if other excellences are equal, the audience will not always rise better pleased from the final triumph of persecuted virtue."

It is not, I hope, necessary for me to add that I am not claiming for the detective story all possible virtues; I am not, as a matter of fact, actually claiming any except the very specific ones alluded to. Indeed, I am so far from urging all writers to write such stories or all readers to read nothing else that my remarks are really intended to be rather more about novels of a different sort than they are about the detective story itself. The serious novelist, it seems to me, is ill-advised either to rail against or remain indifferent to the vast popularity of what he is inclined to regard as a subliterary genre. I am suggesting that he might be well-advised to consider whether it would be possible for him to incorporate into his own novels certain of the virtues which have won so many readers for works which, often enough, have no virtues except those which the "serious" novelist has come increasingly to scorn.

The Dangerous Edge

by Gavin Lambert

> Our interest's on the dangerous edge of things.
> The honest thief, the tender murderer,
> The superstitious atheist...
>
> *Bishop Blougram's Apology*

In his autobiography, *A Sort of Life,* Graham Greene writes that he would choose Browning's lines as an epigraph for all his novels. When he first read them as a student, they promised and warned of a particular world—violent, mysterious, conflicted. Today they sum up an obsession that he shares with many writers who are driven to interpret life in terms of melodrama. Raymond Chandler has most accurately defined melodrama as "an exaggeration of violence and fear beyond what one normally experiences in life." Yet all art exaggerates some kind of experience. The mystery of the crime-artist... is why he chooses this distinctive method and what it means to us and to him.

It begins with the discovery of a country in which the dominant reality is criminal. To reach the dangerous edge is to find a point of no return. The same obsession grips the atheist as well as the Roman Catholic, the public figure and the recluse. It becomes a protest against defying the will of society or the will of God. It uncovers impulses at war within the self. It betrays fear of social change and fear of the existing order. Whatever the protest or the fear, a dark cloud is always moving nearer. External mystery of plot—flight and pursuit, riddle and warning—creates a metaphor for the deeper mystery of the threat itself.

The first map of the country was made halfway through the nineteenth century by Wilkie Collins. Although he didn't invent the detective or the mystery novel, he was the first to grasp its expressive possibilities. The genre became personal with *The Woman in White* and mechanical soon afterwards. But a few genuine explorers persisted, of whom Greene, Simen-

Gavin Lambert, "Prologue" from Lambert, *The Dangerous Edge* (London: Barrie & Jenkins, 1975), pp. ix-xv. Reprinted by permission of A. D. Peters & Co. Ltd., and Viking Penguin Inc.

on, Eric Ambler, and Hitchcock in films, still survive. It seems likely that
they will be the last. [Truman Capote's] *In Cold Blood* signalled the end
of one direction and the beginning of another. For this reason the moment
is apt for a summing up.

To trace the separate lives of crime-artists is like trying to find the vital
but submerged link between the different travellers who passed each other
on *The Bridge of Sun Luis Rey*. Relating the biographical material to the
work and looking for figures in both carpets, I decided to follow one of
Sherlock Holmes's favourite principles of detection: Truth is usually a
matter of seizing the correct improbability.

To be seduced by fear and to convey it so fanatically, one must have felt
its power some time before the end of childhood. Adolescents are not quite
vulnerable enough. Uncertainty is one of the hardest things for a child to
bear—and suspense, as the adult imagination conceives it, is still based on
that vivid apprehensive need to know what's going to happen next. Most
children have moments of paranoia when the world seems in monstrous
conspiracy against them. Everyone then becomes potentially murderer,
pursuer, enemy, and life a struggle between hunters and hunted. So many
childhood games project that situation. For the adult unable to shake off
early influences, the division of hunter and hunted remains and the pattern of identification with victim or killer grows set. Then curiousity and
dread interact. The quarry must finally be cornered and the antagonist's
motive unlocked. The climax of most crime stories is ritualistic, almost
dreamlike—Holmes face to face with Moriarty at the Reichenbach falls,
Buchan's Richard Hannay transfixed by his own prey across the precipice
in Scotland, the Hitchcock hero lured to confrontation on Mount Rush-
more or the isolated bell-tower, Chandler's Marlowe in the empty room as
he waits for the last door to open.

We are not led gradually in this world to a point of no return, but begin
on the edge. The cold sweat is a condition of daily life and Buchan's "How
thin is the protection of civilization" the warning that hangs in the air. This
appeal to an immediate sense-response of panic and excitement creates a
wrinkle in the fastidious nose. But doesn't the nose fail to see further than
itself? The record contradicts all the familiar charges of sensationalism, lack
of depth, escape from reality. When asked why he so often chose to write
thrillers, Greene pointed out that subjects choose writers. "It sometimes
seems as though our whole planet has swung into the fog belt of melodrama. . . ." His answer echoes the most compelling crime stories since 1850,
which are touched with prophecy, not evasion. The charge of sensationalism
becomes the escape from reality. A glance at the newspaper refutes it.

Only one recent crime story is the imaginative equal of Chandler's last
novel, and it re-creates an actual happening and "invents" nothing at all.
To illuminate the facts of *In Cold Blood,* Truman Capote chooses the crime

novelist's basic apparatus of suspense, betrayal and pursuit. On one level he recognizes today's fact through yesterday's fiction. On another he detects a link with his own early life in the deprived and wretched childhood of a young murderer. The shared experience produces both a creative and a destructive person, and leads one to become obsessed with the other....

An increasingly regulated society not only arouses in many people the desire to escape, but makes escape more difficult. Until the First World War dissatisfaction could be relaxed by drugs, since laudanum was freely available in many countries. The occult offered the stimulus of ghosts and mediums, a trip to the irrational. Travel books provided transportation to exotic and primitive ways of life, dime novels and penny dreadfuls released fantasies of sex and aggression. A priviledged few could even live like outlaws, rejecting established conventions without ending up in jail. They could even end up as heroes. Explorers like Burton, creative adventurers as different as Gauguin, Rimbaud and Isadora Duncan, even gunfighters like Wyatt Earp, confronted danger, loneliness, ridicule—but they freed themselves from the pressure of the human crack. Their lives might be cut short and yet they remained somehow complete, faithful to the idea of a private destiny. Some died unhappy, but perhaps this was the least unconventional thing about them.

When exits begin to close, the possibilities of release are narrowed. T. E. Lawrence typifies the new dilemma, driven to escape from himself but uncertain where to go. A private freedom slips away when almost everywhere is on the map. The next explorers of a totally untouched region, the astronauts, are no longer individual agents but uniformed servants of the state. Other mysteries are pre-empted by the middle class, mediums employed for assurance that the next world is friendly and respectable, astrologers contacting the silent planets for tips on investments. All kinds of vicarious escape—books, movies, the new mass availability of travel— inevitably confront the law of diminishing returns.

One route has remained open. For the double man interned with his obsessions, the criminal life has always been the most democratic choice, accessible in some form to all. In the end it offers only a new set of pressures, but so intense and fantastic that they can be glamourized by the name of risk. The successful criminal aims for freedom by celebrating the death of conscience, which means defining "right" and "good" as whatever he wants. But after this act of self-assertion he must settle for a masked and anonymous life. To get away literally with murder he has to abandon any hope of recognition and satisfy his vanity in secret. He will be safer if not too intellectual or gifted with a sense of theatre, for here again the temptation to show off is strong. (Vanity and carelessness, a by-product of vanity, are the flaws that most often lead to capture.) Most important of all, he commits himself to the situation of the hunted man, in which any close human involvement is an invitation to betrayal. The prescription for secrecy, mistrust and remoteness is not far from Joyce's motto for survival as an artist: "Silence, exile, cunning." An implicit point of departure for this book is the criminal act as a gesture of the imagination, equally appealing to criminal and artist.

When Wilkie Collins developed the idea of writing novels "with a secret," he was thinking not only of the puzzle element in detective stories but of something traumatically buried and seeking release. The ideal mystery, Chandler has written, is "one you would read if the end was missing!" The crime-artist, as opposed to the technician of the genre, uses the devices of melodrama to discover "the strange coincidences, the plannings, the cross purposes, the wonderful chain of events...leading to the most *outre* results," as Conan Doyle expressed it through Holmes. Shock, with its threat of the alien and inexplicable, is his basic weapon. "There was no *because,*" one of Simenon's murderers insists, "it was a word for fools."

"Those extraordinary accidents and events which happen to few men" seemed to Wilkie Collins "legitimate materials for fiction to work with," just as much as "the ordinary accidents and events which may and do, happen to us all." When an extraordinary accident happens to someone he becomes, instantly, an outsider. He is placed in a situation where he either rejects everyday beliefs and assumptions or they cease to be helpful. The whole ordinary world is a long cry away. The accident transforms him into an archetypal character—murderer, victim, spy, hunted man—whose predicament is a metaphor of isolation. In Collins's best novels, and those of his successors, crimes lead like underground passages to a discovery about the foundations of the world above.

The idea of a story "with a secret" leads back, by way of Poe, to the autobiography of a French detective. Eugène Vidocq was a criminal who became a successful police spy and then the first chief of the Paris Sûreté in 1811. Later he returned to crime and ended where he began, in obscure respectability. His *Memoires* were probably dramatized with the aid of a ghost-writer, like those of Mafia figures today, but Collins and Conan Doyle, as well as Poe, found them a rich source of mythology and fact. Vidocq had an unquestioned genius for disguise which enabled him to give the first insider's account of both the detective and the criminal world. Hunter and hunted, working for both sides, he proved that established authority and crime could be opposite faces of the same coin. Here his shadow reaches forward as far as Chandler, whose novels are dedicated to this proposition. The most spectacular anecdote in the *Memoires* comes from Vidocq's period as a police spy. Assigned (in disguise) to track down and liquidate an elusive criminal, only Vidocq knows that the quarry is himself.

It seems likely that the situation inspired Poe's *"William Wilson." "In me thou didst exist,"* says the dying man to his assailant, *"and, in my death, see by this image, which is thine own, how utterly thou hast murdered thyself."* Certainly Vidocq's methods sparked Poe's creation of the puzzle story with a fictional detective. Dupin, though on the side of the law, is "perhaps of a diseased intelligence." *"The Murders in the Rue Morgue"* (1841) is the first and most ingenious of these stories, none of which shows Poe's imagination at its freest. Thinly characterized essays in deductive logic, they contain puzzles too laboured to be dramatic. Poe's symbolic pieces are much more arresting, and one of them, influenced by the persona rather than the techniques of Vidocq, projects a powerful vision of the criminal as hunted man. The Man of the Crowd is old and decrepit, but something in his appearance suggests ideas of "vast mental power, of caution, of penuriousness, of avarice, of coolness, of malice, of blood-thirstiness, of triumph, of merriments, of excessive terror..." Following him as he wanders through a city, the narrator discovers someone who cannot bear to be alone. Perpetually on the run, he is unable to make contact with the crowd and yet terrified of not being part of it. In this estrangement from himself and alienation from the World Poe senses "the type and genius of deep crime."

At this point the narrator gives up the chase. Face to face for a moment with his quarry, he has his intuition and deliberately turns away. Some secrets, he feels, never reveal themselves. The essence of all crime remains "undivulged." The hunted creature is allowed to escape and disappear again into the vast unknowing crowd.

The detection of crime, Poe implies, lies beyond the criminologist's grasp and has nothing to do with the technical solution of a problem. The Man of the Crowd symbolizes everything that Dupin will never decode. Having invented the puzzle story, Poe defines its limitations. Chandler echoes him when he describes the ideal mystery as a story without an end. Most crime-artists are haunted by the idea that solving a puzzle involves dishonesty or anticlimax. To fool the reader is to cheat him. In fact the only detective novels that go beyond a mechanical puzzle to the creative puzzle of life are *The Moonstone* and some of Simenon's Maigret series: the only detective stories, the Sherlock Holmes cycle and a few of Father Brown's adventures. In each case the writer is concerned with raising questions, not answering them. The crime-artist's solution is a stimulant, the technician's a sedative.

The history and ingenuity of the detective novel has been well studied by its devotees, but their approach is inevitably the opposite of mine. They look at Collins, Conan Doyle, Simenon and others as superior exponents of a fixed genre. They subdivide Greene, Chandler and the rest into writers of spy stories and thrillers. But to fix a genre is to make it academic. The creative approach starts from scratch. Collins switches from the labyrinth of the puzzle to the stretched-out line of pursuit and suspense. Conan Doyle and Simenon find innumerable variations within a precisely structured world. Chandler is impatient with structure. ...

For Greene [the criminal] is one of the damned. For Eric Ambler he is beyond normal feeling and "emotionally *un*disturbed." For Simenon he is his own victim and for Chandler he embodies "the simplest and yet most complete pattern of the tensions on which we live." In every case he emerges as a private fear made public. A crime may or may not be detected, as Collins wrote, but its *raison d'être* lies in the fact that it was committed.

The Omnibus of Crime

by Dorothy L. Sayers

The art of self-tormenting is an ancient one, with a long and honourable literary tradition. Man, not satisfied with the mental confusion and un-happiness to be derived from contemplating the cruelties of life and the riddle of the universe, delights to occupy his leisure moments with puzzles and bugaboos. The pages of every magazine and newspaper swarm with cross-words, mathematical tricks, puzzle-pictures, enigmas, acrostics, and detective-stories, as also with stories of the kind called "powerful" (which means unpleasant), and those which make him afraid to go to bed. It may be that in them he finds a sort of catharsis or purging of his fears and self-questionings. These mysteries made only to be solved, these horrors which he knows to be mere figments of the creative brain, comfort him by subtly persuading that life is a mystery which death will solve, and whose horrors will pass away as a tale that is told. Or it may be merely that his animal faculties of fear and inquisitiveness demand more exercise than the daily round affords. Or it may be pure perversity. The fact remains that if you search the second-hand bookstalls for his cast-off literature, you will find fewer mystery stories than any other kind of book. Theology and poetry, philosophy and numismatics, love-stories and biography, he discards as easily as old razor-blades, but Sherlock Holmes and Wilkie Collins are cherished and read and reread, till their covers fall off and their pages crumble to fragments.

Both the detective-story proper and the pure tale of horror are very ancient in origin. All native folk-lore has its ghost tales,...from the Jewish Apocrypha, Herodotus, and the Aeneid. But, whereas the tale of horror has flourished in practically every age and country, the detective-story has had a spasmodic history, appearing here and there in faint, tentative sketches and episodes, until it suddenly burst into magnificent flower in the middle of the last century.

Dorothy L. Sayers, "Introduction," from her *The Omnibus of Crime.* New York: Payson and Clarke, Ltd., 1929), pp. 9-44. Reprinted by permission of David Higham Associates Ltd. on behalf of the estate of Dorothy L. Sayers, and Victor Gallancz Ltd.

Early History of Detective Fiction

Between 1840 and 1845 the wayward genius of Edgar Allan Poe (himself a past-master of the horrible) produced five tales, in which the general principles of the detective-story were laid down for ever. In "The Murders in the Rue Morgue" and, with a certain repulsive facetiousness, in "Thou Art the Man" he achieved the fusion of the two distinct genres and created what we may call the story of mystery, as distinct from pure detection on the one hand and pure horror on the other. In this fused genre, the reader's blood is first curdled by some horrible and apparently inexplicable murder or portent; the machinery of detection is then brought in to solve the mystery and punish the murderer. Since Poe's time all three branches—detection, mystery, and horror—have flourished. We have such pleasant little puzzles as Conan Doyle's "Case of Identity," in which there is nothing to shock or horrify; we have mere fantasies of blood and terror—human, as in Conan Doyle's "The Case of Lady Sannox,"[1] or supernatural, as in Marion Crawford's "The Upper Berth,"[2] most satisfactory of all, perhaps, we have such fusions as "The Speckled Band,"[3] or "The Hammer of God,"[4] in which the ghostly terror is invoked only to be dispelled.

It is rather puzzling that the detective-story should have had to wait so long to find a serious exponent. Having started so well, why did it not develop earlier? The Oriental races, with their keen appreciation of intellectual subtlety, should surely have evolved it. The germ was there. "Why do you not come to pay your respects to me?" says Aesop's lion to the fox. "I beg your Majesty's pardon," says the fox, "but I noticed the track of the animals that have already come to you; and, while I see many hoof-marks going in, I see none coming out. Till the animals that have entered your cave come out again, I prefer to remain in the open air." Sherlock Holmes could not have reasoned more lucidly from the premises.

Cacus the robber, be it noted, was apparently the first criminal to use the device of forged footprints to mislead the pursuer, though it is a long development from his primitive methods to the horses shod with cow-shoes in Conan Doyle's "Adventure of the Priory School."[5] Hercules's methods of investigation, too, were rather of the rough and ready sort, though the reader will not fail to observe that this early detective was accorded divine honours by his grateful clients.

The Jews, with their strongly moral preoccupation, were, as our two

[1]Conan Doyle: *Round the Red Lamp.*
[2]Marion Crawford: *Uncanny Tales.*
[3]Conan Doyle: *Adventures of Sherlock Holmes.*
[4]G. K. Chesterton: *The Innocence of Father Brown.*
[5]Conan Doyle: *Return of Sherlock Holmes.*

Apocryphal stories show, peculiarly fitted to produce the *roman policier*. The Romans, logical and given to law-making, might have been expected to do something with it, but they did not. In one of the folk-tales collected by the Grimms, twelve maidens disguised as men are set to walk across a floor strewn with peas, in the hope that their shuffling feminine tread will betray them; the maidens are, however, warned, and baffle the detectives by treading firmly. In an Indian folk-tale a similar ruse is more successful. Here a suitor is disguised as a woman, and has to be picked out from the women about him by the wise princess. The princess throws a lemon to each in turn, and the disguised man is detected by his instinctive action in clapping his knees together to catch the lemon, whereas the real women spread their knees to catch it in their skirts. Coming down to later European literature, we find the *Bel-and-the-Dragon* motif of the ashes spread on the floor reproduced in the story of Tristan. Here the king's spy spreads flour between Tristan's bed and that of Iseult; Tristan defeats the scheme by leaping from one bed to the other. The eighteenth century also contributed at least one outstanding example, in the famous detective chapter of Voltaire's *Zadig*.

It may be, as Mr. E. M. Wrong has suggested in a brilliant little study,[6] that throughout this early period "a faulty law of evidence was to blame, for detectives cannot flourish until the public has an idea of what constitutes proof, and while a common criminal procedure is arrest, torture, confession, and death." One may go further, and say that, though crime stories might, and did, flourish, the detective-story proper could not do so until public sympathy had veered round to the side of law and order. It will be noticed that, on the whole, the tendency in early crime-literature is to admire the cunning and astuteness of the criminal.[7] This must be so while the law is arbitrary, oppressive, and brutally administered.

We may note that, even to-day, the full blossoming of the detective-stories is found among the Anglo-Saxon races. It is notorious that an English crowd tends to side with the policeman in a row. The British legal code, with its tradition of "sportsmanship" and "fair play for the criminal" is particularly favourable to the production of detective fiction, allowing, as it does, sufficient rope to the quarry to provide a ding-dong chase, rich in up-and-down incident. In France, also, though the street policeman is less honoured than in England, the detective-force is admirably organised and greatly looked up to. France has a good output of detective-stories, though considerably smaller than that of the English-speaking races. In the Southern States of

[6]Preface to *Tales of Crime and Detection.* World's Classics. (Oxford University Press, 1926.)
[7]e.g. *The Story of Rhampsinitus; Jacob and Esau; Reynard the Fox; Ballads of Robin Hood,* etc.

Europe the law is less loved and the detective story less frequent. We may not unreasonably trace a connection here.

Some further light is thrown on the question by a remark made by Herr Lion Feuchtwanger when broadcasting during his visit to London in 1927. Contrasting the tastes of the English, French, and German publics, he noted the great attention paid by the Englishman to the external details of men and things. The Englishman likes material exactness in the books he reads; the German and the Frenchman, in different degrees, care little for it in comparison with psychological truth. It is hardly surprising, then that the detective-story, with its insistence on footprints, bloodstains, dates, times, and places, and its reduction of character-drawing to bold, flat outline, should appeal far more strongly to Anglo-Saxon taste than to that of France or Germany.

Taking these two factors together, we begin to see why the detective-story had to wait for its full development for the establishment of an effective police organisation in the Anglo-Saxon countries. This was achieved—in England, at any rate—during the early part of the nineteenth century[8] and was followed about the middle of that century by the first outstanding examples of the detective-story as we know it to-day.[9]

To this argument we may add another. In the nineteenth century the vast, unexplored limits of the world began to shrink at an amazing and unprecedented rate. The electric telegraph circled the globe; railways brought remote villages into touch with civilisation; photographs made known to the stay-at-homes the marvels of foreign landscapes, customs, and animals; science reduced seeming miracles to mechanical marvels; popular education and improved policing made town and country safer for the common man than they had ever been. In place of the adventurer and the knight errant, popular imagination hailed the doctor, the scientist, and the policeman as saviours and protectors. But if one could no longer hunt the manticora, one could still hunt the murderer; if the armed escort had grown less necessary, yet one still needed the analyst to frustrate the wiles of the poisoner; from this point of view, the detective steps into his right place as the protector of the weak—the latest of the popular heroes, the true successor of Roland and Lancelot.

[8]In a letter to W. Thornbury, dated February 18, 1862, Dickens says: "The Bow Street Runners ceased out of the land soon after the introduction of the new police. I remember them very well. ...They kept company with thieves and such-like, much more than the detective police do. I don't know what their pay was, but I have no doubt their principal complements were got under the rose. It was a very slack institution, and its head-quarters were the Brown Bear, in Bow Street, a public house of more than doubtful reputation, opposite the police-office." The first "peelers" were established in 1829.

[9]The significance of footprints, and the necessity for scientific care in the checking of alibis, were understood at quite an early date, though, in the absence of an effective detective police, investigations were usually carried out by private persons at the instigation of the coroner. A remarkable case, which reads like a Freeman Wills Crofts novel, was that of R. *v.* Thornton (1818).

Edgar Allan Poe: Evolution of the Detective

Before tracing further the history of detective fiction, let us look a little more closely at those five tales of Poe's, in which so much of the future development is anticipated. Probably the first thing that strikes us is that Poe has struck out at a blow the formal outline on which a large section of detective fiction has been built up. In the three Dupin stories, . . . we have the formula of the eccentric and brilliant private detective whose doings are chronicled by an admiring and thick-headed friend. From Dupin and his unnamed chronicler springs a long and distinguished line: Sherlock Holmes and his Watson; Martin Hewitt and his Brett; Raffles and his Bunny (on the criminal side of the business, but of the same breed); Thorndyke and his various Jardines, Ansteys, and Jervises; Hanaud and his Mr. Ricardo; Poirot and his Captain Hastings; Philo Vance and his Van Dine.[10] It is not surprising that this formula should have been used so largely, for it is obviously a very con-formula should have been used so largely, for it is obviously a very convenient one for the writer. For one thing, the admiring satellite may utter expressions of eulogy which would be unbecoming in the mouth of the author, gaping at his own colossal intellect. Again, the reader, even if he is not, in R. L. Stevenson's phrase, "always a man of such vastly greater ingenuity than the writer," is usually a little more ingenious than Watson. He sees a little further through the brick wall; he pierces, to some extent, the cloud of mystification with which the detective envelops himself. "Aha!" he says to himself, "the average reader is supposed to see no further than Watson. But the author has not reckoned with me. I am one too many for him." He is deluded. It is all a device of the writer's for flattering him and putting him on good terms with himself. For though the reader likes to be mystified, he also likes to say, "I told you so," and "I spotted that." And this leads us to the third great advantage of the Holmes-Watson convention: by describing the clues as presented to the dim eyes and bemused mind of Watson, the author is enabled to preserve a spurious appearance of frankness, while keeping to himself the special knowledge on which the interpretation of those clues depends. This is a question of paramount importance, involving the whole artistic ethic of the detective-story. We shall return to it later. For the moment, let us consider a few other interesting types and formulae which make their first appearance in Poe.

The personality of Dupin is eccentric, and for several literary generations eccentricity was highly fashionable among detective heroes. Dupin, we are informed, had a habit of living behind closed shutters, illumined by "a couple of tapers which, strongly perfumed, threw out only the ghastliest and feeblest of rays." From this stronghold he issued by night, to promenade the

---

[10][This point has been further developed in several articles in *The Armchair Detective,* Editor's note.]

streets and enjoy the "infinity of mental excitement" afforded by quiet observation. He was also given to startling his friends by analysing their thought-processes, and he had a rooted contempt for the methods of the police.

Sherlock Holmes modelled himself to a large extent upon Dupin, substituting cocaine for candlelight, with accompaniments of shag and fiddle-playing. He is a more human and endearing figure than Dupin, and has earned as his reward the supreme honour which literature has to bestow— the secular equivalent of canonisation. He has passed into the language. He also started a tradition of his own—the hawk-faced tradition, which for many years dominated detective fiction.

So strong, indeed, was this domination that subsequent notable eccentrics have displayed their eccentricities chiefly by escaping from it. "Nothing," we are told, "could have been less like the traditional detective than"—so-and-so. He may be elderly and decrepit, like Baroness Orczy's Old Man in the Corner, whose characteristic habit is the continual knotting of string. Or he may be round and innocent-looking, like Father Brown or Poirot. There is Sax Rohmer's Moris Klaw,[11] with his bald, scholarly forehead; he irrigates his wits with a verbena spray, and carries about with him an "odically-sterilised" cushion to promote psychic intuition. There is the great Dr. Thorndyke, probably the handsomest detective in fiction; he is outwardly bonhomous, but spiritually detached, and his emblem is the green research-case, filled with miniature microscopes and scientific implements. Max Carrados has the distinction of being blind; Old Ebbie wears a rabbit-skin waistcoat; Lord Peter Wimsey (if I may refer to him without immodesty) indulges in the buying of incunabula and has a pretty taste in wines and haberdashery. By a final twist of the tradition, which brings the wheel full circle, there is a strong modern tendency to produce detectives remarkable for their ordinariness; they may be well-bred walking gentlemen, like A. A. Milne's Antony Gillingham, or journalists, like Gaston Leroux's Rouletabille, or they may even be policemen, like Freeman Wills Crofts' Inspector French, or the heroes of Mr. A. J. Rees's sound and well-planned stories.[12]

There have also been a few women detectives,[13] but on the whole, they have not been very successful. In order to justify their choice of sex, they are

---

[11]Sax Rohmer: *The Dream Detective.*

[12]A. J. Rees: *The Shrieking Pit; The Hand in the Dark;* (with J. R. Watson) *The Hampstead Mystery; The Mystery of the Downs,* etc. Messrs. Rees and Watson write of police-affairs with the accuracy born of inside knowledge, but commendably avoid the dullness which is apt to result from a too-faithful description of correct official procedure.

[13]e.g. Anna Katharine Green: *The Golden Slipper;* Baroness Orczy; *Lady Molly of Scotland Yard;* G. R. Sims: *Dorcas Dene;* Valentine: *The Adjusters;* Richard Marsh: *Judith Lee;* Arthur B. Reeve: *Constance Dunlap;* etc.

obliged to be so irritatingly intuitive as to destroy that quiet enjoyment of the logical which we look for in our detective reading. Or else they are active and courageous, and insist on walking into physical danger and hampering the men engaged on the job. Marriage, also, looms too large in their view of life; which is not surprising, for they are all young and beautiful. Why these charming creatures should be able to tackle abstruse problems at the age of twenty-one or thereabouts, while the male detectives are usually content to wait till their thirties or forties before setting up as experts, it is hard to say. Where do they pick up their wordly knowledge? Not from personal experience, for they are always immaculate as the driven snow. Presumably it is all intuition.

Better use has been made of women in books where the detective is strictly amateur—done, that is, by members of the family or house-party themselves, and not by a private consultant. Evelyn Humblethorne[14] is a detective of this kind, and so is Joan Cowper, in *The Brooklyn Murders*.[15] But the really brilliant woman detective has yet to be created.[16]

While on this subject, we must not forget the curious and interesting development of detective fiction which has produced the *Adventures of Sexton Blake*, and other allied cycles. This is the Holmes tradition, adapted for the reading of the board-school boy and crossed with the Buffalo Bill adventure type. The books are written by a syndicate of authors, each one of whom uses a set of characters of his own invention, grouped about a central and traditional group consisting of Sexton Blake and his boy assistant, Tinker, their comic landlady Mrs. Bardell, and their bulldog Pedro. As might be expected, the quality of the writing and the detective methods employed vary considerably from one author to another. The best specimens display extreme ingenuity, and an immense vigour and fertility in plot and incident. Nevertheless, the central types are pretty consistently preserved throughout the series. Blake and Tinker are less intuitive than Holmes, from whom however, they are directly descended, as their address in Baker Street shows. They are more careless and reckless in their methods; more given to displays of personal heroism and pugilism; more simple and human in their emotions. The really interesting point about them is that they present the nearest modern approach to a national folk-lore, conceived as the centre for a cycle of loosely connected romances in the Arthurian manner. Their significance in popular literature and education would richly repay scientific investigation.

[14]Lord Gorell: *In the Night.*
[15]G. D. H. & M. Cole.
[16]Wilkie Collins—who was curiously fascinated by the "strong-minded" woman—made two attempts at the woman detective in *No Name* and *The Law and the Lady*. The spirit of the time was, however, too powerful to allow these attempts to be altogether successful.

Edgar Allan Poe: Evolution of the Plot

As regards plot also, Poe laid down a number of sound keels for the use of later adventurers. Putting aside his instructive excursion into the psychology of detection—instructive, because we can trace their influence in so many of Poe's successors down to the present day—putting these aside, and discounting that atmosphere of creepiness which Poe so successfully diffused about nearly all he wrote, we shall probably find that to us, sophisticated and trained on an intensive study of detective fiction, his plots are thin to transparency. But in Poe's day they represented a new technique. As a matter of fact, it is doubtful whether there are more than half a dozen deceptions in the mystery-monger's bag of tricks, and we shall find that Poe has got most of them, at any rate in embryo.

Take, first, the three Dupin stories. In "The Murders in the Rue Morgue," an old woman and her daughter are found horribly murdered in an (apparently) hermetically sealed room. An innocent person is arrested by the police. Dupin proves that the police have failed to discover one mode of entrance to the room, and deduces from a number of observations that the "murder" was committed by a huge ape. Here is, then, a combination of three typical motifs: the wrongly suspected man, to whom all the superficial evidence (motive, access, etc.) points; the hermetically sealed death-chamber (still a favourite central theme); finally, the *solution by the unexpected means*. In addition, we have Dupin drawing deductions, which the police have overlooked, from the evidence of witnesses (superiority in inference), and discovering clues which the police have not thought of looking for owing to obsession by an *idée fixe* (superiority in observation based on inference). In this story also are enunciated for the first time those two great aphorisms of detective science: first, that when you have eliminated all the impossibilities, then, whatever remains, *however improbable,* must be the truth; and, secondly, that the more *outré* a case may appear, the easier it is to solve. Indeed, take it all round, "The Murders in the Rue Morgue" constitutes in itself almost a complete manual of detective theory and practice.

In "The Purloined Letter," we have one of those stolen documents on whose recovery hangs the peace of mind of a distinguished personage. It is not, indeed, one of the sort whose publication would spread consternation among the Chancelleries of Europe, but it is important enough. The police suspect a certain minister of taking it. They ransack every corner of his house, in vain. Dupin, arguing from his knowledge of the minister's character, decides that subtlety must be met by subtlety. He calls on the minister and discovers the letter, turned inside out and stuck in a letter-rack in full view of the casual observer.

Here we have, besides the reiteration, in inverted form,[17] of aphorism No. 2 (above), the method of *psychological deduction* and the solution by the formula of the *most obvious place*. This trick is the forerunner of the diamond concealed in the tumbler of water, the man murdered in the midst of a battle, Chesterton's "Invisible Man" (the postman, so familiar a figure that his presence goes unnoticed)[18] and a whole line of similar ingenuities.

The third Dupin story, "The Mystery of Marie Rogêt," has fewer imitators, but is the most interesting of all to the connoisseur. It consists entirely of a series of newspaper cuttings relative to the disappearance and murder of a shopgirl, with Dupin's comments thereon. The story contains no solution of the problem, and, indeed, no formal ending—and that for a very good reason. The disappearance was a genuine one, its actual heroine being one Mary Celia Rogers, and the actual place New York. The newspaper cuttings, were also, *mutatis mutandis,* genuine. The paper which published Poe's article dared not publish his conclusion. Later on it was claimed that his argument was, in substance, correct; and though this claim has, I believe, been challenged of late years,[19] Poe may, nevertheless, be ranked among the small band of mystery-writers who have put their skill in deduction to the acid test of a problem which they had not in the first place invented.[20]

Of the other Poe stories, one, "Thou Art the Man," is very slight in theme and unpleasantly flippant in treatment. A man is murdered; a hearty person, named, with guileless cunning, Goodfellow, is very energetic in fixing the crime on a certain person. The narrator of the story makes a repulsive kind of jack-in-the-box out of the victim's corpse, and extorts a confession of guilt from—Goodfellow! Of course. Nevertheless, we have here two more leading motifs that have done overtime since Poe's day: the trail of false clues laid by the real murderer[21] and the *solution by way of the most unlikely person.*

[17]"The business is very simple indeed, and I make no doubt that we can manage it sufficiently well ourselves; but then I thought Dupin would like to hear of it because it is so excessively *odd.*"

"Simple and odd," said Dupin.

"Why, yes; and not exactly that either. The fact is, we have all been a good deal puzzled because the affair *is* so simple, and yet baffles us altogether."

"Perhaps it is the very simplicity of the thing which puts you at fault," said Dupin.

The psychology of the matter is fully discussed in Poe's characteristic manner a few pages further on.

[18]G. K. Chesterton: *The Innocence of Father Brown.*

[19][There is now a substantial literature on this subject. See, in particular, the journal *Poe Studies* and two books, Raymond Paul, *Who Murdered Mary Rogers?* (New York, 1971) and John Walsh, *Poe the Detective: The Curious Circumstances Behind The Mystery of Marie Rogêt* (New Brunswick, N.J., 1968). Editor's note].

[20]Sir Arthur Conan Doyle's successful efforts on behalf of George Edalji and Oscar Slater deserve special mention.

[21]See also "The Story of Susanna."

The fifth story is "The Gold Bug." In this a man finds a cipher which leads him to the discovery of a hidden treasure. The cipher is of the very simple one-sign-one-letter type, and its solution, of the mark-where-the-shadow-falls-take-three-paces-to-the-east-and-dig variety. In technique this story is the exact opposite of "Marie Rogêt"; the narrator is astonished by the antics of his detective friend, and is kept in entire ignorance of what he is about until *after* the discovery of the treasure; only then is the cipher for the first time either mentioned or explained. Some people think that "The Gold Bug" is Poe's finest mystery-story.

Now, with "The Gold Bug" at the one extreme and "Marie Rogêt" at the other, and the other three stories occupying intermediate places, Poe stands at the parting of the ways for detective fiction. From him go the two great lines of development—the Romantic and the Classic, or, to use terms less abraded by ill-usage, the purely Sensational and the purely Intellectual. In the former, thrill is piled on thrill and mystification on mystification; the reader is led on from bewilderment to bewilderment, till everything is explained in a lump in the last chapter.[22] This school is strong in dramatic incident and atmosphere; its weakness is a tendency to confusion and a dropping of links—its explanations do not always explain; it is never dull, but it is sometimes nonsense. In the other—the purely Intellectual type—the action mostly takes place in the first chapter or so; the detective then follows up quietly from clue to clue till the problem is solved, the reader accompanying the great man in his search and being allowed to try his own teeth on the material provided. The strength of this school is its analytical ingenuity; its weakness is its liability to dullness and pomposity, its mouthing over the infinitely little, and its lack of movement and emotion.

Intellectual and Sensational Lines of Development

The purely Sensational thriller is not particularly rare—we may find plenty of examples in the work of William Le Queux, Edgar Wallace, and others. The purely Intellectual is rare indeed; few writers have consistently followed the "Marie Rogêt" formula of simply spreading the *whole* evidence before the reader and leaving him to deduce the detective's conclusion from it if he can.[23]

M. P. Shiel, indeed, did so in his trilogy, *Prince Zaleski,* whose curious and elaborate beauty recaptures in every arabesque sentence the very accent of Edgar Allan Poe. Prince Zaleski, "victim of a too importunate, too unfortunate Love, which the fulgor of the throne itself could not abash,"

---

[22][See, more recently, the work of Helen MacInnes. Editor's note.]

[23][It is interesting to note that Miss Sayers then goes on to write precisely the kinds of books she observes, in this essay, have not been written. Editor's note.]

sits apart in his ruined tower in "the semi-darkness of the very faint green-ish lustre radiated from an open censer-like *lampas* in the centre of the doomed encausted roof," surrounded by Flemish sepulchral brasses, runic tablets, miniature paintings, winged bulls, Tamil scriptures on lacquered leaves of the talipot, mediaeval reliquaries richly gemmed, Brahmin gods, and Egyptian mummies, and lulled by "the low, liquid tinkling of an invisible musical-box." Like Sherlock Holmes, he indulges in a drug—"the narcotic *cannabis sativa:* the base of the *bhang* of the Mohammedans." A friend brings to him the detective problems of the outside world, which he proceeds to solve from the data given and (except in the final story) without stirring from his couch. He adorns his solutions with philosophical discourses on the social progress of mankind, all delivered with the same melancholy grace and remote intellectual disdain. The reasoning is subtle and lucid, but the crimes themselves are fantastic and incredible—a fault which these tales have in common with those of G. K. Chesterton.

Another writer who uses the "Marie Rogêt" formula is Baroness Orczy. Her *Old Man in the Corner* series is constructed precisely on those lines, and I have seen a French edition in which, when the expository part of the story is done, the reader is exhorted to: "Pause a moment and see if you can arrive at the explanation yourself, before you read the Old Man's solution." This pure puzzle is a formula which obviously has its limitations. Nearest to this among modern writers comes Freeman Wills Crofts, whose painstaking sleuths always "play fair" and display their clues to the reader as soon as they have picked them up. The intellectually minded reader can hardly demand more than this. The aim of the writer of this type of detective-story is to make the reader say at the end, neither: "Oh well, I knew it must be that all along," nor yet: "Dash it all! I couldn't be expected to guess that"; but: "Oh, of course! What a fool I was not to see it! Right under my nose all the time!" Precious tribute! How often striven for! How rarely earned!

On the whole, however, the tendency is for the modern educated public to demand fair play from the writer, and for the Sensational and Intellectual branches of the story to move further apart.

Before going further with this important question, we must look back once more to the middle of the last century, and see what development took place to bridge the gap between Dupin and Sherlock Holmes.

Poe, like a restless child, played with his new toy for a little while, and then, for some reason, wearied of it. He turned his attention to other things, and his formula lay neglected for close on forty years. Meanwhile a somewhat different type of detective-story was developing independently in Europe. In 1848 the elder Dumas, always ready to try his hand at any novel and ingenious thing, suddenly inserted into the romantic body of the *Vicomte de Bragelonne* a passage of pure scientific deduction. This pas-

sage is quite unlike anything else in the Musketeer cycle, and looks like
the direct outcome of Dumas' keen interest in actual crime.[24]

But there is another literary influence which, though the fact is not generally recognised, must have been powerfully exerted at this date upon
writers of mystery fiction. Between 1820 and 1850 the novels of Fenimore
Cooper began to enjoy their huge popularity, and were not only widely
read in America and England, but translated into most European languages. In *The Pathfinder, The Deerslayer, The Last of the Mohicans,* and
the rest of the series, Cooper revealed to the delighted youth of two hemi-
spheres the Red Indian's patient skill in tracking his quarry by footprints,
in interrogating a broken twig, a mossy trunk, a fallen leaf. The imagination of childhood was fired; every boy wanted to be an Uncas or a Chingach-
gook. Novelists, not content with following and imitating Cooper on his
own ground, discovered a better way, by transferring the romance of the
woodland tracker to the surroundings of their native country. In the sixties
the generation who had read Fenimore Cooper in boyhood turned, as
novelists and readers, to tracing the spoor of the criminal upon their own
native heath.[25] The enthusiasm for Cooper combined magnificently with
that absorbing interest in crime and detection which better methods of communication and an improved police system had made possible. While, in
France, Gaboriau and Fortuné du Boisgobey concentrated upon the police
novel pure and simple, English writers, still permeated by the terror and
mystery of the romantic movement, and influenced by the "Newgate novel"
of Bulwer and Ainsworth, perfected a more varied and imaginative genre,
in which the ingenuity of the detective problem allied itself with the sombre
terrors of the weird and supernatural.

The Pre-Doyle Period

Of the host of writers who attempted this form of fiction in the sixties and
seventies, three may be picked out for special mention.

That voluminous writer, Mrs. Henry Wood, represents, on the whole,
melodramatic and adventurous development of the crime-story as distinct
from the detective problem proper. Through *East Lynne,* crude and sentimental as it is, she exercised an enormous influence on the rank and file of
sensational novelists, and at her best, she is a most admirable spinner of
plots. Whether her problem concerns a missing will, a vanished heir, a
murder, or a family curse, the story spins along without flagging, and,
though she is a little too fond of calling in Providence to cut the knot of

---

[24]He published a great collection of famous crimes.

[25][This point is explored at greater length by George Grella in the second of his two essays
reprinted here. Editor's note.]

intrigue with the sword of coincidence, the mystery is fully and properly unravelled, in a workmanlike manner and without any loose ends. She makes frequent use of supernatural thrills. Sometimes these are explained away: a "murdered" person is seen haunting the local churchyard, and turns out never to have been killed at all. Sometimes the supernatural remains supernatural, as, for instance, the coffin-shaped appearance in *The Shadow of Ashlydyat*. Her morality is perhaps a little oppressive, but she is by no means without humour, and at times can produce a shrewd piece of characterisation.

Melodramatic, but a writer of real literary attainment, and gifted with a sombre power which has seldom been equalled in painting the ghastly and the macabre, is Sheridan Le Fanu.[26] Like Poe, he has the gift of investing the most mechanical of plots with an atmosphere of almost unbearable horror. Take, for example, that scene in *Wylder's Hand* where the aged Uncle Lorne appears—phantom or madman? we are not certain which—to confront the villainous Lake in the tapestried room.

"Mark Wylder is in evil plight," said he.

"Is he?" said Lake with a sly scoff, though he seemed to me a good deal scared. "We hear no complaints, however, and fancy he must be tolerably comfortable notwithstanding."

"You know where he is," said Uncle Lorne.

"Aye, in Italy; everyone knows that," answered Lake.

"In Italy," said the old man reflectively, as if trying to gather up his ideas, "Italy.... He has had a great tour to make. It is nearly accomplished now; when it is done, he will be like me, *humano major*. He has seen the places which you are yet to see."

"Nothing I should like better; particularly Italy," said Lake.

"Yes," said Uncle Lorne, lifting up slowly a different finger at each name in his catalogue. "First, Lucus Mortis; then Terra Tenebrosa; next, Tartarus; after that Terra Oblivionis; then Herebus; then Barathrum; then Gehenna, and then Stagnum Ignis."

"Of course," acquiesced Lake, with an ugly sneer....

"Don't be frightened—but he's alive; I think they'll make him mad. It is a frightful plight. Two angels buried him alive in Vallombrosa by night; I saw it, standing among the lotus and hemlocks. A negro came to me, a black clergyman with white eyes, and remained beside me; and the angels imprisoned Mark; they put him on duty forty days and forty nights, with his ear to the river listening for voices; and when it was over we blessed them; and the clergyman walked with me a long while, to-and-fro, to-and-fro upon the earth, telling me the wonders of the abyss."

"And is it from the abyss, sir, he writes his letters?" enquired the Town Clerk, with a wink at Lake.

"Yes, yes, very diligent; it behoves him; and his hair is always standing

---

[26][Pronounced "lef-noo." In the 1930s Dorothy Sayers would set one of her principal characters, Harriet Vane, to work on a biography of Le Fanu. Editor's note.]

straight on his head for fear. But he'll be sent up again, at last, a thousand, a
hundred, ten and one, black marble steps, and then it will be the other one's
turn. So it was prophesied by the black magician."

This chapter leads immediately to those in which Larkin, the crooked
attorney, discovers, by means of a little sound detective work of a purely
practical sort, that Mark Wylder's letters have indeed been written "from
the abyss." Mark Wylder has, in fact, been murdered, and the letters are
forgeries sent abroad to be despatched by Lake's confederate from various
towns in Italy. From this point we gradually learn to expect the ghastly
moment when he is "sent up again at last" from the grave, in the Black-
berry Dell at Gylingden.

> In the meantime the dogs continued their unaccountable yelling close by.
> "What the devil's that?" said Wealden.
> Something like a stunted, blackened branch was sticking out of the peat,
> ending in a set of short, thickish twigs. This is what it seemed. The dogs were
> barking at it. It was, really, a human hand and arm....

In this book the detection is done by private persons, and the local police
are only brought in at the end to secure the criminal. This is also the case
in that extremely interesting book *Checkmate* (1870), in which the plot
actually turns upon the complete alteration of the criminal's appearance by
a miracle of plastic surgery. It seems amazing that more use has not been
made of this device in post-war days, now that the reconstruction of faces has
become comparatively common and, with the perfecting of aseptic surgery,
infinitely easier than in Le Fanu's day. I can only call to mind two recent
examples of this kind: one, Mr. Hopkins Moorhouse's *Gauntlet of Alceste;*
the other, a short story called "The Losing of Jasper Virel," by Beckles
Willson[27] In both stories the alterations include the tattooing of the criminal's eyes from blue to brown.

For sheer grimness and power, there is little in the literature of horror to
compare with the trepanning scene in Le Fanu's *The House by the Church-
yard.* Nobody who has ever read it could possibly forget that sick chamber,
with the stricken man sunk in his deathly stupor; the terrified wife; the
local doctor, kindly and absurd—and then the pealing of the bell, and the
entry of the brilliant, brutal Dillon "in dingy splendours and a great drag-
gled wig, with a gold-headed cane in his bony hand...diffusing a reek of
whisky-punch, and with a case of instruments under his arm," to perform
the operation. The whole scene is magnificently written, with the surgeon's
muttered technicalities heard through the door, the footsteps—then the
silence while the trepanning is proceeding, and the wounded Sturk's voice,
which no one ever thought to hear again, raised as if from the grave to

denounce his murder. The chapter in itself would entitle Le Fanu to be called a master of mystery and horror.

Most important of all during this period we have Wilkie Collins. An extremely uneven writer, Collins is less appreciated today than his merits and influence deserve.[28] He will not bear comparison with Le Fanu in his treatment of the weird, though he was earnestly ambitious to succeed in this line. His style was too dry and inelastic, his mind too legal. Consider the famous dream in *Armadale,* divided into seventeen separate sections, each elaborately and successively fulfilled in laborious detail! In the curious semi-supernatural rhythm of *The Woman in White* he came nearer to genuine achievement, but, on the whole, his eeriness is wire-drawn and unconvincing. But he greatly excels Le Fanu in humour, in the cunning of his rogues[29] in character-drawing, and especially in the architecture of his plots. Taking everything into consideration, *The Moonstone* is probably the very finest detective story ever written. By comparison with its wide scope, its dove-tailed completeness and the marvellous variety and soundness of its characterisation, modern mystery fiction looks thin and mechanical. Nothing human is perfect, but *The Moonstone* comes about as near perfection as anything of its kind can be.

In *The Moonstone* Collins used the convention of telling the story in a series of narratives from the pens of the various actors concerned. Modern realism—often too closely wedded to externals—is prejudiced against this device. It is true that, for example, Betteredge's narrative is not at all the kind of thing that a butler would be likely to write; nevertheless, it has an ideal truth—it is the kind of thing that Betteredge might think and feel, even if he could not write it. And, granted this convention of the various narratives, how admirably the characters are drawn! The pathetic figure of Rosanna Spearman, with her deformity and her warped devotion, is beautifully handled, with a freedom from sentimentality which is very remarkable. In Rachel Verinder, Collins has achieved one of the novelist's hardest tasks; he has depicted a girl who is virtuous, a gentlewoman, and really interesting, and that without the slightest exaggeration or deviation from naturalness and probability. From his preface to the book it is clear that he took especial pains with this character, and his success was so great as almost to defeat itself. Rachel is so little spectacular that we fail to realise what a singularly fine and truthful piece of work she is.

[28]In the British Museum catalogue only two critical studies of this celebrated English mystery-monger are listed: one is by an American, the other by a German.

[29]Collins made peculiarly his own the art of plot and counter-plot. Thus we have the magnificent duels of Marion Halcombe and Count Fosco in *The Woman in White;* Captain Wragge and Mrs. Lecount in *No Name;* the Pedgifts and Miss Gwilt in *Armadale.* Move answers to move as though on a chessboard (but very much more briskly), until the villain is manoeuvred into the corner where a cunningly contrived legal checkmate has been quietly awaiting him from the beginning of the game.

The detective part of the story is well worth attention. The figure of Sergeant Cuff is drawn with a restraint and sobriety which makes him seem a little colourless beside Holmes and Thorndyke and Carrados, but he is a very living figure. One can believe that he made a success of his rose-growing when he retired; he genuinely loved roses, whereas one can never feel that the great Sherlock possessed quite the right feeling for his bees. Being an official detective, Sergeant Cuff is bound by the etiquette of his calling. He is never really given a free hand with Rachel, and the conclusion he comes to is a wrong one. But he puts in a good piece of detective work in the matter of Rosanna and the stained nightgown; and the scenes in which his shrewdness and knowledge of human nature are contrasted with the blundering stupidity of Superintendent Seagrave read like an essay in the manner of Poe.

It is, of course, a fact that the Dupin stories had been published fifteen years or so when *The Moonstone* appeared. But there is no need to seek in them for the original of Sergeant Cuff. He had his prototype in real life, and the whole nightgown incident was modelled, with some modifications, upon a famous case of the early sixties—the murder of little William Kent by his sixteen-year-old sister, Constance. Those who are interested in origins will find an excellent account of the "Road murder," as it is called, in Miss Tennyson Jesse's *Murder and its Motives,* or in Atkey's *Famous Trials of the Nineteenth Century,* and may compare the methods of Sergeant Cuff with those of the real Detective Whicher.

Wilkie Collins himself claimed that nearly all his plots were founded on fact; indeed, this was his invariable answer when the charge of improbability was preferred against him.

> "I wish," he cries angrily to a friend, "before people make such assertions, they would think what they are writing or talking about. I know of very few instances in which fiction exceeds the probability of reality. I'll tell you where I got many of my plots from. I was in Paris, wandering about the streets with Charles Dickens, amusing ourselves by looking into the shops. We came to an old book stall—half-shop and half-store—and I found some dilapidated volumes and records of French crime—a sort of French Newgate Calendar. I said to Dickens "Here is a prize!" So it turned out to be. In them I found some of my best plots"[30]

Not that Collins was altogether disingenuous in his claim never to have o'erstepped the modesty of nature. While each one of his astonishing contrivances and coincidences might, taken separately, find its parallel in real life, it remains true that in cramming a whole series of such improbabilities into the course of a single story he does frequently end by staggering all belief. But even so, he was a master craftsman, whom many modern mystery-mongers might imitate to their profit. He never wastes an incident; he

[30]Wybert Reeve: "Recollections of Wilkie Collins," *Chambers Journal,* Vol. IX, p. 458.

never leaves a loose end; no incident, however trivial on the one hand or sensational on the other, is ever introduced for the mere sake of amusement or sensation. Take, for example, the great "sensation-scene" in *No Name*, where for half an hour Magdalen sits, with the bottle of laudanum in her hand, counting the passing ships. "If, in that time, an even number passed her—the sign given should be a sign to live. If the uneven number prevailed, the end should be—death." Here, you would say, is pure sensationalism; it is a situation invented deliberately to wring tears and anguish from the heart of the reader. But you would be wrong. That bottle of laudanum is brought in because it will be wanted again, later on. In the next section of the story it is found in Magdalen's dressing-case, and this discovery, by leading her husband to suppose that she means to murder him, finally induces him to cut her out of his will, and so becomes one of the most important factors in the plot.

In *The Moonstone*, which of all his books comes nearest to being a detective-story in the modern sense, Collins uses with great effect the formula of the most unlikely person[31] and the unexpected means in conjunction. Opium is the means in this case—a drug with whose effects we are tolerably familiar to-day, but which in Collins's time was still something of an unknown quantity, de Quincey notwithstanding. In the opium of *The Moonstone* and the plastic surgery of *Checkmate* we have the distinguished forebears of a long succession of medical and scientific mysteries which stretches down to the present day.

During the 'seventies and early 'eighties the long novel of marvel and mystery held the field, slowly unrolling its labyrinthine complexity through its three ample volumes crammed with incident and leisurely drawn characters.[32]

Sherlock Holmes and His Influence

In 1887 *A Study in Scarlet* was flung like a bombshell into the field of detective fiction, to be followed within a few short and brilliant years by the

---

[31]Franklin Blake—the actual, though unconscious thief. By an ingenious turn, this discovery does not end the story. The diamond is still missing, and a further chase leads to the really guilty party (Godfrey Ablewhite). The character of this gentleman is enough to betray his villainy to the modern reader, though it may have seemed less repulsive to the readers in the sixties. His motive, however, is made less obvious, although it is quite honourably and fairly hinted at for the observant reader to guess.

[32]We must not leave this period without mentioning the stories of Anna Katharine Green, of which the long series begins with *The Leavenworth Case* in 1883, and extends right down to the present day. They are genuine detective-stories, often of considerable ingenuity, but marred by an uncritical sentimentality of style and treatment which makes them difficult reading for the modern student. They are, however, important by their volume and by their influence on other American writers. [Anna Green died in 1935. Miss Sayers is in error here; *The Leavenworth Case* was first published in 1898. Editor's note.]

marvellous series of Sherlock Holmes short stories. The effect was electric. Conan Doyle took up the Poe formula and galvanised it into life and popularity. He cut out the elaborate psychological introductions, or re-stated them in crisp dialogue. He brought into prominence what Poe had only lightly touched upon—the deduction of staggering conclusions from trifling indications in the Dumas-Cooper-Gaboriau manner. He was sparkl-ing, surprising, and short. It was the triumph of the epigram.

A comparison of the Sherlock Holmes tales with the Dupin tales shows clearly how much Doyle owed to Poe, and, at the same time, how greatly he modified Poe's style and formula. Read, for instance, the opening pages of "The Murders in the Rue Morgue," which introduce Dupin, and compare them with the first chapter of *A Study in Scarlet.* Or merely set side by side the two passages which follow and contrast the relations between Dupin and his chronicler on the one hand, and between Holmes and Watson on the other:

> I was astonished, too, at the vast extent of his reading; and, above all, I felt my soul enkindled within me by the wild fervour, and the vivid freshness of his imagination. Seeking in Paris the objects I then sought, I felt that the society of such a man would be to me a treasure beyond price; and this feeling I frankly confided to him. It was at length arranged that we should live to-gether...and as my worldly circumstances were somewhat less embarrassed than his own, I was permitted to be at the expense of renting, and furnishing in a style which suited the rather fantastic gloom of our common temper, a time-eaten and grotesque mansion...in a retired and desolate portion of the Faubourg Saint Germain...It was a freak of fancy in my friend (for what else shall I call it?) to be enamoured of the Night for her own sake; and into this *bizarrerie,* as into all his others, I quietly fell, giving myself up to his wild whims with a perfect abandon.[33]
>
> An anomaly which often struck me in the character of my friend Sherlock Holmes was that, though in his methods of thought he was the neatest and most methodical of mankind, and although also he affected a certain quiet primness of dress, he was none the less in his personal habits one of the most untidy men that ever drove a fellow-lodger to distraction. Not that I am in the least conventional in that respect myself. The rough-and-tumble work in Afghanistan, coming on the top of a natural Bohemianism of disposition, has made me rather more lax than befits a medical man. But with me there is a limit, and when I find a man who keeps his cigars in the coal-scuttle, his tobacco in the toe-end of a Persian slipper, and his unanswered correspon-dence transfixed by a jackknife into the very centre of his wooden mantel-piece, then I begin to give myself virtuous airs. I have always held, too, that pistol-practice should distinctly be an open-air pastime; and when Holmes in one of his queer humours would sit in an arm-chair, with his hair-trigger and a hundred Boxer cartridges, and proceed to adorn the opposite wall with a patriotic V.R. done in bullet-pocks, I felt strongly that neither the atmosphere nor the appearence of our room was improved by it.[34]

[33]"The Murders in the Rue Morgue."
[34]"The Musgrave Ritual."

See how the sturdy independence of Watson adds salt and savour to the eccentricities of Holmes, and how flavourless beside it is the hero-worshipping self-abnegation of Dupin's friend. See, too, how the concrete details of daily life in Baker Street lift the story out of the fantastic and give it a solid reality. The Baker Street menage has just that touch of humorous commonplace which appeals to British readers.

Another pair of parallel passages will be found in "The Purloined Letter" and "The Naval Treaty." They show the two detectives in dramatic mood, surprising their friends by their solution of the mystery. In "The Adventure of the Priory School," also, a similar situation occurs, though Holmes is here shown in a grimmer vein, rebuking wickedness in high places.

Compare, also, the conversational styles of Holmes and Dupin, and the reasons for Holmes's popularity become clearer than ever. Holmes has enriched English literature with more than one memorable aphorism and turn of speech.

> "You know my methods, Watson."
> "A long shot, Watson—a very long shot."
> "—a little monograph on the hundred-and-fourteen varieties of tobacco-ash."
> "These are deep waters, Watson."
> "Excellent" cried Mr. Action.—"But very superficial," said Holmes.
> "Excellent" I cried.—"Elementary," said he.
> "It is of the highest importance in the art of detection to be able to recognise out of a number of facts which are incidental and which vital."
> "You mentioned your name as if I should recognise it, but beyond the obvious fact that you are a bachelor, a solicitor, a Freemason and an asthmatic, I know nothing whatever about you."
> "Every problem becomes very childish when once it is explained to you."

Nor must we forget that delightful form of riposto which Father Ronald Knox has wittily christened the "Sherlockismus":

> "I would call your attention to the curious incident of the dog in the night-time."
> "The dog did nothing in the night-time."
> "That was the curious incident."

So, with Sherlock Holmes, the ball—the original nucleus deposited by Edgar Allan Poe nearly forty years earlier—was at last set rolling. As it went, it swelled into a vast mass—it set off others—it became a spate—a torrent—an avalanche of mystery fiction. It is impossible to keep track of all the detective-stories produced to-day. Book upon book, magazine upon magazine pour out from the Press, crammed with murders, thefts, arsons, frauds, conspiracies, problems, puzzles, mysteries, thrills, maniacs, crooks, poisoners, forgers, garrotters, police, spies, secret-service men, detectives, until it seems that half the world must be engaged in setting riddles for the other half to solve.

The Scientific Detective

The boom began in the 'nineties, when the detective short story, till then rather neglected, strode suddenly to the front and made the pace rapidly under the aegis of Sherlock Holmes. Of particular interest is the long series which appeared under various titles from the pens of L. T. Meade and her collaborators. These struck out a line—not new, indeed, for, as we have seen, it is as old as Collins and Le Fanu, but important because it was paving the way for great developments in a scientific age—the medical mystery story. Mrs. L. T. Meade opened up this fruitful vein with *Stories from the Diary of a Doctor* in 1893,[35] and pursued it in various magazines almost without a break to *The Sorceress of the Strand*[36] in 1902. These tales range from mere records of queer cases to genuine detective-stories in which the solution has a scientific or medical foundation. During this long collaboration, the authors deal with such subjects as hypnotism, catalepsy (so-called—then a favourite disease among fiction-writers), somnambulism, lunacy, murder by the use of X-rays and hydrocyanic acid gas, and a variety of other medical and scientific discoveries and inventions.

More definitely in the Holmes tradition is the sound and excellent work of Arthur Morrison in the "Martin Hewitt" books. Various authors such as John Oxenham and Manville Fenn also tried their hands at the detective-story, before turning to specialise in other work. We get also many lively tales of adventure and roguery, with a strong thread of detective interest, as, for example, the "African Millionaire" series by Grant Allen.

Now in the great roar and rush of enthusiasm which greeted Sherlock Holmes, the detective-story became swept away on a single current of development. We observed, in discussing the Poe tales, that there were three types of story—the Intellectual ("Marie Rogêt"), the Sensational ("The Gold Bug"), and the Mixed ("Murders in the Rue Morgue"). "Sherlock Holmes" tales, as a rule, are of the mixed type. Holmes—I regret to say it—does not always play fair with the reader. He "picks up," or "pounces upon," a "minute object," and draws a brilliant deduction from it, but the reader, however brilliant, cannot himself anticipate that deduction because he is not told what the "small object" is. It is Watson's fault, of course—Holmes, indeed, remonstrated with him on at least one occasion about his unscientific methods of narration.

An outstanding master of this "surprise" method is Melville Davisson Post. His tales are so admirably written, and his ideas so ingenious, that we fail at first reading to realise how strictly sensational they are in their method. Take, for instance, "An Act of God" from *Uncle Abner* (1911). In

---

[35]In collaboration with "Clifford Halifax."

[36]In collaboration with Robert Eustace. In these stories the scientific basis was provided by Robert Eustace, and the actual writing done, for the most part, by L. T. Meade.

this tale, Uncle Abner uses the phonetic mis-spelling in a letter supposed to be written by a deaf mute to prove that the letter was not, in fact, written by him. If the text of the letter were placed before the reader, and he were given a chance to make his deduction for himself, the tale would be a true detective-story of the Intellectual type; but the writer keeps this clue to himself, and springs the detective's conclusions upon us like a bolt from the blue.

The Modern "Fair-Play" Method

For many years, the newness of the genre and the immense prestige of Holmes blinded readers' eyes to these feats of legerdemain. Gradually, however, as the bedazzlement wore off, the public became more and more exacting. The uncritical are still catered for by the "thriller," in which nothing is explained, but connoisseurs have come, more and more, to call for a story which puts them on an equal footing with the detective himself, as regards all clues and discoveries.[37]

Seeing that the demand for equal opportunities is coupled today with an insistence on strict technical accuracy in the smallest details of the story, it is obvious that the job of writing detective-stories is by no means growing easier. The reader must be given every clue—but he must not be told, surely, all the detective's deductions, lest he should see the solution too far ahead. Worse still, supposing, even without the detective's help, he interprets all the clues accurately on his own account, what becomes of the surprise? How can we at the same time show the reader everything and yet legitimately obfuscate him as to its meaning?

Various devices are used to get over the difficulty. Frequently the detective, while apparently displaying his clues openly, will keep up his sleeve some bit of special knowledge which the reader does not possess. Thus, Thorndyke can cheerfully show you all his finds. You will be none the wiser, unless you happen to have an intimate acquaintance with the fauna of local ponds; the effect of belladonna on rabbits; the physical and chemical properties of blood; optics; tropical diseases; metallurgy; hieroglyphics, and a few other trifles. Another method of misleading is to tell the reader what the detective has observed and deduced—but to make the observations and deductions turn out to be incorrect, thus leading up to a carefully manufactured surprise-packet in the last chapter.[38]

[37]Yet even to-day the naughty tradition persists. In *The Crime at Diana's Pool*, for instance (1927), V. L. Whitechurch sins notably, twice over, in this respect, in the course of an otherwise excellent tale. But such crimes bring their own punishment, for the modern reader is quick to detect and resent unfairness, and a stern, though kindly letter of rebuke is presently despatched to the erring author.

[38]E. C. Bentley: *Trent's Last Case;* Lord Gorell: *In the Night;* George Pleydell: *The Ware Case;* etc.

Some writers, like Mrs. Agatha Christie, still cling to the Watson formula. The story is told through the mouth, or at least through the eyes, of a Watson.[39] Others, like A. A. Milne in his *Red House Mystery,* adopt a mixed method. Mr. Milne begins by telling his tale from the position of a detached spectator; later on, we find that he has shifted round, and is telling it through the personality of Bill Beverley (a simple-minded but not unintelligent Watson); at another moment we find ourselves actually looking out through the eyes of Anthony Gillingham, the detective himself.

Importance of the Viewpoint

The skill of a modern detective novelist is largely shown by the play he makes with these various viewpoints.[40] Let us see how it is done in an acknowledged masterpiece of the genre. We will examine for the purpose a page of Mr. E. C. Bentley's *Trent's Last Case.* Viewpoint No. 1 is what we may call the Watson viewpoint; the detective's external actions only are seen by the reader. Viewpoint No. 2 is the middle viewpoint; we see what the detective sees, but are not told what he observes. Viewpoint No. 3 is that of close intimacy with the detective; we see all he sees, and are at once told his conclusions.

WE BEGIN FROM VIEWPOINT NO. 2.

Two bedroom doors faced him on the other side of the passage. He opened that which was immediately opposite, and entered a bedroom by no means austerely tidy. Some sticks and fishing-rods stood confusedly in one corner, a pile of books in another. The housemaid's hand had failed to give a look of order to the jumble of heterogeneous objects left on the dressing-table and on the mantel-shelf — pipes, penknives, pencils, keys, golf-balls, old letters, photographs, small boxes, tins, and bottles. Two fine etchings and some water-colour sketches hung on the walls; leaning against the end of the wardrobe, unhung, were a few framed engravings.

FIRST SHIFT: VIEWPOINT NO. 1.

A row of shoes and boots were ranged beneath the window. Trent crossed the room and studied them intently; then he measured some of them with his

[39]An exceptional handling of the Watson theme is found in Agatha Christie's *Murder of Roger Ackroyd,* which is a *tour de force.* Some critics, as, for instance, Mr. W. H. Wright in his introduction to *The Great Detective Stories* (Scribner's, 1927), consider the solution illegitimate. I fancy, however, that this opinion merely represents a natural resentment at having been ingeniously bamboozled. All the necessary data are given. The reader ought to be able to guess the criminal, if he is sharp enough, and nobody can ask for more than this. It is, after all, the reader's job to keep his wits about him, and, like the perfect detective, to suspect *everybody.*

[40]For a most fascinating and illuminating discussion of this question of viewpoint in fiction, see Mr. Percy Lubbock: *The Craft of Fiction.*

tape, whistling very softly. This done, he sat on the side of the bed, and his eyes roamed gloomily about the room.

Here we observe Trent walking, studying, measuring, whistling, looking gloomy; but we do not know what was peculiar about the boots, nor what the measurements were. From our knowledge of Trent's character we may suppose that his conclusions are unfavourable to the amiable suspect, Marlowe, but we are not ourselves allowed to handle the material evidence.

SECOND SHIFT: BACK TO VIEWPOINT NO. 2.

The photographs on the mantel-shelf attracted him presently. He rose and examined one representing Marlowe and Manderson on horseback. Two others were views of famous peaks in the Alps. There was a faded print of three youths — one of them unmistakably his acquaintance of the haggard blue eyes [i.e. Marlowe] — clothed in tatterdemalion soldier's gear of the sixteenth century. Another was a portrait of a majestic old lady, slightly resembling Marlowe. Trent, mechanically taking a cigarette from an open box on the mantel-shelf, lit it and stared at the photographs.

Here, as at the opening of the paragraph, we are promoted to a more privileged position. We see all the evidence, and have an equal opportunity with Trent of singling out the significant detail — the fancy-costume portrait — and deducting from it that Marlowe was an active member of the O.U.D.S.,[41] and, by inference, capable of acting a part at a pinch.

THIRD SHIFT: VIEWPOINT NO. 3

Next he turned his attention to a flat leathern case that lay by the cigarette-box. It opened easily. A small and light revolver, of beautiful workmanship, was disclosed, with a score or so of loose cartridges. On the stock were engraved the initials "J. M." ...

With the pistol in its case between them, Trent and the Inspector looked into each other's eyes for some moments. Trent was the first to speak. "This mystery is all wrong," he observed. "It is insanity. The symptoms of mania are very marked. Let us see how we stand."

Throughout the rest of this scene we are taken into Trent's confidence. The revolver is described, we learn what Trent thinks about it from his own lips.

Thus, in a single page, the viewpoint is completely shifted three times, but so delicately that, unless we are looking for it, we do not notice the change.

In a later chapter, we get the final shift to a fourth viewpoint — that of complete mental identification with the detective:

[41][Oxford Union Dramatic Society.]

Mrs. Manderson had talked herself into a more emotional mood than she had yet shown to Trent. Her words flowed freely, and her voice had begun to ring and give play to a natural expressiveness that must hitherto have been dulled, he thought, by the shock and self-restraint of the past few days.

Here the words "had yet shown to Trent" clinch the identification of viewpoint. Throughout the book, we always, in fact, see Mrs. Manderson through Trent's emotions, and the whole second half of the story, when Trent has abandoned his own enquiries and is receiving the true explanation from Marlowe and Cupples, is told from Viewpoint No. 4.

The modern evolution in the direction of "fair play"[42] is to a great extent a revolution. It is a recoil from the Holmes influence and a turning back to *The Moonstone* and its contemporaries. There is no mystification about *The Moonstone*—no mystification of the reader, that is. With such scrupulous care has Collins laid the clues that the "ideal reasoner" might guess the entire outline of the story at the end of the first ten chapters of Betteredge's first narrative.[43]

Artistic Status of the Detective-Story

As the detective ceases to be impenetrable and infallible and becomes a man touched with the feeling of our infirmities, so the rigid technique of the art necessarily expands a little. In its severest form, the mystery-story is a pure analytical exercise, and, as such, may be a highly finished work of art, within its highly artificial limits. There is one respect, at least, in which the detective-story has an advantage over every other kind of novel. It possesses an Aristotelian perfection of beginning, middle, and end. A definite and single problem is set, worked out, and solved; its conclusion is

[42]It is needless to add that the detectives must be given fair play, too. Once they are embarked upon an investigation, no episode must ever be described which does not come within their cognisance. It is artistically shocking that the reader should be taken into the author's confidence behind the investigator's back. Thus, the reader's interest in *The Deductions of Colonel Gore* (Lynn Brock) is sensibly diminished by the fact of his knowing (as Gore does not) that it was Cecil Arndale who witnessed the scene between Mrs. Melhuish and Barrington near the beginning of the book. Those tales in which the action is frequently punctuated by eavesdropping of this kind on the reader's part belong to the merely Sensational class of detective-story, and rapidly decline into melodrama.

[43]Poe performed a similar feat in the case of *Barnaby Rudge*, of which he correctly prognosticated the whole development after reading the first serial part. Unhappily, he was not alive to perform the same office for *Edwin Drood!* Dickens came more and more to hanker after plot and mystery. His early efforts in this style are crude, and the mystery as a rule pretty transparent. In *Edwin Drood* he hoped that the "story would turn upon an interest suspended until the end," and the hope was only too thoroughly fulfilled. Undoubtedly his close friendship with Collins helped to influence him in the direction of mystery fiction; in the previous year (1867) he had pronounced *The Moonstone:* "Much better than anything he [Collins] has done."

not arbitrarily conditioned by marriage or death.[44] It has the rounded (though limited) perfection of a triolet. The farther it escapes from pure analysis, the more difficulty it has in achieving artistic unity.

It does not, and by hypothesis never can, attain the loftiest level of literary achievement. Though it deals with the most desperate effects of rage, jealousy, and revenge, it rarely touches the heights and depths of human passion. It presents us only with the *fait accompli,* and looks upon death and mutilation with a dispassionate eye. It does not show us the inner workings of the murderer's mind—it must not; for the identity of the murderer is hidden until the end of the book.[45] The victim is shown rather as a subject for the dissecting-table than as a husband and father. A too violent emotion flung into the glittering mechanism of the detective-story jars the movement by disturbing its delicate balance. The most successful writers are those who contrive to keep the story running from beginning to end upon the same emotional level, and it is better to err in the direction of too little feeling than too much. Here, the writer whose detective is a member of the official force has an advantage: from him a detached attitude is correct; he can suitably retain the impersonal attitude of the surgeon. The sprightly amateur must not be sprightly all the time, lest at some point we should be reminded that this is, after all, a question of somebody's being foully murdered, and that flippancy is indecent. To make the transition from the detached to the human point of view is one of the writer's hardest tasks. It is especially hard when the murderer has been made human and sympathetic. A real person has then to be brought to the gallows, and this must not be done too lightheartedly. Mr. G. K. Chesterton deals with this problem by merely refusing to face it. His Father Brown (who looks at sin and crime from the religious point of view) retires from the problem before the arrest is reached. He is satisfied with a confession. The sordid details take place "off." Other authors permit sympathetic villains to commit suicide. Thus, Mr. Milne's Gillingham, whose attitude starts by being flippant and ends by being rather sentimental, warns Cayley of his approaching arrest, and Cayley shoots himself, leaving a written confession. Monsters of villainy can, of course, be brought to a bad end without compunction; but modern

[44]This should appeal to Mr. E. M. Forster, who is troubled by the irrational structure of the novel from this point of view. Unhappily, he has openly avowed himself "too priggish" to enjoy detective stories. This is bad luck, indeed.

[45]An almost unique example of the detective-story told from the point of view of the hunted instead of the hunter is *Ashes to Ashes* by Isabel Ostrander. This shows the clues being left by the murderer, who is then compelled to look on while they are picked up, one after the other, by the detectives, despite all his desperate efforts to cover them. It is a very excellent piece of work which, in the hands of a writer of a little more distinction, might have been a powerful masterpiece. Isabel Ostrander, who also wrote under the name of Robert Orr Chipperfield and other pseudonyms, was a particularly competent spinner of yarns. Her straight-forward police-detective, McCarty, is always confounding the conclusions of Terhune—a "scientific" private detective, who believes in modern psycho-analytical detective apparatus.

taste rejects monsters, therefore the modern detective-story is compelled to achieve a higher level of writing, and a more competent delineation of character. As the villain is allowed more good streaks in his composition, so the detective must achieve a tenderer human feeling beneath his frivolity or machine-like efficiency.

Love Interest

One fettering convention, from which detective fiction is only very slowly freeing itself, is that of the "love interest." Publishers and editors still labour unless the delusion that all stories must have a nice young man and woman who have to be united in the last chapter. As a result, some of the finest detective stories are marred by a conventional love-story, irrelevant to the action and perfunctorily worked in. The most harmless form of this disease is that taken, for example, in the works of Mr. Austin Freeman. His secondary characters fall in love with distressing regularity, and perform a number of conventional antics suitable to persons in their condition, but they do not interfere with the course of the story. You can skip the love-passages if you like, and nothing is lost. Far more blameworthy are the heroes who insist on fooling about after young women when they ought to be putting their minds on the job of detection. Just at the critical moment when the trap is set to catch the villain, the sleuth learns that his best girl has been spirited away. Heedlessly he drops everything, and rushes off to Chinatown or to the lonely house on the marshes or wherever it is, without even leaving a note to say where he is going. Here he is promptly sand-bagged or entrapped or otherwise made a fool of, and the whole story is impeded and its logical development ruined.

The instances in which the love-story is an integral part of the plot are extremely rare.[46] One very beautiful example occurs in *The Moonstone.* Here the entire plot hangs on the love of two women for Franklin Blake. Both Rachel Verinder and Rosanna Spearman know that he took the diamond, and the whole mystery arises from their efforts to shield him. Their conduct is, in both cases, completely natural and right, and the characters are so finely conceived as to be entirely convincing. E. C. Bentley, in *Trent's Last Case,* has dealt finely with the still harder problem of the detective in love. Trent's love for Mrs. Manderson is a legitimate part of the plot; while it does not prevent him from drawing the proper conclusion from the evidence before him, it does prevent him from acting upon his conclusions, and

---

[46][Here again Miss Sayers is predicting her own story line, since many critics consider her books, *Strong Poison* (1930), *Gaudy Night* (1935), and *Busman's Honeymoon* (1937), to be distinguished love stories as well as mysteries. Editor's note.]

so prepares the way for the real explanation. Incidentally, the love-story is handled artistically and with persuasive emotion.

In *The House of the Arrow* and, still more strikingly, in *No Other Tiger*, A. E. W. Mason has written stories of strong detective interest which at the same time have the convincing psychological structure of the novel of character. The characters are presented as a novelist presents them — romantically, it is true, but without that stark insistence on classifying and explaining which turns the persons of the ordinary detective-story into a collection of museum exhibits.

Apart from such unusual instances as these, the less love in a detective-story, the better. *"L'amour au théâtre,"* says Racine, *"ne peut pas être en seconde place,"* and this holds good of detective fiction. A casual and perfunctory love-story is worse than no love-story at all, and, since the mystery must, by hypothesis, take the first place, the love is better left out.

Lynn Brock's *The Deductions of Colonel Gore* affords a curious illustration of this truth. Gore sets out, animated by an unselfish devotion to a woman, to recover some compromising letters for her, and, in so doing, becomes involved in unravelling an intricate murder plot. As the story goes on, the references to the beloved woman become chillier and more perfunctory; not only does the author seem to have lost interest, but so does Colonel Gore. At length the author notices this, and explains it in a paragraph:

> There were moments when Gore accused himself — or, rather, felt that he ought to accuse himself — of an undue coldbloodedness in these speculations of his. The business was a horrible business. One ought to have been decently shocked by it. One ought to have been horrified by the thought that three old friends were involved in such a business.
>
> But the truth was — and his apologies to himself for that truth became feebler and feebler — that the thing had now so caught hold of him that he had come to regard the actors in it as merely pieces of a puzzle baffling and engrossing to the verge of monomania.

There is the whole difficulty about allowing real human beings into a detective-story. At some point or other, either their emotions make hay of the detective interest, or the detective interest gets hold of them and makes their emotions look like pasteboard. It is, of course, a fact that we all adopt a detached attitude towards "a good murder" in the newspaper. Like Betteredge in *The Moonstone*, we get "detective fever," and forget the victim in the fun of tracking the criminal. For this reason, it is better not to pitch the emotional key too high at the start; the inevitable drop is thus made less jarring.

Future Developments: Fashion and Formula

Just at present, therefore, the fashion in detective fiction is to have characters credible and lively; not conventional, but, on the other'hand, not too profoundly studied—people who live more or less on the *Punch* level of emotion. A little more psychological complexity is allowed than formerly; the villain may not be a villain from every point of view; the heroine, if there is one, is not necessarily pure; the falsely accused innocent need not be a sympathetic character.[47] The automata—the embodied vices and virtues—the weeping fair-haired girl—the stupid but manly young man with the biceps—even the colossally evil scientist with the hypnotic eyes—are all disappearing from the intellectual branch of the art, to be replaced by figures having more in common with humanity.

An interesting symptom of this tendency is the arrival of a number of books and stories which recast, under the guise of fiction, actual murder cases drawn from real life. Thus, Mrs. Belloc Lowndes and Mrs. Victor Rickard have both dealt with the Bravo Poisoning Mystery. Anthony Berkeley has retold the Maybrick case; Mr. E. H. W. Meyerstein has published a play based on the Seddon poisoning case, and Mr. Aldous Huxley, in "The Gioconda Smile," has reinterpreted in his own manner another famous case of recent years.[48]

We are now in a position to ask ourselves the favourite question of modern times: What next? Where is the detective-story going? Has it a future? Or will the present boom see the end of it?

The Most Unlikely Person

In early mystery fiction, the problem tends to be, *who* did the crime? At first, while readers were still unsophisticated, the formula of the Most Unlikely Person had a good run. But the reader soon learned to see through this. If there was a single person in the story who appeared to have no motive for the crime and who was allowed to amble through to the penultimate chapter free from any shadow of suspicion, that character became a marked man or woman. "I knew he must be guilty because nothing was said about him," said the cunning reader. Thus we come to a new axiom, laid down by Mr. G. K. Chesterton in a brilliant essay in the *New Statesman:* the

---

[47]e.g. in J. J. Connington's *The Tragedy at Ravensthorpe*, where the agoraphobic Maurice is by no means an agreeable person to have about the house.

[48]*What Really Happened*, by Mrs. Belloc Lowndes; *Not Sufficient Evidence*, by Mrs. Victor Rickard; *The Wychford Poisoning Drama*, by the Author of *The Layton Court Mystery; Heddon*, by E. H. W. Meyerstein; *Mortal Coils*, by Aldous Huxley.

real criminal must be suspected at least once in the course of the story. Once he is suspected, and then (apparently) cleared, he is made safe from future suspicion. This is the principle behind Mr. Wills Crofts' impregnable alibis, which are eventually broken down by painstaking enquiry. Probably the most baffling form of detective-story is still that in which suspicion is distributed equally among a number of candidates, one of whom turns out to be guilty. Other developments of the Most Unlikely Person formula make the guilty person a juror at the inquest or trial; the detective himself; the counsel for the prosecution; and, as a supreme effort of unlikeliness, the actual narrator of the story. Finally, resort has been made to the double-cross, and the person originally suspected turns out to be the right person after all.

The Unexpected Means

There are signs, however, that the possibilities of the formula are becoming exhausted, and of late years much has been done in exploring the solution by the unexpected means. With recent discoveries in medical and chemical science, this field has become exceedingly fruitful, particularly in the provision of new methods of murder. It is fortunate for the mystery-monger that, whereas, up to the present, there is only one known way of getting born, there are endless ways of getting killed. Here is a brief selection of handy short cuts to the grave: Poisoned tooth-stoppings; licking poisoned stamps; shaving-brushes inoculated with dread diseases; poisoned boiled eggs (a bright thought); poison-gas; a cat with poisoned claws; poisoned mattresses; knives dropped through the ceiling; stabbing with a sharp icicle; electrocution by telephone; biting by plague-rats and typhoid-carrying lice; boiling lead in the ears (much more effective than cursed hebanon in a vial): air-bubbles injected into the arteries; explosion of a gigantic "Prince Rupert's drop"; frightening to death; hanging head-downwards; freezing to atoms in liquid air; hypodermic injections shot from air-guns; exposure, while insensible, to extreme cold; guns concealed in cameras; a thermometer which explodes a bomb when the temperature of the room reaches a certain height; and so forth.

The methods of disposing of inconvenient corpses are also varied and peculiar; burial under a false certificate obtained in a number of ways; substitution of one corpse for another (very common in fiction, though rare in real life); mummification; reduction to bone-dust; electro-plating; arson; "planting" (not in the church-yard, but on innocent parties)—a method first made famous by R. L. Stevenson.[49] Thus, of the three ques-

[49]*The Wrong Box.*

tions, "Who?" "How?" and "Why?" "How" is at present the one which offers most scope for surprise and ingenuity, and is capable of sustaining an entire book on its own, though a combination of all three naturally provides the best entertainment.[50]

The mystery-monger's principal difficulty is that of varying his surprises. "You know my methods, Watson," says the detective, and it is only too painfully true. The beauty of Watson was, of course, that after thirty years he still did not know Holmes's methods; but the average reader is sharper-witted. After reading half a dozen stories by one author, he is sufficiently advanced in Dupin's psychological method[51] to see with the author's eyes. He knows that, when Mr. Austin Freeman drowns somebody in a pond full of water-snails, there will be something odd and localised about those snails; he knows that, when one of Mr. Wills Crofts's characters has a cast-iron alibi, the alibi will turn out to have holes in it; he knows that if Father Knox casts suspicion on a Papist, the Papist will turn out to be innocent; instead of detecting the murderer, he is engaged in detecting the writer. That is why he gets the impression that the writer's later books are seldom or never "up to" his earlier efforts. He has become married to the writer's muse, and marriage has destroyed the mystery.

There certainly does seem a possibility that the detective-story will some time come to an end, simply because the public will have learnt all the tricks. But it has probably many years to go yet, and in the meantime a new and less rigid formula will probably have developed, linking it more closely to the novel of manners and separating it more widely from the novel of adventure. The latter will, no doubt, last as long as humanity, and while crime exists, the crime thriller will hold its place. It is, as always, the higher type that is threatened with extinction.

At the time of writing (1928) the detective-story is profiting by a reaction against novels of the static type. Mr. E. M. Forster is indeed left murmuring regretfully, "Yes, ah! yes—the novel tells a story"; but the majority of the public are rediscovering that fact with cries of triumph. Sexual abnormalities are suffering a slight slump at the moment; the novel of passion still holds the first place, especially among women, but even women seem to be growing out of the simple love-story. Probably the cheerful cynicism of the detective-tale suits better with the spirit of the times than the sentimentality which ends in wedding bells. For, make no mistake about it, the detective-story is part of the literature of escape, and not of expression. We read tales of domestic unhappiness because that is the kind of thing which hap-

---

[50] Mr. Austin Freeman has specialised in a detective-story which rejects all three questions. He tells the story of the crime first, and relies for his interest on the pleasure afforded by following the ingenious methods of the investigator. *The Singing Bone* contains several tales of this type. Mr. Freeman has had few followers, and appears to have himself abandoned the formula, which is rather a pity.

[51] As outlined in "The Purloined Letter."

pens to us; but when these things gall too close to the sore, we fly to mystery and adventure because they do not, as a rule, happen to us. "The detective-story," says Philip Guedalla, "is the normal recreation of noble minds." And it is remarkable how strong is the fascination of the higher type of detective-story for the intellectually-minded, among writers as well as readers. The average detective-novel to-day is extremely well written, and there are few good living writers who have not tried their hand at it at one time or another.[52]

[52]Among men of letters distinguished in other lines who have turned their attention to the detective-story may be mentioned A. E. W. Mason, Eden Phillpotts, "Lynn Brock" (whose pseudonym protects the personality of a well-known writer)/[not very well, actually; this was Alister McAllister, not in fact so distinguished], Somerset Maugham, Rudyard Kipling, A. A. Milne, Father R. Knox, J. D. Beresford.

It is owing to the work of such men as these that the detective-novel reaches a much higher artistic level in England than in any other country. At every turn the quality of the writing and the attention to beauty of form and structure betray the hand of the practised novelist.

Miss Sayer's original essay included a section on "Tales of Mystery and Horror," omitted here. On the matter of "sensational novels," see an especially useful short study by P. D. Edwards, *Some Mid-Victorian Thrillers: The Sensation Novel, Its Friends and Foes* (Brisbane, Australia: University of Queensland Press, 1971). Editor's note.]

The Formal Detective Novel

by George Grella

The formal detective novel, the so called "pure puzzle" or "whodunit," is the most firmly established and easily recognized version of the thriller. Sharing sources with the novel proper, boasting a tradition dating from Poe, and listing among its practitioners a number of distinguished men of letters, the detective novel has enjoyed a long, though slightly illicit, relationship with serious literature. As with literary study, historians and bibliographers of the form, discovering incunabula, repudiating apocrypha, and tracing sources and lineage, have published their findings in a multitude of books and essays, in somewhat learned journals and para-scholarly periodicals. And almost since its inception, critics have been denouncing the rise and announcing the demise of the whodunit. But the detective novel has survived the vicissitudes of literary taste and the sometimes suffocating paraphernalia of scholarship; though it attained its greatest heights of production and consumption in the 1920's and 1930's —the so called Golden Age of the detective story—the best examples of the type retain a remarkable longevity. The whodunit, in fact, has become a kind of classic in the field of popular fiction.

One commentator has rather loosely defined the detective story as "a tale in which the primary interest lies in the methodical discovery, by rational means, of the exact circumstances of a mysterious event or series of events,"[1] which could describe a number of literary works, including *Oedipus Rex, Hamlet, Tom Jones,* and *Absalom, Absalom!.* In reality the form, in Raymond Chandler's words, has "learned nothing and forgotten nothing."[2] It subscribes to a rigidly uniform, virtually changeless combination of characters, setting, and events familiar to every reader in the English speaking world. The typical detective story presents a group of people assembled at an isolated place—usually an English country house—

George Grella, "Murder and Manners: The Formal Detective Novel." From Larry N. Landrum, Pat Browne, and Ray B. Browne, eds., *Dimensions of Detective Fiction* (Bowling Green, Ohio) : Popular Press, 1976), pp. 37-57. Reprinted by permission of the author, and of *Novel: A Forum on Fiction*, the journal in which the essay originally appeared.

[1]A. E. Murch, *The Development of the Detective Novel* (London, 1958), p. 11.

[2]"The Simple Art of Murder," *The Art of the Mystery Story*, ed. Howard Haycraft (New York, 1947), p. 230.

who discover that one of their number has been murdered. They summon the local constabulary, who are completely baffled; they find either no clues or entirely too many, everyone or no one has had the means, motive, and opportunity to commit the crime, and nobody seems to be telling the truth. To the rescue comes an eccentric, intelligent, unofficial investigator who reviews the evidence, questions the suspects, constructs a fabric of proof, and in a dramatic final scene, names the culprit. This sequence describes almost every formal detective novel, the best as well as the worst; whatever the variations, the form remains, as Chandler says,

> ...Fundamentally...the same careful grouping of suspects, the same utterly incomprehensible trick of how somebody stabbed Mrs. Pottington Postlethwaite III with the solid platinum poniard just as she flatted on the top note of the "Bell Song" from *Lakme* in the presence of fifteen ill-assorted guests; the same ingénue in fur-trimmed pajamas screaming in the night to make the company pop in and out of doors and ball up the timetable; the same moody silence the next day as they sit around sipping Singapore slings and sneering at each other, while the flatfeet crawl to and fro under the Persian rugs, with their derby hats on.[3]

It is one of the curiosities of literature that an endlessly reduplicated form, employing sterile formulas, stock characters, and innumerable clichés of method and construction, should prosper in the two decades between the World Wars and continue to amuse even in the present day. More curious still, this unoriginal and predictable kind of entertainment appealed to a wide and varied audience, attracting not only the usual public for popular fiction but also a number of educated readers. ... This dual appeal raises an obvious question: why should both ordinary and sophisticated readers enjoy a hackneyed and formula-ridden fiction devoid of sensation or titillation, and frequently without significant literary distinction?

Most readers and writers of detective fiction claim that the central puzzle provides the form's chief appeal. Every reasoning man, they say, enjoys matching his intellect against the detective's, and will quite happily suspend his disbelief in order to play the game of wits. Accordingly, detective novelists have drawn up regulations for their craft forbidding unsportsmanlike conduct of any kind; all relevant facts must be revealed to the reader and, though misdirection is allowed, fair play must be observed at all times. Adherents of the puzzle theory assume that the average reader conscientiously catalogues the alibis, checks the timetables, sifts through the clues, and concludes with the detective that only one person could have caught the 4:17 from Stoke Pogis in time to put the cyanide in the crumpets, maladjust the hands of the grandfather clock, incriminate the nice young gentleman who quite innocently left a 12EEE footprint in the rose garden, and

[3]*Ibid.* [Gore Vidal has satirized this formula particularly well in the three novels he wrote as Edgar Box, Editor's note.]

arrive home just in time for high tea. That person is the murderer, no matter how guiltless he may have seemed.

In fact, though many readers discover the murderer—usually that old standby, the Least Likely Person—they do so by guesswork or intuition rather than by following the detective's frequently improbable methods. Because the reader seldom possesses the detective's exotic knowledge and superior reason, the important clues often mean little to him. Since he doesn't know the killing distance of a South American blowgun, the rate at which curare is absorbed into the bloodstream, or the effects of an English summer on the process of *rigor mortis,* he cannot duplicate the sleuth's conclusions.

The writers of the Ellery Queen stories (Frederick Dannay and Manfred B. Lee) so firmly accepted the puzzle theory that at one time they inserted near the end of their books a "challenge to the reader," who now possessed all the information necessary to solve the case himself. Since the Queen novels presented some of the most abstruse problems in detective fiction, few readers, if any, rose to the challenge. (The writers have not used the device for more than twenty years.) In *The Chinese Orange Mystery,* for example, one must figure out why a murderer would turn his victim's clothes back-to-front and how a room could be locked from the outside by a complicated arrangement of weights, strings, and thumbtacks. Similarly, few would arrive at Hercule Poirot's dazzling conclusion, in Agatha Christie's *Murder in the Calais Coach,* that since no single person on a train could have committed a murder, all the passengers must have done it together. "Only a halfwit could guess it," commented Raymond Chandler. The fanciful methods and incredible ingenuity of most fictional murderers elude everyone but the detective. Only he is granted the power to arrive at the correct deduction from the most tenuous or ambiguous evidence; thus, the box of spilled pins in John Dickson Carr's *Till Death Do Us Part* immediately suggests to Gideon Fell yet another method of re-locking a room, while to the reader it suggests nothing at all extraordinary. Fell solves another difficult case in *Death Turns the Tables* because he happens to know that Canadian taxidermists stuff mooseheads with red sand, a fact unlikely to be known by the reader and equally unlikely to be thought important.

The puzzle theory demands some credence, if only because so many readers and writers espouse it. It seems clear, however, that although the puzzle is central to the detective novel, it does not in fact provide the chief source of appeal; the reader generally cannot solve it by the detective's means, and thus derives his chief pleasure not from duplicating but from observing the mastermind's work. The novels do not so much challenge human ingenuity as display it to its furthest limits. The reader does not share the detective's ability, rather he marvels at it.

Other, more subtle, readers of detective fiction reject the puzzle theory for a psychological and literary explanation. Edmund Wilson argues that in the 1920's and 1930's the world was "ridden by an all-pervasive feeling of guilt and by a fear of impending disaster,"[4] which led to the production and enjoyment of detective fiction: everyone sought release from anxiety in the identification of the scapegoat-criminal, who "is not, after all, a person like you and me." W. H. Auden carries Wilson's thesis a step further, suggesting a literary basis for the whodunit's chief appeal. In his penetrating essay, "The Guilty Vicarage," Auden finds a timelessness in the detective story, derived from its resemblance to Greek tragedy. Its interest, he claims, lies "in the dialectic of innocence and guilt." He identifies as "demonic pride" the murderer's belief that his own intelligence will permit him to elude the punishment of a just universe. Since the murderer's action has implicated a whole society, the detective's task is to locate and expel the particular cause of a general guilt. The expulsion has a cathartic effect, liberating the reader's own latent *hubris* and guilty desires. Auden concludes that "the typical reader of detective stories is, like myself, a person who suffers from a sense of sin."

Both critics, though persuasive, fail to account for the peculiar elements of the detective novel. Wilson does not consider the fact that though the whodunits of the Golden Age remain popular, they no longer dominate light fiction, or that very few classic detective novels are currently written. In the present era, haunted by memories of global conflict and menaced by the spectre of nuclear holocaust, man may well labor under the greatest burden of guilt and anxiety since the Fall; logically, the detective novel should now be enjoying unprecedented popularity, but this is not the case. Wilson carelessly identifies the typical villain of the novels as a criminal ("known to the trade as George Gruesome"). Even a casual reader of detective fiction will recognize Wilson's error: the typical villain is not a criminal but an ordinary and superficially acceptable citizen, "a person like you and me," which, in Wilson's terms, would imply condemnation rather than exculpation of the society. Wilson also fails to account for the peculiar nonviolence of the form. It is not, as he implies, a manhunt, but rather an exploration of a posh and stylized milieu; further, the final accusation is less an attempt to fix guilt than a means of expelling a social offender.

Perhaps because he is a confessed "addict" of detective fiction, Auden comes closer to the truth in recognizing the relevance of the novel's society, but errs in identifying its structure and significance as tragic. Since the reader never learns the murderer's identity until he is revealed, and since the criminal's method is described through an intellectual reconstruction, there is no opportunity to identify with him or sympathize with whatever

---

[4]"Why Do People Read Detective Stories?" *The New Yorker* (October 14, 1944), p. 76.

hubris, fear, remorse, or guilt he may suffer. Though the detective novel deals in the materials of human disaster, it steadfastly avoids presenting them in emotional terms, and thus prevents the characteristically emotional engagement of tragedy. It presents no violent disruptions of the social fabric, no sense of universal culpability, but rather a calm and virtually unruffled world, where everything turns out, after all, for the best. With the intellectualization of potentially sensational matters, without any direct involvement, knowledge of the murderer's character, or sense of doom, the reader neither experiences complicity nor requires catharsis. A closer examination of the nature of the detective novel reveals something far different from the conclusions of Wilson and Auden.

As Auden implies, the detective novel's true appeal is literary. Neither a picture of actual crime, a pure game of wits, nor a popular but degenerate version of tragedy, it is a comedy. More specifically, it remains one of the last outposts of the comedy of manners in fiction. Once the comic nature of the detective story is revealed, then all of its most important characteristics betray a comic function. The central puzzle provides the usual complication, which the detective hero must remove; and its difficulty insures a typically comic engagement of the intellect. The whodunit's plot, full of deceptions, red herrings, clues real and fabricated, parallels the usually intricate plots of comedy, which often depend upon mistaken motives, confusion, and dissembling; it also supports the familiar romantic subplot. And the upper class setting of the detective story places it even more precisely in the tradition of the comedy of manners. Like the fiction of Jane Austen, George Meredith, and Henry James, the detective novel presents the necessary "stable and numerous society...in which the moral code can in some way be externalized in the more or less predictable details of daily life."[5] The *haut monde* of the whodunit provides not only the accepted subject of the comedy of manners, but also furnishes the perfect place for the observable variations of human behavior to be translated into the significant clues of criminal investigation. The detective thriller maintains the necessary equivalence between the social and the moral code: a minute flaw in breeding, taste, or behavior—the wrong tie, the wrong accent, "bad form" of any sort—translates as a violation of an accepted ethical system and provides grounds for expulsion or condemnation. Because of this system the unofficial investigator succeeds where the police fail. They are ordinary, bourgeois citizens who intrude into a closed, aristocratic society; unable to comprehend the complex and delicate social code, they are invariably stymied. The amateur detective, conversely, always is socially acceptable and comprehends the code of the society he investigates—he can question with

[5]John Williams, "The 'Western': Definition of a Myth," *The Popular Arts,* ed. Irving and Harriet A. Deer (New York, 1967), p. 202. [By far the most important book on this subject is John G. Cawelti, *Six-Gun Mystique* (Bowling Green, Ohio: Bowling Green University Popular Press, 1971. Editor's note.]

delicacy, notice "bad form," or understand lying like a gentleman to the police; therefore, he always triumphs over the mundane ways of the official forces of law and order. In fact, although the most frequent types of detective hero derive superficially from the brilliant eccentrics of nineteenth century detective stories, in reality they owe more to the archetypal heroes of comedy. There is more of Shakespeare, Congreve, and Sheridan than Poe, Conan Doyle, and Chesterton in their creation. Even the characters who dwell in the usual settings of detective fiction share close relationships with the humors characters of literary comedy, which may be why they are so often criticized as mere puppets and stereotypes. Finally, in theme, value, and structure, the formal detective novel displays a close alliance with some of the great works of comic literature of the past; both its peculiar, often-criticized nature and its great popularity result from the attributes and attractions of a particular, stylized, and aristocratic type. Consequently, it would be more appropriate to call the detective novel the "thriller of manners."

The most important personage in any comedy, of course, is the hero, who may not necessarily involve himself, except as a problem solver, in the chief romantic plot, but usually deserves credit for clearing up the obstacles to happiness which comedy traditionally presents. Characters like Prospero, Brainworm, and Tony Lumpkin, for example, are the problem-solvers of their plays, but do not share the romantic hero's rewards. The comic hero of the detective story is the sleuth, often distinctive and pre-possessing enough to earn the title of Great Detective, who initially develops from the Poe-Conan Doyle tradition, which may at first seem an unlikely beginning for the comedy of manners.

Poe, it is generally agreed, invented the detective story and established its basic conventions—the murky atmosphere, the insoluble problem, the *outré* method, the incredible deductions, the adoring Boswell, and the gifted being who unravels the most difficult crimes.[6] His prototypical detective, C. Auguste Dupin, possesses a dual temperament, "both creative and...resolvent," combining the intuition of the poet with the analytical ability of the mathematician; the fusion gives him extraordinary deductive powers, enabling him, for example, to reconstruct his companion's chain of thought from a few penetrating physical observations ("The Murders in the Rue Morgue"). "Enamored of the Night," he shares unusual tastes with his deferential narrator-stooge—they dwell in a "time-eaten and grotesque mansion" which suits "the rather fantastic gloom of [their] common temper." Not at all a comic figure, Dupin exhibits the striking characteristics of intellectual brilliance and personal eccentricity which indelibly mark all later detective heroes.

[6]This is the consensus of an overwhelming majority of historians, critics, writers, and readers. For pre-Poe detective themes and types (known to initiates as the incunabula) see Miss Murch's book, Note 1.

From Dupin, with some slight influence from Gaboriau and Wilkie Collins,[7] springs Sherlock Holmes, the most important and beloved sleuth in literature, whose creator took the Poe character and formula, condensed the pompous essays on the ratiocinative faculties, added a more concrete sense of life, dispelled the romantic gloom and substituted a lovingly detailed picture of late Victorian England. Like Dupin, Holmes displays extraordinary deductive powers, inferring an entire life history from the most trivial items (a hat in "The Blue Carbuncle," a watch in *The Sign of Four,* a pipe in "The Yellow Face"). Though endowed with the Dupin-esque dual temperament—Wilson calls Holmes a "romantic personality possessed by the scientific spirit"—Holmes is considerably less morbid and more endearing than his prototype; his foibles are the understandable eccentricities of a man of genius. He lives in a state of Bohemian disorder, smokes foul tobacco, relieves his chronic melancholia by playing the violin or taking cocaine, and even shoots a patriotic V. R. on his walls with a heavy calibre pistol. Conan Doyle developed Poe's inventions further, giving his detective varied abilities and wide and exotic interests, especially in the sciences of criminology. (Holmes, for example, is the author of a pamphlet on the one hundred and forty varieties of tobacco ash and of a "trifling monograph" analyzing one hundred and sixty separate ciphers.) He established the convention of singular knowledge symbolizing great knowledge: the unusual, with a certain sleight of hand, passed for the universal. Conan Doyle also expressed in conversational, epigrammatic form his detective's peculiar personality and superior intellect: Holmes caps one solution, for example, with "There were twenty-three other deductions which would be of more interest to experts than to you" ("The Reigate Puzzle"). He compresses into one sentence the principle of all fictional detectives: "Eliminate all other factors, and the one which remains must be the truth" *(The Sign of Four).* ...

Whatever their individual differences, all other fictional detectives derive from the Dupin-Holmes tradition. Though many later sleuths may seem eminently unSherlockian in appearance, methods, and personality, they all exhibit the primary qualities of the Great Detective. They generally possess a physical appearance as distinctive as Holmes's hawklike profile—they may be either very tall or very short, very fat or very thin, or they may

[7]For detailed accounts of this development, see Murch, *op. cit.,* Haycraft, *Murder for Pleasure* (New York: D. Appleton-Century, 1941) and *The Art of the Mystery Story,* and Julian Symons, *The Detective Story in Britain* (London: Longmans, Green, 1962). [The literature on Collins has grown enormously. An entire issue of *Nineteenth-Century Fiction* has been devoted to him. Serious students should read, in particular, Walter M. Kendrick, "The Sensationalism of *The Woman in White,"ibid.,* XXXII (June, 1977), 18-34; John R. Reed, "English Imperialism and the Unacknowledged Crime of *The Moonstone," Clio,* II (June, 1973), 281-89; and Ian Ousby, *Bloodhounds of Heaven: The Detective in English Fiction from Godwin to Doyle* (Cambridge, Mass., 1976), which is particularly strong on Collins and Charles Dickens. Editor's note.]

affect unusual attire. They are usually pronounced eccentrics, enjoying odd hobbies, interests, or life styles, and frequently overindulging in what Auden calls the "solitary oral vices" of eating, drinking, smoking, and boasting. Above all, whatever his particular method of detection, the sleuth is blessed with a penetrating observation, highly developed logical powers, wide knowledge, and a brilliantly synthetic imagination: the detective story, unlike most kinds of popular literature, prizes intellectual gifts above all others.

But to change the Great Detective of short fiction to the comic hero of the novel required more than the Dupin-Holmes tradition. The anti-social bachelor with cranky and exotic interests could not adapt well to the large and complex world of the longer form. The detective of the novel demanded a fuller personal background, a greater cast of characters, a more gradual and intricate development of his investigation than the short story provided. The book that effectively transformed the short detective story into the novel of detection is E. C. Bentley's *Trent's Last Case,* published in 1913, while Sherlock Holmes was still practicing at 221B Baker Street. It is probably the most important work of detective fiction since Conan Doyle began writing in 1887, and has been much praised by critics and practitioners as a nearly perfect example of its type. In her historical study, *The Development of the Detective Novel,* A. E. Murch states the usual view of the book:

> *Trent's Last Case,* a novel written at a period when the short detective story was still the most popular form of the genre, brought to fiction of this kind a more spacious atmosphere, time to consider and reconsider the implications of the evidence, and a new literary excellence.

More important, *Trent's Last Case* is the most influential source for the comedy of manners which came to dominate the formal detective novel. It introduced that favorite English detective, the gentleman amateur, in the person of Philip Trent—artist, popular journalist, lover of poetry, and dabbler in crime—the progenitor of all the insouciant dilettantes who breeze gracefully through detective fiction for the next thirty years. Because Trent is an obvious gentleman—immediately apparent by his whimsical speech and shaggy tweeds—he can succeed where the official police cannot: the characters accept him socially, and his accomplishments (an artist's keen eye, well-bred sympathy, the ability to interrogate the French maid in her native tongue) give him greater mobility. Most important, he understands the social code of the world he investigates; in a significant exchange with the secretary of a murdered millionaire, Trent points the direction of later detective fiction:

> "Apropos of nothing in particular...were you at Oxford?"
> "Yes," said the young man. "Why do you ask?"

"I just wondered if I was right in my guess. It's one of the things you can very
often tell about a man, isn't it?"   (ch. vii)

Trent's sensitivity to those indecipherable things that characterize the Oxford man (by definition a gentleman) emphasizes his own gentlemanly
status; moreover, a value system is established—no Oxford man, naturally,
could be a murderer. Following Bentley, the detective novel largely abandoned its atmosphere of gloom and menace—a heritage of the Poe influence
—and turned to the comic milieu of the traditional English novel. Its
favorite detectives, settings, and characters resembled less and less their
subliterary models and showed ever closer relationships with the favorite
characters and types of traditional comedy. The Great Detective became a
comic hero, as well as a transcendent and infallible sleuth; his solution of
a difficult problem became the task of releasing a whole world from the
bondage of suspicion and distrust. His task allied him with the archetypal
problem-solvers of comedy—the tricky slave, the benevolent elf, the
Prospero figure.

After *Trent's Last Case* the gentleman amateur dominates the full-length
novel of detection. Although this character exhibits the Holmesian conventions of arcane knowledge, personal eccentricity, and idiosyncratic
speech, these traits are diluted in the popular conception of the English
gentleman. The sardonic savant becomes the witty connoisseur: wide re-
searches are replaced by dilettantism, and the ironic Sherlockian speech is
translated into bright and brittle badinage. Some of the best-known examples of this extremely popular detective are H. C. Bailey's Reginald
Fortune, A. A. Milne's Antony Gillingham, Phillip MacDonald's Anthony
Gethryn, Anthony Berkeley's Roger Sheringham, Margery Allingham's
Albert Campion, Nicholas Blake's Nigel Strangeways, and the Oxonian
policemen John Appleby and Roderick Alleyn, the creations of Michael
Innes and Ngaio Marsh. The only important American versions of the
type, which does not travel well, are S. S. Van Dine's Philo Vance and
Ellery Queen's Ellery Queen.

The fusion of gentleman and detective reaches its zenith (some think its
nadir) in Dorothy L. Sayers' noble sleuth, Lord Peter Wimsey, a full-fledged
aristocrat as well as a fop, a bibliophile, and a gourmet.

> He was a respectable scholar in five or six languages, a musician of some skill
> and more understanding, something of an expert in toxicology, a collector of
> rare editions, an entertaining man-about-town, and a common sensationalist.
>   (*Clouds of Witness*, ch. iv)

Lord Peter combines the Great Detective with a familiar comic character.
His varied abilities, recondite interests, and high intelligence derive of
course from the Holmesian genius; but his attire, languid air, and silly-ass
speech ally him with the *gracioso* or dandy figure of comedy. Wimsey is

partly a version of Jung's archetypal Wonderful Boy (or, as Auden calls him, "the priggish superman"), partly the "tricky slave" of Roman comedy (as Northrop Frye points out), partly the fop of Restoration comedy. As a detective he is, needless to say, a gentleman, a graduate of the proper schools (Eton and Oxford), aware of the subtle code of the thriller of manners. His consistent desire to make things come right—he is always rescuing people from themselves—translates him from the ludicrous dandy figure of satire to the intelligent mechanic of human complications.

Although the gentleman amateur overshadows all other detective heroes, some important sleuths derive from other comic archetypes. Agatha Christie's Hercule Poirot, perhaps the most famous detective since Sherlock Holmes, combines something of the Holmesian tradition with that of the dandy, yet stands apart from both. Lacking the formidable personality of the Sherlockian genius and the airy manner of the *gracioso*, Poirot is an elf.

> Poirot was an extraordinary looking little man. He was hardly more than five feet, four inches, but carried himself with great dignity. His head was exactly the shape of an egg, and he always perched it a little on one side. His moustache was very stiff and military. The neatness of his attire was almost incredible, I believe a speck of dust would have caused him more pain than a bullet wound.   (*The Mysterious Affair at Styles*, ch. ii)

In Poirot individuality of utterance becomes a rather tiresome difficulty with English idioms; his major eccentricity is an overweening faith in his "little gray cells." His short stature, pomposity, avuncular goodness, and his foreign, otherworldly air, place him with the kindly elves of the fairytale, as well as with Puck and Ariel. (Miss Christie's elderly spinster detective, Miss Jane Marple, is a kind of universal aunt or fairy godmother, a female Poirot.) Other elf types, of whom Poirot is the major representative, are G. K. Chesterton's Father Brown and Anthony Gilbert's Arthur Crook. Poirot, naturally, always employs his magic for good purposes, insuring that the fabric of society will be repaired after the temporary disruption of murder. It is not surprising that he especially tries to establish or restore conjugal happiness, a symbol of a newly reintegrated society and the traditional goal of all comedy.

Neither a dandy nor an elf, the third major problem-solver is the wizard. The detectives in this category retain the powerful physical presence and the convincing infallibility of the Sherlockian tradition. Rex Stout's curmudgeonly genius, Nero Wolfe, and John Dickson Carr's Sir Henry Merrivale and, above all, Dr. Gideon Fell, are the most successful examples and closest to the Great Detective. A scholar and lexicographer specializing in Satanism and witchcraft, Dr. Fell usually encounters the "impossible" murder, committed in the traditional hermetically sealed room. In addition to his wizardry, he radiates an immense benevolence and a Falstaffian gusto:

There was the doctor, bigger and stouter than ever. He wheezed. His red face shone, and his small eyes twinkled over eyeglasses on a broad black ribbon. There was a grin under his bandit's moustache, and chuckling upheavals animated his several chins. On his head was the inevitable black shovel-hat; his paunch projected from a voluminous black cloak. Filling the stairs in grandeur he leaned on an ash cane with one hand and flourished another cane with the other. It was like meeting Father Christmas or Old King Cole. Indeed, Dr. Fell had frequently impersonated Old King Cole at garden pageants, and enjoyed the role immensely.

(*The Mad Hatter Mystery*, ch. i)

His love for the ancient British virtues and his enormous capacity for beer combine in his magnum opus, *The Drinking Customs of England from the Earliest Days*. When not outwitting evildoers, Dr. Fell assiduously pursues research for this book through all the novels in which he appears. His joviality, his resemblance to the kindly father figures of legend, and his expertise in the supernatural ally him with an archetypal wizard, Jung's Wise Old Man, the good magician or Prospero figure.

The usual settings of detective fiction serve a comic as well as a functional purpose. The novel invariably presents murder in isolated and luxurious surroundings, combining the necessities of the whodunit with the manners tradition. The setting limits the suspects to a manageable number and establishes an aura of wealth and gentility, the aristocratic atmosphere of high comedy. The ubiquitous English Country house, whose attraction is confirmed by a glance at titles—*The Red House Mystery, Crooked House, Peril at End House, The Mysterious Affair at Styles, Scandal at High Chimneys, The House at Satan's Elbow*—separates a small, homogeneous, elite group from the rest of the world, performing the same function as the *mise en scène* of writers like Goldsmith, Sheridan, Jane Austen, George Meredith, and Henry James. Other settings serve the same purpose; the charity bazaars, men's clubs, card parties, hunting lodges, university common rooms, and snowbound resort hotels of the detective novel withstand the intrusions of the bourgeois policemen and the tramp who is always initially suspect. This posh and pedigreed society, remote from criminal reality, often irritates detective novel readers, but it offers social forms for the novelist of manners and within those forms, the observable clues to human behavior by which the detective hero can identify the culprit.

Though basically homogeneous, this society does contain variety. Its members, though roughly equal in social standing, are not of the same class, family background, or profession. Within a limited range they comprise an English microcosm. There is always at least one representative of the squirearchy, one professional man—commonly a doctor, but sometimes a lawyer, professor, or schoolmaster—a cleancut young sporting type, and a military man (never below the rank of major), usually a veteran of colonial service. An English vicar, often a muscular Christian, frequently hovers about, providing a link with the Established Church. Like the vicar, the other characters serve an emblematic function, the beef-witted squire speaks for the rural aristocratic virtues, "huntin', shootin', and fishin'," the sporting type exemplifies the "Barbarian" graces of good looks, athletic skill, and intellectual deficiency, and the military man stands for the Empire, bluff British honesty, the officer class.

One of the major criticisms of the detective novel is that its characters are merely stereotyped, cardboard constructions, serving the contrivances of a highly artificial method. Though the novelist often creates mere puppets, he errs in good company: his characters generally are modern versions of the humors characters of Roman, Renaissance, and Restoration comedy, people governed by an emblematic function, a single trait, or a necessity of plot. The cast, for example, usually includes a "smashing," decent girl (poor, but of good family) and a spirited young man, to provide the traditional romantic plot. The circumstances of the murder frequently implicate the girl, so the young man covers up for her by destroying or manufacturing evidence, providing false alibis, and generally behaving like a gentleman. The detective sympathizes with such actions and avoids embarrassing the pair. In addition, he clears up the obstacle of criminal suspicion so that they can marry: they furnish the objective means by which the detective can benefit society. They are usually a pallid and uninteresting pair who possess little intrinsic appeal, but exist largely to reflect the powers of the comic hero.

Another favorite stock character is the obsessed philosopher or comic pedant, a man defined wholly in terms of his ruling passion, like "my uncle Toby" or Emma Woodhouse's father. He appears as Pastor Venables in Dorothy L. Sayers' *The Nine Tailors;* perhaps the most extreme example of the type, Venables' ruling passion is campanology. Others include the mechanically minded hobbyists of *The Problem of the Wire Cage* and *The Problem of the Green Capsule* (John Dickson Carr) and the physician of Agatha Christie's *The Murder of Roger Ackroyd*. Often these hobbyists use their unusual knowledge to fashion infernal machines or strange methods of murder, another example of a respectable comic tradition usefully adapted to functional detective purposes.

The military man owes to his comic archetype, the *miles gloriosus* or braggart soldier, a latent ridiculousness: easily recognizable by his phlegmatic temperament, brusque manner, and peculiar habits of speech, he often provides an object of satire. Sometimes he is used solely for humorous effect, as in Major Blunt's embarrassed wooing in *The Murder of Roger Ackroyd*. His stiff upper lip emphasizes his class and his interests, as Colonel Marchbanks demonstrates while regretting the imprisonment on a murder charge of his host, the Duke of Denver, in Dorothy L. Sayers'

Clouds of Witness: "'Awfully unpleasant for him, poor chap, and with the birds so good this year'" (ch. ii). Like the obsessed philosopher or the military man, most of the other characters achieve an almost archetypal level themselves, derived both from their frequent appearance in detective stories and their constant use in comedy. Usually they are defined only by their function, e.g., the young man is no more than a suitor or the squire no more than the conventional *senex iratus.* Just as part of the pleasure of comedy results from the author's skilful handling of his stock characters, so too the enjoyment of a mystery comes from the author's tampering with his stereotypes—the reader wonders which of the perennial group will be the murderer this time.

The comedy of manners generally contains an expulsion of the socially undesirable which insures the continued happiness of those remaining. Similarly, the detective novel features two expulsions of "bad" or socially unfit characters: the victim and the murderer. Because only unlikeable characters are made to suffer permanently in comedy, pains are taken to make the victim worthy of his fate: he must be an exceptionally murderable man. This prevents regret and also insures that all characters have sufficient motive. The favorite victim of the mystery is also the favorite unsympathetic character of comedy—the blocking character, who works against such natural and desirable ends as joining the correctly matched young couple. A frequent victim, therefore, is the negative father or mother (a common comic obstacle) who opposes a marriage, makes an unfair will, or refuses to act his or her age, all actions which cause distress to the young. The squire, being elderly, stupid, and irascible, makes an excellent murderee. His fictional archetype is probably Squire Western, who wouldn't have lasted long if *Tom Jones,* a notable comedy of manners, had also been a detective novel. The victim of *The Murder of Roger Ackroyd* is a *senex iratus* who forces an engagement on his stepson, impeding the path of true love and earning his doom. Old General Fentiman is murdered in Miss Sayers' *The Unpleasantness at the Bellona Club* because he has made a bad will. Sigsbee Manderson in *Trent's Last Case* dies because he is much older than his wife, and a brute besides. The negative mothers, like the gross, evil Mrs. Boynton of Agatha Christie's *Appointment with Death,* also make expendable obstacles: Mrs. Boynton prevents her children from marrying, thus causing her death. Similarly, Mrs. Cavendish of Christie's *The Mysterious Affair at Styles* pays dearly for marrying a man much younger than herself and making an unfair will. All of these victims have hindered the natural course of events, chiefly by obstructing the path of true love. Such obstruction in any form of comedy means eventual defeat of exclusion: and in the exacting code of the detective novel, that exclusion means murder.

Another favorite victim is the ineligible mate, whose impending marriage to the decent young girl would interfere with her natural preference for the eligible young man. Since he is young, this victim is burdened with an even more specific sin: under his attractive exterior he conceals the personality of a bounder, a rotter, and a cad. The young victim of Carr's *The Problem of the Wire Cage* reveals his caddishness by taking advantage of a working class girl and cheating at tennis, offenses implicitly equivalent. Philip Boyes of Miss Sayers' *Strong Poison* earns expulsion by espousing free love, writing experimental novels, and making himself "an excrescence and a public nuisance," and (kiss of death) in being "a bit of a cad" (ch. iv). In another Sayers novel, *Clouds of Witness*, the dead man seems at first an inappropriate victim—handsome, dashing, an officer with a distinguished war record. But the coroner's inquest establishes his unfitness: he cheated at cards, which "was regarded as far more shameful than such sins as murder and adultery" (ch. i). Another rotter of the worst sort, Paul Alexis in *Have His Carcase*, meets an untimely end because he is a gigolo who preys on lonely, vulnerable women, a professional cad.

Other common fatal flaws, often indirectly related to the social ethic of the comedy of manners, merit violent exclusion. The victim may be guilty of exploiting the ritual of his society, posing as a gentleman, but hiding a dark, unacceptable secret. Mr. Shaitana of Agatha Christie's *Cards on the Table* exudes evil; in her *Murder in the Calais Coach* the victim is an American kidnapper posing as a philanthropist. The victim in Carr's *The Crooked Hinge* is a false claimant to a considerable country estate, neither a gentleman nor a true squire. Because he may have risen from humble beginnings to achieve the doctor's high status, the professional man — generally the only character who actually works for a living—is also a potential victim. On the rare occasions that a young woman is murdered, she is always revealed as a secret sinner under a respectable façade, like the murdered adulteress in Carr's *The Sleeping Sphinx*. (If she is not an adulteress masquerading as a respectable woman, she will then be an actress, never a very desirable occupation for a woman in English literature.) One other damning trait is a fatal un-Englishness. Foreigners lead dangerous lives in detective novels, and men otherwise exemplary die for merely ethnic reasons. The Mediterraneans of the detective novel never seem true gentlemen, perhaps a result of the Italian villainy of Elizabethan revenge tragedies and Gothic fiction. Anthony Morell is condemned on the fourth page of John Dickson Carr's *Death Turns the Tables*, where the reader is told "you would have taken him for an Italian." Since he is indeed an Italian, a businessman, and a symbol of lower class virility, Morell meets his doom three chapters later. The wealthy peer of *Whose Body?* loses his life because he is a Jew; Paul Alexis of *Have His Carcase* compounds his caddishness by being Russian; and in *Clouds of Witness*, Denis Cathcart's French blood explains his inadequacy. (Hercule Poirot is a rare foreigner, tolerated by his society because he is faintly laughable and—like all detectives—represents no sexual threat.)

Virtually all victims, then, suffer their violent expulsion because of some breach of the unwritten social or ethical code of the thriller of manners. Even minute infractions, like ungentlemanliness, incur tremendous penalties. Violations of accepted morality, particularly adultery, are capital crimes; both immoral and ungentlemanly (or unladylike), infidelity usually demands the most rigorous penalty that society can apply. The offense of foreign birth or blood seems too trifling to be murdered for, but Englishmen in general distrust the foreigner, and the comedy of manners, which seems the quintessential representation of a ruling class, follows the prejudices of the society it depicts. The dark, handsome, charming man with gleaming white teeth and glossy black hair (all characteristic of the Latin in the whodunit) is generally marked for murder. Since he attempts also to woo the young girl, he serves a blocking function as well. Murder initiates the action of the detective novel, but its real purpose is to indicate the nature of the society in which it occurs, to provide a complication which requires the abilities of a comic hero, and to exclude a social undesirable.

The murderer, though technically a criminal, is more interesting than his victim and consequently occupies an ambivalent position. On the one hand, he has removed an obstacle, destroyed a rotter posing as a gentleman, or expelled a social evil. On the other hand, he has committed the gravest human crime, an offense against both society and God, and has placed the other members of his group under suspicion. In short, he has created a complication which demands his own dismissal. Because he is intelligent enough to commit an ingenious crime and elude detection for most of the novel, he earns a certain admiration. However, since "good" (*i.e.*, socially valuable) people cannot permanently suffer in comedy, the murderer must turn out to be somehow undesirable himself. Usually the culprit is a more acceptable person than his victim, because he comprehends the elaborate social ritual well enough to pose as an innocent. This sustained pretense of innocence culminates, however, in the unveiling of the murderer's true character; the detective exposes him as an imposter, the *alazon*, a familiar comic figure who, Northrop Frye says, "pretends or tries to be something more than he is." His crime is not the true cause of his defeat, only a symptom of it: like his victim, the murderer has guaranteed his doom by committing some earlier comic, social, or ethical mistake. ...

Once the murderer leaves, the world of the novel begins to approach its former peacefulness. The last chapter resembles the final scene of almost every traditional comedy. The successful sleuth presides over a feast of some kind in an appropriately convivial place and explains his reasoning, to the accompaniment of admiring comments from those assembled. The group usually consists of all the major characters in the novel—minus murderer and victim—who represent their society as it should be, cleansed of guilt, free of complication and obstacles, recreated anew from the shambles of a temporary disorder. They gather around a table in the library, at a pub, a dinner party, or even at a wedding: the rightly matched couple have finally married or made plans to marry, their relationship symbolizing the happy and orderly end toward which the detective has been working. Poirot, for example, manages a happy marriage in *The Mysterious Affair at Styles,* causing his Watson, Captain Hastings, to comment, "Who on earth but Poirot would have thought of a trial for murder as a restorer of conjugal happiness" (ch. xiii). At this feast the detective also explains red herrings, forgives those who (through the best of motives) have misled him, and offers advice for the future. The comic hero employs his greatest gifts: he is an engineer of destiny, with the power to recreate a new society from the ruins of the old. Moreover, his acuity and perception, which had enabled him to penetrate both a social code and a complex mystery, now function as abilities even more magical: he presides over a festival of innocence celebrating a return to the usual normative state, and he distributes the miraculous gift of absolution by establishing the essential goodness and worth of the society that survives. As the tricky slave, the benevolent elf, or the Prospero of a particular world, the detective has rearranged human relationships to insure the reintegration and harmony of an entire social order. This conventional ending re-emphasizes the comic structure and function of the formal detective novel.

Often, in fact, the detective novel moves over into purely comic realms. This movement results quite naturally from the whodunit's origins in the manners traditions. In his book on Henry James, *The Expense of Vision,* Laurence Bedwell Holland has remarked of the novel of manners, "That the genre tends toward stylization is suggested by some of the predecessors which on the surface it most resembles: the literature of courtship, Shakespeare's idyllic comedies, Restoration comedy, and the literature of sensibility." As a highly conventionalized version of the thriller and a further stylization of a highly stylized form, the whodunit frequently exhibits a conscious tampering with conventions and becomes sophisticated self-parody. Anthony Berkeley has produced a number of startling variations on the normal whodunit, all of them skilful and individual: in *Trial and Error,* the murderer finds himself forced to prove his own guilt; in *Before the Fact,* the victim helps plan her own demise; in *The Poisoned Chocolates Case,* six different and utterly plausible solutions for one murder are suggested by six different amateur detectives. Agatha Christie has written one book, *Ten Little Indians,*[8] in which all of the characters, including the murderer, are victims. Her best novel, *The Murder of Roger*

---

[8][This book is an interesting example of titles that move with the times. Originally it was called *Ten Little Niggers,* then *Ten Little Indians,* and finally *And Then There were None.* Editor's note.]

Ackroyd, serves a number of purposes: it provides the staple attributes of the detective story, satirizes the tiny rural village of King's Abbot, "rich in unmarried ladies and retired military officers...whose hobbies and recreations can be summed up in one word, 'gossip'" (ch. ii), and "tricks" the reader by...a departure from convention that aroused considerable critical controversy.

Dorothy L. Sayers often wholly subordinates her mystery to a purely literary purpose. *The Nine Tailors* is less a detective novel than a nostalgic picture of life in the fen country of East Anglia. In *Gaudy Night,* Lord Peter plays Mirabell to Harriet Vane's Millamant against the Oxford landscape of a "straight" academic comedy devoted to a rather repellent intellectual-feminist thesis.[9] Though her *Clouds of Witness* seems at first a very complicated and satisfying novel of detection, it actually serves to vindicate the aristocratic way of life: Lord Peter defends his brother, the Duke of Denver, before the House of Lords, redeems the honor of his family, and selects the right mate for his flighty sister, who has a penchant for unsuitable men. Along the way he excludes the socially unfit—bohemians, Socialists, "conchies," and cads—while bringing the right people together; the only complete villain in the novel, which has no murderer, is a lout of a farmer who is conveniently run over by a taxicab. Michael Innes also employs the detective story for comic purposes—a satirical look at academic life in *Seven Suspects,* a humorous picture of the art world in *One Man Show,* a sly Jamesian parody in *Comedy of Terrors;* the highly literate Innes manages to satirize his characters, their world, and the mystery itself, all within the normal framework of the whodunit. Most of these works display not only the usual conditioning exerted by the comedy of manners on the whodunit, but also normal comedy of manners masquerading as the detective novel, further demonstrating the reciprocity between the two forms. ...

The formal detective novel may succeed best in England because of its dependence on the mainstreams of the national literary heritage. Its use of the heroes, the characters, the archetypes and patterns of fictional comedy of manners for its major sources of theme and meaning is fully appropriate to that heritage. English fiction most often avoids and condemns the extremes of violence, disorder, or anti-social action, favoring instead wholeness, harmony, and social integration, the stable virtues of an essentially benevolent and correct society. Firmly in the mainstream of English literature, the detective novel shares a strong affinity with the "great tradition" identified by F. R. Leavis as central to British fiction. Since it also favors rural settings and rural (though upper-class) people, the formal detective novel shares with the novels of Jane Austen, George Eliot, Anthony Trol-

---

[9][As editor, I cannot forbear to remark that no one today, reading *Gaudy Night,* would consider the penultimate scene, which clearly deals with a feminist issue, "repellent." This is another excellent indication of how Miss Sayers moved ahead of her readers. Editor's note.]

lope, and George Meredith a tinge of the pastoral. This pastoralism explains in part the whodunit's characteristic distance from ordinary life: like the conventional pastorals of Spenser or Sydney, the detective novel should be judged in terms of its form, rather than in reference to the life that teems outside its quiet, genteel world.

Again like other forms of English fiction, the whodunit assumes a benevolent and knowable universe. In part imitating Conan Doyle's ability to illuminate and transform the ordinary details of life, detective novelists liberally sprinkle charts, diagrams, timetables, maps, plans, and other concrete evidence throughout their books, indicating the English tradition of empirical thought. This penchant for the tangible implies a world that can be interpreted by human reason, embodied in the superior intellect of the detective. His penetration of facts and clues shows his power to apprehend particular reality and attach significance to the trivial residue of any human action. Finding a meaning in the tiniest clue enables the detective to know the truth; thus, his universe seems explainable, the typical cosmos of English fiction, unlike the extravagant and grotesque realities of the American novel. Like the Gothic novel, which treats the seemingly irrational and inexplicable, the detective novel always provides a plausible and rational explanation of even the most perplexing chain of events.

Though the whodunit lacks verisimilitude, it practices the specific literary realism of its major tradition, not so much true to all observable life, as true to its stylized segment of life and its own assumed vision. Having confined his vision to a particular complex of conventions, the detective novelist attempts only to meet the requirements of those conventions, with no reference to the realities of criminal behavior. The highly artificial nature of the form, combined with its pastoral tendencies, isolates it from the facts of life—a detective novel of thirty or forty years ago seems only slightly dated, if at all. The detective novels of the Golden Age never mention the tensions and dangers that threatened the precarious stability of the Twenties and Thirties. They say nothing of the Depression, the social, economic, and political unrest of that time, but choose to remain within the genteel luxury of an aristocratic world, suffering the intrusions of the police and the initially suspected nameless vagabond before the detective hero turns suspicion on society. Except for these brief intrusions, themselves conventional, the great concern of the detective novel is centripetal; it is a formal minuet leading to an inescapable conclusion, as mannered and unreal as the masque, the sonnet, or the drawing room farce.

Aside from its interest as a disappearing vestige of the comedy of manners, perhaps the most important question that remains involves the reasons for the form's flourishing at its particular moment in history. Its profoundly English nature and heritage supply one answer: the detective novel demonstrates perhaps the last identifiable place where traditional, genteel, British fashions, assumptions, and methods triumph in the

twentieth century novel. Another answer to the enigma of the detective
novel has been advanced by John Paterson, who feels the form answered a
profound cultural need in the troubled times of the Golden Age:

> In the age of the Boom, the Great Depression, flappers and gangsterism, and
> the Fascist Solution, it recalls the sober gentility and crude optimism of an
> earlier and more complacent generation; it asserts the triumph of a social
> order and decorum that have all but passed away.[10]

In that sense, perhaps, the detective novel fulfills not only the functions of
comedy, but also the purposes of works like the sonnet or the pastoral
eclogue, both of which flourished in an age of violence and rapid change.
Just as the Elizabethans often found solace in rigidly conventional, peace-
ful, and essentially unreal literary forms, so too the twentieth-century
Briton apparently longed for the aristocratic aura, knowable universe, and
unerring truth-teller of the detective novel when poverty threatened the
established social order, when the cosmos had lost its infinite meaning,
and when the Big Lie drowned out all attempts at truth. Dreaming of
luxury, longing for stability, desiring the security of formal rigidity,
readers of all classes turned toward the detective story, where significant
truth lurked behind the arrangement of cigars in an ashtray, where a time-
less society re-established its innocence anew, where nubility triumphed
over senility, where a wizard disposed of the bad parent, the impostor, the
parvenu, the outsider, and bestowed his magical blessings on decent young
women and deserving young men. The twentieth-century reader, like the
Elizabethan, could turn his back on the ugly reality around him and retreat
into the stylized world of literary art. The kind of art that most satisfied
him and most fully answered the deepest needs of his nation and time was,
not surprisingly, comic.

---

[10]"A Cosmic View of the Private Eye," *Saturday Review of Literature* (August 22, 1963), p. 7.

The Hard-Boiled Detective Novel

by George Grella

In America the formal detective novel has never found a proper home. Though read widely, and practiced by such authors as S. S. Van Dine, Rex Stout, and Ellery Queen, the form has never really flourished here. Conditions do not favor the comedy of manners. Where in England a society with recognizable class distinctions provides a propitious background for isolating a select number of privileged characters, American society is vast, polyglot, and heterogeneous, difficult to capsulize. In a culture characterized by diversity rather than homogeneity, microcosms demand at least platoon strength. The United States still lacks the traditions and institutions that Cooper, Hawthorne, and James envied: a ruling class, a landed gentry, an Established Church, the great gentleman-producing public schools and universities, in short, all the developed structures of a venerable history. Where the English are fond of eccentrics, Americans regard the Great Detective as more fatuous than acute. Nero Wolfe's massive misanthropy and misogyny seem more psychopathic than endearing. The gentleman amateur is even more incongruous in a society where "gentleman" connotes far less than in England, and where languid, airy-mannered young men seldom play heroic roles. Ellery Queen and Philo Vance appear prissy, unmasculine, and at times, insufferable. (Ogden Nash's comment, "Philo Vance needs a kick in the pance," is a typical, healthy American reaction.) Finally, where the formal detective novel displays the charm and manner, the generally polished and solid techniques of English fiction, American attempts at the whodunit usually lack style and distinction. As Raymond Chandler remarked, "The English may not always be the best writers in the world, but they are incomparably the best dull writers."

The form that dominates American practice is the "hard-boiled" detective story, radically different from the classic whodunit. Rejecting the established patterns, it drew its materials from the indigenous life of America, including its major literary tradition. If the dominant American novel

George Grella, "Murder and the Mean Streets: The Hard-Boiled Detective Novel." From Dick Allen and David Chacko, eds. *Detective Fiction: Crime and Compromise* (New York: Harcourt Brace Jovanovich, 1974), pp. 411-28. Reprinted with permission of the author. This essay first appeared in the journal *Contempora*, I (March, 1970), 6-15.

is, as has been maintained, a romance, so is the American detective story, and for the same reasons. Where the English novel is notable for its mental, moral, and spiritual health, and as Richard Chase points out, "gives the impression of absorbing all extremes into a normative view of life," the American novel has a "penchant for the marvelous, the sensational, the legendary, and in general, the heightened effect." The American novel is "less interested in incarnation and reconciliation that in alienation and disorder." Since the American novel derives from a mixed tradition, encompassing folk tales, medieval literature, Gothic novels, and the works of writers like Scott and Cooper, it reflects a variety of romance elements— pastoral, melodrama, legend, and myth. Influenced by the Puritan imagination, it tends to see life as a Manichean struggle between good and evil; its vision, moreover, is usually obsessed with sin. Energized by the self-reliance of the frontier, it customarily establishes its moral norm within the consciousness of an individual man. The quest motif often supplies its structure, as in the medieval and mythic romance. The hard-boiled detective novel thus employs a characteristically American hero and world view, which it translates into the framework of a twentieth century mystery story. Its central problem is a version of the quest, both a search for truth and an attempt to eradicate evil.

The American detective novel, paradoxically, combines its romance themes and structures with a tough, realistic surface and a highly sensational content, both in part a heritage of its origin in popular cheap magazines. The hard-boiled stories appeared soon after World War I in the "action" pulps, where they shared space with Westerns, hunting and fishing yarns, war stories, and adventure fiction of all kinds. Constrained by the limited education of their audience and performing in the bloody arena of a low-brow medium, the hard-boiled writers rejected the sometimes constricting formulas of the formal detective novel. Abandoning the static calm, the intricate puzzle, the ingenious deductions, they wrote an entirely different detective story, characterized by rapid action, colloquial language, emotional impact, and the violence that pervades American fiction. The most important magazine, the famous *Black Mask*, rose to prominence under the gifted editorship of Joseph T. Shaw, who outlined his requirements for detective fiction. "We wanted simplicity for the sake of clarity, plausibility, and belief," Shaw wrote. "We wanted action, but held that action is meaningless unless it involves recognizable human character in three-dimensional form." This credo, which appealed to a great many writers and readers, inspired such successful competitors as *Dime Detective, Thrilling Detective, Detective Fiction Weekly*, and *Action Detective. Black Mask*, however, was the acknowledged leader in its field, attracting a specific group of writers—among them Dashiell Hammett, Carroll John Daly, Lester Dent, Raoul Whitfield, Peter Ruric, Thomas Walsh, Reuben Jennings Shay—

most of whom are now remembered only by nostalgic buffs. But for two decades the pulps prospered, providing cheap, easily available entertainment when comparatively few popular media existed. *Black Mask*, which outlived its era, finally succumbed in 1953; copies of the magazine are now highly prized collectors' items.

Postwar America provided the hard-boiled school with an abundance of subjects. Undergoing the disorder that accompanies explosive social change, the nation coped unsuccessfully with a variety of problems—the Boom of the twenties, Prohibition, the national spiritual hangover of the Depression, and gangsterism on a spectacular scale. In an era of scandalous municipal and federal corruption, crime flourished in the mean streets of America's great cities. Criminals like Al Capone, John Dillinger, Prettyboy Floyd, Babyface Nelson, Clyde Barrow, and Bonnie Parker achieved national notoriety. The country was suffering through a period of turmoil and savagery, a chaotic violence which the hard-boiled writers mirrored in their work. Populated by real criminals and real policemen, reflecting some of the tensions of the time, endowed with considerable narrative urgency, and imbued with the disenchantment peculiar to postwar American writing, the hard-boiled stories were considered by their writers and readers honest, accurate portraits of American life.

In reality, however, the pulp detective stories were often crudely and naively written, as an examination of Joseph T. Shaw's *The Hard-Boiled Omnibus* and Ron Goulart's *The Hardboiled Dicks* demonstrates. A kind of realistic melodrama, they attest to the power of a variety of literary influences. Since the magazines inherited much of the spirit as well as the audience of the nineteenth century Dime Novels, they seldom strayed very far from the primitive manner and matter of their ancestors: the Wild West flavored a great many supposedly urban mystery stories. The tough stance—a blend of sentiment and cynicism—and scrupulously unadorned prose style of the hard-boiled writers stemmed most directly from Ernest Hemingway; both formed part of the standard literary equipment of the 1920's and '30's. In addition, like most of their contemporaries, the *Black Mask* writers were indebted to naturalism, from which, Matthew Bruccoli says, they acquired their interest in "documentary verisimilitude, social stratification, sexual force, and the unpretty aspects of American life."

Today the hard-boiled school is largely forgotten. Only one member of the original *Black Mask* group survived the transition from the pulp story to the novel and outlived his era—Dashiell Hammett, the most important American detective story writer since Poe. In fact, Hammett, who published his five novels and several dozen short stories from 1922 to 1934, made the form internationally famous; he is often given cridit for inventing it. Raymond Chandler, perhaps the most distinguished practitioner of the genre, belongs to the second generation of hard-boiled novelists. Chandler began publishing in *Black Mask* and similar magazines in 1933; his first novel, *The Big Sleep,* appeared in 1939, his last, *Playback,* in 1959. The most significant inheritor of the hard-boiled tradition is Ross Macdonald (Kenneth Millar), whose first Lew Archer novel was published in 1949. ... A fourth figure, roughly contemporaneous with Macdonald, Mickey Spillane, grows out of the hard-boiled tradition but represents the perversion it has undergone in the hands of the inept and the unthinking. Hammett, Chandler, and Macdonald constitute a continuum of achievement from the beginning of the hard-boiled school to the present. This solid tradition is the enduring accomplishment of the American detective story.

In addition to founding a truly American detective story, the hard-boiled writers created an appropriate hero, the private eye. They took the professional investigator of real life—usually considered a seedy voyeur—and transformed him into a familiar figure of the popular media, inspiring countless books, magazines, movies, and radio and television shows. Though superficially an altogether new kind of folk hero, the private detective is actually another avatar of that prototypical American hero, Natty Bumppo, also called Leatherstocking, Hawkeye, Deerslayer, and Pathfinder. As Henry Bambord Parkes has noticed, the Leatherstocking archetype possesses qualities which fit the requirements of detective fiction:

> Technical skill, along with physical courage and endurance; simplicity of character, with a distrust of intellectualism; an innate sense of justice; freedom from all social or family ties except those of loyalty to male comrades; and above all a claustrophobic compulsion to escape from civilization, supported by a belief that social organization destroys natural virtue and by a generally critical attitude toward all established institutions.

The American detective hero has his archetype's pronounced physical ability, dealing out and absorbing great quantities of punishment. Like Hawkeye, he is proficient with his gun and seldom goes anywhere without it. Like the lonely man of the forests, he works outside the established social code, preferring his own instinctive justice to the often tarnished justice of civilization. The private detective always finds the police incompetent, brutal, or corrupt, and therefore works alone. He replaces the subtleties of the deductive method with a sure knowledge of his world and a keen moral sense. Finding the social contract vicious and debilitating, he generally isolates himself from normal human relationships. His characteristic toughness and his redeeming moral strength conflict with the values of his civilization and cause him, like Natty Bumppo or Huckleberry Finn,[1] to flee the society which menaces his personal integrity and spiritual freedom.

The three great writers of the hard-boiled tradition employ the Leatherstocking archetype, but treat him in significantly different ways. Hammett's

---

[1][Anyone unfamiliar with the argument of Leslie Fiedler in *Love and Death in the American Novel* (New York, 1968) should investigate that analysis now. Editor's note.]

best known detectives, the nameless Continental Op (i.e., an operative for the Continental Detective Agency) and Sam Spade, are the least complex, basically the sleuths of the pulps. The Op is tough, unemotional, a thorough professional. Spade, younger and more attractive, is a cold, almost cruel man whose code of loyalty redeems him from an otherwise total amorality. Raymond Chandler embellishes the toughness of his Philip Marlowe with compassion, honesty, and wit, and a dimension of nobility that Spade and the laconic Op lack. Lew Archer, named for Spade's partner and modeled on Marlowe, is distinguished, beyond the others, for natural goodness. Perhaps the most sympathetic of the hard-boiled dicks, his forte is neither cynicism nor toughness, but a limitless capacity for pity. The central archetype of the frontiersman remains in all three writers but it evolves from the simple Op into the almost Christ-like Archer, paralleling the development of another Leatherstocking hero, the movie cowboy, from inarticulate roughneck to the smooth and stylized knight of the plains.

Living in a lawless world, the private eye, like the frontier hero, requires physical rather than intellectual ability. The short, fat Op is tough enough to tame a lawless city virtually singlehanded *(Red Harvest)* and tough enough to shoot a woman when he must, though he regrets it: "I had never shot a woman before. I felt queer about it" ("The Gutting of Couffignal"). Handy with both fists and firearms, in *The Maltese Falcon,* Sam Spade holds his own against experienced gunmen and international gangsters. Chandler and Macdonald relate their detectives even more closely to their archetype. Philip Marlowe and Lew Archer occasionally shoot and brawl, but more often absorb alarming physical punishment, being variously slugged, beaten, and battered by criminals and police, invariably recovering to continue their investigation. They display the stoic resistance to physical suffering which typifies Leatherstocking. Their insults and wisecracks are the badge of their courage; refusing to show pain or fear, they answer punishment with flippancy. After Captain Gregorius beats him in *The Long Goodbye,* Marlowe refuses to break: "'I wouldn't betray an enemy into your hands. You're not only a gorilla, you're an incompetent'" (ch. vii). After a sheriff pistol-whips him in *The Doomsters,* Archer answers, "'It takes more than a Colt revolver to change a Keystone Kop into an officer'" (ch. xvi).

An almost painful honesty accompanies the private eye's toughness and stamina; however imperfect or limited he may be, he acts according to his apprehension of the truth. No matter what it may cost him, the detective follows his moral code. For Hammett, the code is chiefly professional. Turning down a tempting bribe in "The Gutting of Couffignal," the Continental Op explains, "…I like being a detective, like the work. And liking work makes you want to do it as well as you can. Otherwise there'd be no sense to it." In fact, the Op has little interest in anything else. Unconcerned with moral judgments, he cares only about completing his task; as Frederick

Garner points out, "to the Op each case is just a job, not a moral crusade." Sam Spade is even less concerned with questions of morality. In *The Maltese Falcon* he carries on affairs with his partner's wife and his client and even participates temporarily in the criminal schemes of Caspar Gutman and Joel Cairo. But Spade also has a code; he turns in Brigid O'Shaughnessy, with whom he has fallen in love, because he owes a certain loyalty to his partner, his profession, and his organization:

> "When one of your organization gets killed it's bad business to let the killer get away with it…bad for that one organization, bad for detectives everywhere…I'm a detective and expecting me to run criminals down and then let them go free is like asking a dog to catch a rabbit and let it go. It can be done, all right,…but it's not the natural thing."   (ch. xx)

Philip Marlowe fuses personal integrity with professional ethics. He often endures the third-degree tactics of the police rather than reveal a client's business or, as in *The Long Goodbye*, betray a friend. Above all, he is honorable; he doesn't do all kinds of detection, "'Only the fairly honest kinds'" (*The Lady in the Lake*, ch. 1). His personal code prevents his accepting tainted money, even for doing the right thing: "'I've got a five-thousand dollar bill in my safe but I'll never spend a nickel of it. Because there was something wrong with the way I got it.'" (*The Long Goodbye*, ch. xxxix). Similarly, because he is loyal, Lew Archer suffers for his clients, whether they deserve it or not. Like Marlowe, he refuses tainted money: offered a thousand dollars to gather information for a gambler, he replies, "'I wasn't planning to hire myself out as a finger'" (*Black Money*, ch. xxvi).

The detective's code is developed even further in Marlowe and Archer. In addition to a sense of duty, compassion motivates them. Marlowe tells a friend:

> "I'm a romantic, Bernie. I hear voices crying in the night and I go see what's the matter. You don't make a dime that way. You got sense, you shut your windows and turn up more sound on the TV set…Stay out of other people's troubles. All it can get you is the smear…You don't make a dime that way."
> (*The Long Goodbye*, ch. xxxix)

Morally concerned, Marlowe and Archer are drawn to the outcast, the vulnerable, the miserable, often working only for what they conceive as justice. Archer is often fired by his clients, yet feels compelled to carry the investigation through to its end. He sees his job in almost Christ-like terms:

> The problem was to love people, to serve them, without wanting anything from them. I was a long way from solving that one.
> (*The Barbarous Coast*, ch. xvi)

Unlike the Op, unlike Spade, he often hates being a detective because of the evil in which he finds himself immersed. And, unlike Spade, he can let the murderer go, as in *The Drowning Pool*, where the criminal is a victim of circumstances. From the Op through Archer, the detective's moral code develops from the simple notion of professionalism to the complex realization of the depth of human need.

The moral code often exacts severe personal sacrifice. The detective generally finds that the beautiful and available girl is also the source of guilt; consequently, he is compelled to arrest a woman he desires or even loves. The particular terms of this sacrifice suggest the marked tendency of American fiction to depict women as potentially destructive, and demonstrate the detective's ambivalence toward them. The Op rejects Princess Zhukovski in "The Gutting of Couffignal." Spade refuses to yield to the entreaties of Brigid O'Shaughnessy in *The Maltese Falcon*, though he suffers for it ("'I'll have some rotten nights'"). Philip Marlowe and Lew Archer ironically discover that the desirable woman is corrupt, a bitch or a murderess, too evil to deserve their compassion. Chandler's *The Little Sister* most fully develops the hero's ambiguous attitudes. Marlowe rejects three women in the book; two of them, Mavis Weld and Dolores Gonzales, always appear together and are paired like Scott's Rowena and Rebecca or Hawthorne's Priscilla and Zenobia, as the Perfect Blonde and the Seductive Brunette. Marlowe refuses the blonde because she has the movie star's professional unreality. "In a little while she will drift off into a haze of glamor and expensive clothes and muted sex." He resists the brunette because she is "utterly beyond the moral laws of this or any world I could imagine" (ch. xxiv). He rejects the little sister of the title because, though she appears to be an innocent virgin from Kansas, she is a blackmailer and an accessory to murder. The conception of a detective surrounded by pliant females is a latter-day perversion of a major motif in the hard-boiled novel. Even the familiar ideal of masculine companionship, implicit in Cooper, Melville, and Whitman, is denied the detective; a good friend often is the criminal, like Albert Graves in Macdonald's *The Moving Target*. Terry Lennox, with whom Marlowe shares an inarticulate homoerotic friendship, turns out to be unworthy of the detective's devotion. Marlowe rejects him for his innate amorality:

> "...You had standards and you lived up to them, but they were personal. They had no relation to any kind of ethics or scruples. You were a nice guy because you had a nice nature. But you were just as happy with mugs or hoodlums as with honest men. ... You're a moral defeatist."
>
> (*The Long Goodbye*, ch. liii)

This loss of a friend, a girl, a colleague, intensifies the private eye's essential loneliness. His successful investigation becomes a kind of defeat. As John Paterson points out:

> There is always at the end of the hard-boiled novel a moment of depression
> when the mission is completed, the enterprise ended, as if this little victory
> had cost too much in terms of human suffering.

More than a defeat of the spirit, the moment of depression is a symptom of
the detective's personal sacrifice, the sadness that accompanies his adherence to his code. His loneliness is characteristic of the Leatherstocking
hero, who must proceed through moral entanglements unencumbered by
the impedimenta of social or sexual alliances. Nothing, not even love, must
prevent the detective from finishing his quest. Without antecedents, unmarried, childless, he is totally alone. Archer's symbolic maladjustment as
a divorced man emphasizes this alienation from human beings and human
institutions. The physical exhaustion at the end of the hard-boiled novel is
a sign of *accidie,* which even the Op experiences: "I felt tired, washed out"
("106,000 Blood Money"), an eloquent speech, for him, about the demands
of his profession.

The detective is finally alone, not only because the romantic hero is
doomed to solitude, but because he is too good for the society he inhabits.
Although not a perfect man, he is the best man in his world. The hard-
boiled novel's vision usually approximates the prevailing vision of American fiction. Its world, implied in Hammett's works, and fully articulated in
Chandler and Macdonald, is an urban chaos, devoid of spiritual and moral
values, pervaded by viciousness and random savagery. Because its laws and
regulations endanger the integrity of the hero, this world resembles the
settlements of the Leatherstocking novels and the "civilization" of *Huckleberry Finn.* Because its customs are often evil and its denizens degraded, it
is allied with the dreary towns along Huck Finn's Mississippi and the joy-
less civilization symbolized in *The Great Gatsby's* Valley of Ashes. No one
is immune to its pernicious influence. The initial crime of murder has a
way of proliferating in the hard-boiled novel, entrapping everyone by
association. The complicated plots of Ross Macdonald, with their intricate
blood and marital relationships, often symbolize the extent of complicity,
a universal guilt which spares no one.

> The circuit of guilty time was too much like a snake with its tail in its mouth,
> consuming itself. If you looked too long, there'd be nothing left of it, or you.
> We had to learn to live with it.   (*The Doomsters,* ch. xxxv)

Symbolic sins infest the American thriller. The homosexual gunman, since
Joel Cairo of *The Maltese Falcon,* has been a conventional character. Rape,
incest, and fratricide further indicate the perversion of all normal human
connections. Though the detective is compelled to work in this chaotic and
sinful society, he does not share its values; instead, he is always in conflict
with or in flight from civilization. He finds no fruitful human relationship

possible; his condemnation or rejection of other human beings unites him with the alienated and the lost of American fiction—Ahab, Huck Finn, Nick Adams, Joe Christmas, Holden Caulfield. The private eye observes a moral wasteland and, with no "territory" to flee to (unlike Huck Finn), he retreats into himself.

In the devastated society of the hard-boiled novel, crime is not a temporary aberration, but a ubiquitous fact. In *Red Harvest* the Continental Op fights a small war against an unholy coalition of gangsters, policemen, and politicians. The city of Personville—Poisonville to the *cognoscenti*—even begins to infect the Op, who feels himself "going blood-simple like the natives" (ch. xx). Where the police of the classic whodunit are frequently stupid or incompetent, the American police are brutal and degraded. The detectives of *The Maltese Falcon* continually harass and intimidate Spade, in Chandler's novels they bully and beat the detective. Captain Gregorius of *The Long Goodbye* "solves crimes with the bright light, the soft sap, the kick to the kidneys, the knee to the groin, the fist to the solar plexus, the night stick to the base of the spine" (ch. vii). The detective must work outside the law since its representatives demonstrate the decay of order. He works alone because he cannot compromise as the official detectives must; his faith lies in his own values. Marlowe tells the policemen in *The High Window*, "'Until you guys own your own souls you don't own mine. ... Until you guys can be trusted every time...to seek the truth out... I have a right to listen to my own conscience'" (ch. xv).

Criminals and policemen are not the only moral offenders; culpability often begins at the highest social levels. In Poisonville, for example, the source of disorder is the wealthy and powerful Elihu Wison, who owns "a United States senator, a couple of representatives, the governor, the mayor, and most of the state legislature" (ch. i). The affluent are so often responsible for social problems that a quasi-Marxist distrust of the wealthy becomes a minor motif; the rich are merely gangsters who have managed to escape punishment. A character in *The Long Goodbye* voices the common condemnation:

> "There ain't no clean way to make a hundred million bucks. ... Somewhere along the line guys got pushed to the wall, nice little businesses got the ground cut out from under them...decent people lost their jobs. ... Big money is big power and big power gets used wrong. It's the system"   (ch. xxxix).

In Ross Macdonald's novels the rich seem particularly culpable, perhaps because of this prevailing belief that there is no clean way to make a lot of money. In *The Barbarous Coast* Lew Archer discovers that a wealthy movie producer owes his success to a notorious gangster; in *Black Money* that underworld profits link the honored rich with the hoodlums and gamblers of Las Vegas.

Even the ordinary bourgeois, including the respected professional man, is not immune to the general taint. Because the doctor epitomizes bourgeois values he is suspect; in addition, his education is a target of the Leatherstocking hero's anti-intellectual antipathy. In Chandler's novels there are the crooked Dr. Verringer of *The Long Goodbye* (merely one of three shady doctors in that book), Dr. Sonderborg of *Farewell, My Lovely*, Dr. Almore of *The Lady in the Lake*, Dr. Lagardie of *The Little Sister*. Macdonald's novels are full of corrupt doctors; in addition he attacks the college professor who, like the doctor, has misused his position. In *The Chill*, Lew Archer discovers the academic community can conceal scandal, and in *The Far Side of the Dollar* unmasks a professor-murderer. Crime spreads a general *malaise* through every level of society:

> We've got the big money, the sharp shooters, the percentage workers, the fast-dollar boys, the hoodlums out of New York and Chicago and Detroit—and Cleveland. We've got the flash restaurants and night clubs they run, and the grifters and con men and female bandits that live in them. The luxury trades, the pansy decorators, the Lesbian dress designers, the riff-raff... Out in the fancy suburbs dear old Dad is reading the sports page in front of a picture window, with his shoes off, thinking he is high class because he has a three-car garage. Mom is in front of her princess dresser trying to paint the suitcases out from under her eyes. And Junior is clamped onto the telephone calling up a succession of high school girls that talk pigeon English and carry contraceptives in their make-up kit.   (*The Little Sister*, ch. xxvi)

All hard-boiled novels depict a tawdry world which conceals a shabby and depressing reality beneath its painted facade. Respectable Bay City hides a dreary criminality, "the pick-pockets and grifters and con men and drunk rollers and pimps and queens on the board walk" (*The Lady in the Lake*, ch. xxvi). The general shabbiness is another symptom of society's debilitating influence; wherever human beings gather, evil results. The social contract breeds not happiness but culpability.

The general tawdriness characterizes the urban locale of all hard-boiled fiction; in keeping with the American agrarian bias, the city is a place of wickedness. Unlike most American heroes, however, the detective has no other place to go. A man of the wilderness, he finds the wilderness destroyed, replaced by the urban jungle. The novels of Hammett, Chandler, and Macdonald all take place in California, where the frontier has finally disappeared. The private eye has responded to the national urge; he has completed the Westward trek. The detective novel concerns itself with what happens to the national hero once that trip is over, with what happens to Huck Finn when he runs out of "territory."

He does not find the Edenic land of his dreams, the Great Good Place of the American imagination, but the Great Bad Place. He finds, in short, "California, the department-store state" (*The Little Sister*, ch. xiii), a green and golden land raped of its fecundity and beauty. Where he had expected innocence and love, he finds the pervasive blight of sin, a society fallen from grace, an endless struggle against evil. Instead of a fertile valley, he discovers a cultural cesspool, containing the dregs of a neon-and-plastic civilization. He finds the American Dream metamorphosed into the American Nightmare. Its true capital is not the luminous city or the New Jerusalem, but Hollywood, a place devoted to illusions:

> Hollywood started as a meaningless dream, invented for money. But its colors ran, out through the holes in people's heads, spread across the landscape and solidified. North and south along the coast, east across the desert, across the continent. Now we were stuck with the dream without a meaning. It had become the nightmare we live in.　　　　(*The Barbarous Coast,* ch. xiii)

Natty Bumppo has come to the end of his journey.

Intensifying this dark vision and enriching the romantic associations of the hero, Raymond Chandler and Ross Macdonald employ the conventions and structures of other kinds of romance, giving their novels a further mythic dimension. Philip Durham has characterized Chandler's hero as a knight. In fact, the detectives of both Chandler and Macdonald combine the characteristics of the national hero with those of the knight. Chandler acknowledged that Marlowe's name is an anagram on Malory, and Archer also has medieval connotations. Their loneliness is not only the normal condition of the Leatherstocking hero, but also the celibacy of the pure knight. Chandler and Macdonald scatter numerous romance references throughout their novels to identify their heroes' task with the chivalric quest. Both, for example, employ allusive names. The beautiful Helen Grayle of *Farewell, My Lovely* temporarily distracts the detective from his pursuit of the true Grail. Orfamay Quest initiates the search of *The Little Sister,* another false maiden, her name suggests an association both with the quest and Morgan le Fay. Macdonald, who has a literary background, alludes frequently to medieval romance—he names a character Francis Martel *(Black Money)* and another, who appears at a moment of total disaster in *The Way Some People Die,* Runceyvall. The elegiac tone of the novels, reflected in some of the titles—*The Big Sleep, Farewell, My Lovely, The Long Goodbye, The Way Some People Die*—echoes the autumnal overtones of the Arthurian legends. In *The Lady in the Lake,* Chandler's title refers both to a murder victim and to another important figure from romance.[2]

Chivalric romance serves a more than incidental function, providing not only the hero, but narrative structure and moral judgment as well. The

---

[2][This theme is followed in greater detail in Jonathan Holden, "The Case for Raymond Chandler's Fiction as Romance," *Kansas Quarterly,* X (Fall, 1978), 41-46. Editor's note.]

initial omen of *The Big Sleep* capsulizes the action of the novel. Visiting the Sternwood mansion, Marlowe notices a stained glass panel

> ...showing a knight in dark armor rescuing a lady who was tied to a tree and didn't have any clothes on...I stood there and thought that if I lived in the house, I would sooner or later have to climb up there and help him.
>
> (ch. i)

Marlowe, "the shop-soiled Galahad" (*The High Window*, ch. xxviii), does in fact become the knight of the novel. Hired by the incredibly old, incredibly feeble General Sternwood, an impotent Fisher King, to save his daughter from the Gorgon of blackmail, Marlowe finds the beautiful, depraved girl naked, and saves her, only to discover she is a murderess, the Loathly Lady instead of the fair damsel, the Dark Sister of romance. The detective realizes "It wasn't a game for knights" (*The Big Sleep*, ch. xxiv). His quest is ironic since the hidden truth he discovers is a source of further evil.

One of the most frequently repeated devices of the American thriller is the motif of the magical quack. The detective's investigations lead him to a practitioner of some sort of pseudoscientific or pseudoreligious fakery. Most often, this figure presides over a cult of some kind, practicing faith healing, holding seances, fleecing the credulous. Like many others, the convention seems to begin in Hammett: in *The Dain Curse* the Continental Op encounters apparently supernatural terrors at the Temple of the Holy Grail. Philip Marlowe is temporarily vanquished by the "psychic consultant" Jules Amthor in *Farewell, My Lovely*. In *The Moving Target* Lew Archer visits a self-styled prophet at the Temple of the Clouds, "slipping off the edge of a case into a fairy tale" (ch. xiv). The quackery begins as a reasonable representation of the Southern California setting, where in a richly, though inadvertently, symbolic landscape zany religions proliferate like the orange trees. The device also implies the emptiness of the modern American spiritual condition, enriching the dark vision of the private eye novels by demonstrating the extents to which the faithless will go to find significance in a bleakly dispirited world. Perhaps most important, the bizarre cults and temples lend a quasi-magical element of the Grail romance to the hard-boiled thriller—the detective-knight must journey to a Perilous Chapel where an ambivalent Merlin figure, a mad or evil false priest, presides. His eventual triumph over the charlatan becomes a ritual feat, a besting of the powers of darkness.

Macdonald often demonstrates a sophisticated fusion of myth and legend. He employs variations on the classic identity quests in several books, most notably in *The Far Side of the Dollar*, where a hunt for a runaway boy becomes a multiple search for identity; the boy runs off to find his real parents, his real name, while Archer seeks not only the boy, but also a murderer, an answer to a puzzling series of events in the past, and the son he himself never had. Even Archer's vision of the world and his task employs a familiar romance convention, the visit to the underworld. In *The Moving Target* he imagines "an underground river of filth that ran under the city. There was no turning back. I had to wade the excremental river" (ch. xix). The task of the detective, in chivalric terms, becomes the knight's battle against evil as well as his quest for truth. Because the dragon seems to encompass all society, the detective must accept only partial victories. There is no redemption in the hard-boiled novels because guilt and crime are general and diffuse; the hero cannot simply locate a single source. He sees evil everywhere and can only deal with a small part of it. He wades the excremental river, but is incapable of releasing the wasteland from its blight. In search of the City of the Angels and the Holy Wood, he finds, instead, Los Angeles and Hollywood.

In *Anatomy of Criticism* Northrop Frye characterizes romance as "a sequential and processional form," limiting itself to "a sequence of minor adventures leading up to a major or climacteric adventure." This description, coupled with Richard Chase's statement that the American novel in general "tends to carve out of experience brilliant, highly wrought fragments rather than massive unities," explains the sometimes uncertain plotting of the American thriller. It generally is more preoccupied with the character of its hero, the society he investigates, and the adventures he encounters, than with the central mystery, which gets pushed aside by individual scenes and situations. The detective of the hard-boiled novel generally solves his mystery in a hurried, disordered fashion in the last few pages of his book, with little effort to clear up all points or tie up all loose threads. That the progress of the quest is more interesting than its completion further distinguishes the hard-boiled thriller from the formal detective novel. Because he does not suit his society and its rules and because his quest once again fails to achieve the Grail, the American detective experiences none of the admiration or satisfaction that accompanies the transcendent sleuth's success. He has solved little, he has cured nothing. As Chandler writes of his hero, "I see him always in a lonely street, in lonely rooms, puzzled but never quite defeated."[3] Like Philip Marlowe, he seeks refuge in playing solitary chess against the great masters, where the knights have value and power, and the medieval order of the game has a logic all its own: "beautiful cold remorseless chess, almost creepy in its silent implacability" (*The High Window*, ch. xxxvi). Or like Lew Archer, he is left guilty and alone, contemplating old failures and new disasters.

In the chaotic world of the hard-boiled novel, neither an elegant young man nor a benevolent Prospero can succeed. Its society is too coarse and violent for a languid dilettante of crime; and Prospero's magic is valueless

---

[3][Raymond Chandler's famous essay, "The Simple Art of Murder," is quoted so often by those included in this volume, there seemed little need to include the essay itself. Those who wish to read it will find it in Chandler's volume of that title (Boston, 1950). Editor's note.]

in a civilization governed by Caliban. As Chandler put it, "Down these mean streets a man must go who is not himself mean, who is neither tarnished nor afraid. The detective...must be such a man. He is the hero; he is everything." Though many hard-boiled writers thought their hero a "realistic" detective, his is an imaginative realism, summarizing the subconscious vision of his country, as contained in the conventions of its art. In his relationship to the heroes of the past, the private eye, paradoxically, resembles such types as Lord Peter Wimsey and Gideon Fell, who owe more to literary archetypes than to real life or the conventions of the thriller. As a literary hero he fulfills wishful desires, of his own time and of all times, for courage, competence, and goodness; part fairy tale hero, part culture hero, part national hero. His popular appeal demonstrates the extent of literary penetration into subliterary forms: for people who do not read the classics of American literature, he is a classic American hero. D. H. Lawrence, who probably never read a thriller, could have been describing the hard-boiled detective in his discussion of Cooper's novels:

> True myth concerns itself centrally with the onward adventure of the integral soul. And this, for America, is Deerslayer. A man who turns his back on white society. A man who keeps his moral integrity intact. An isolate, almost selfless, stoic, enduring man, who lives by death, by killing, but who is pure white.

The hard-boiled novel inverts the conventions of both whodunit and romance. Where the formal detective story contains a bucolic setting, an integrated and harmonious social order, and a ritual of absolution, the private eye novel employs an urban locale, a disordered society, and a final dissolution. The city of stone and sterility opposes the fertile garden, the general guilt reverses the establishment of innocence, and incest and homosexuality become demonic parodies of normal human relationships. Its nightmare vision reverses normal wish fulfillment, frustrating rather than gratifying human desires. Romance, generally speaking, is also a wish fulfillment form, but the hard-boiled novel transforms the romance conventions. Though the hero succeeds in his quest for a murderer, his victory is Pyrrhic, costing a great price in the coin of the spirit. The fair maidens turn out to be Loathly Ladies in disguise. And the closer the detective approaches to the Grail, the further away it recedes. In the hard-boiled novel the blessed desires of normally wish-fulfilling literature are all ironically altered; the daydream has given way to nightmare.

Only one writer remains to be discussed, the man who represents the perversion of the American detective novel, Mickey Spillane. In Spillane the wisecrack, the wit, the repartee, the rapid action and pace, the inevitable urgency of event, as well as the stylistic grace and gusto of a Chandler or Macdonald, are absent. What remains of the essence of the American thriller is the toughness, the sexuality, the violence, and a distorted version of its themes, motifs, and values. The detective's solipsistic belief in himself, his unerring rightness, his intensely lonely virtue, all become a vivid argument for a totalitarian moral policeman whose code, no matter how vicious, must be forced upon every man. Mike Hammer is convinced he is the hammer of God, free to torture, maim, or kill all who get in his way. The whodunit's implicit endorsement of a system of justice and the hard-boiled novel's explicit sense of morality are transformed in Spillane into dictatorial apologetics, advance propaganda for the police state. A thug and a brute, Hammer would have been the villain of most mysteries, but in Spillane he is the new superman, a plainclothes Nazi. The titles indicate his character: *My Gun Is Quick, I, the Jury, Vengeance Is Mine.*

Where the knight of the romantic thriller usually finds himself torn between two polar ideals—the etherealized spirit of the Perfect Blonde and the sensual earthiness of the Seductive Brunette—finally settling for neither, Mike Hammer usually manages to sleep with both women, then kills the evil one (sometimes both are guilty; often the innocent one is killed by the enemy), having and eating his cake at the same time. The sexual candor of the American thriller, a departure from the British form, becomes in Spillane a nearly pornographic treatment of lust. The common American literary theme of hostility to women resolves itself into a psychotic destructiveness; Spillane's detective has a pathological fear of women and takes his revenge on them in the most repellent manner. He is not content to turn the guilty woman over to the police, but instead invariably shoots the girl (who is in the final episodes always naked and at her most seductive) with a very large gun, as bloodily and painfully as possible. Perhaps the most revelatory of the Mike Hammer novels, *Vengeance Is Mine* ends in the usual woman-shooting scene, but with a rather unusual twist; Juno, the statuesque beauty who has aroused Hammer's lust throughout the book, turns out to be a male homosexual. The plausibility of such a device is itself questionable, but the inherent brutal homosexuality of Mike Hammer seems transparently obvious.

The sexuality itself is not all that makes the Spillane thriller a perverted version of the romantic thriller; perhaps his novels' most salient characteristic is their sadistic scenes. Not only does Mike Hammer have an unfortunate penchant for shooting women in the belly, but he also finds himself engaging in physical struggles against hoodlums and gangsters, which, like the killings, achieve either the zenith or the nadir of American tough-guy brutality.

> ...I snapped the side of the rod across his jaw and laid the flesh open to the bone. He dropped the sap and staggered into the big boy with a scream starting to come up out of his throat only to get it cut off in the middle as I pounded his teeth back into his mouth with the end of the barrel. The big

guy tried to shove him out of the way. He got so mad he came right at me with his head down and I took my own damn time about kicking him in the face. He smashed into the door and lay there bubbling. So I kicked him again and he stopped bubbling. I pulled the knucks off his hand then went over and picked up the sap. The punk was vomiting on the floor, trying to crawl his way under the sink. For laughs I gave him a taste of his own sap on the back of his hand and felt the bones go into splinters. He wasn't going to be using any tools for a long time.   (*The Big Kill,* ch. iii)

Spillane makes the toughness of Hammett, the insight of Chandler, and the compassion of Macdonald seem like sissified and effeminate stuff indeed.

It is important to remember that Spillane's work flourished in the McCarthyite fifties. His political philosophy—an inversion of the hard-boiled thriller's compassionate identification with liberal political and social thought—smacks strongly of right-wing totalitarianism, of a rabid hatred of anything leftist ("pinko" is his term), of an almost insane fear of "Commies," which parallels his apparent fear of women. The world Spillane describes has no vestige of the failed American Dream or the redemptive hero in it; his streets don't seem particularly mean—except for the fact that they are inhabited by men who resemble Mike Hammer—and his hero is in no way a man of honor. If the private detective of the hard-boiled thriller is yet another version of the cowboy who symbolizes the pastoral dream of America, then in Spillane the death of the good sheriff has finally taken place, and the bad guys walk the streets unhampered by a hero who can rise above his society and exterminate at least a portion of the evil flourishing around him. The private detective story, the romantic thriller, the typically American version of the detective novel, reaches a kind of end in Spillane; though a scant few writers still maintain the form, they are all—except for Ross Macdonald—without the skill, insight, or awareness of the best hard-boiled writers. The private detective has had his day—the shamus, the dick, the peeper, the snooper, who became a powerful American hero in Hammett and Chandler, has descended to the bully, the sadist, the voyeur, no longer a hero at all, but merely a villain who claims the right always to be right.

Although the hard-boiled writers set out to write tough, contemporary mysteries in modern colloquial language, they ultimately wrote romantic rather than realistic fiction. Virtually every major attempt at accurate reporting became a literary device. Their rendering of contemporary reality —Prohibition, gangsterism, corruption—became an expanding metaphor for universal sinfulness, a modern expression of the American Puritan preoccupation with innate depravity. The private detective, born as a plausible substitute for the conventional sleuths of the whodunit and apparently appropriate to his time and place, evolved into a literary hero, nearer to his archetype's imaginative reality than to an actual detective. The prevalence of booze, blondes, and blood, frequently noted by unfriendly critics, not only lent new energy to the detective story, but also entirely suited the romance form: condemnations of the American thriller's violence and depravity recall Roger Ascham's dismissal of *Morte D'Arthur* for its "open manslaughter and bold bawdry" (*The Schoolmaster*, Book I). Even the clipped, slangy style and the first-person objective point of view, which helped justify the adjective, "hard-boiled," were transformed into a literary medium. Hammett's terse, taut style descends from the American tradition of understatement connecting Emily Dickinson, Mark Twain, and Ernest Hemingway. Indeed, Hammett is the detective story's Hemingway, with a comparable influence on his peers. Chandler, on the other hand, seems the Faulkner of the thriller: his prose, richer and more resonant than Hammett's, demonstrates the considerable power and versatility of the hard-boiled style. His vision, too, broadens and intensifies the bleakly vicious world of his predecessor. In Ross Macdonald hard-boiled writing reaches a high point of stylization, full of learned allusions and rich in un-Bumppoish metaphorical flights. This development of hard-boiled prose from the terseness of Hammett to the rococo conceits of Macdonald parallels the evolution of the American detective thriller from the tough action story of the pulps to the very literary novel of the American romance tradition.

The wide success of the American hard-boiled thriller reveals a hitherto unrealized aesthetic sense in the reading public. Though many writers have attempted hard-boiled novels, none has achieved the popularity or longevity of the great practitioners of the romantic tradition. A. A. Fair, Thomas B. Dewey, Brett Halliday, and Richard S. Prather have won only ephemeral success; like the early writers of the hard-boiled school, in all probability they will be forgotten long before Hammett, Chandler, or Macdonald. The very fact that the ordinary public, as well as a few literary critics, seems to prefer the major practitioners to the minor, the skilled writers to the unskilled, the thoughtful and conscious authors to the superficial and imitative, is significant. The best examples of a particular kind, however questionable that kind may seem to some, retain their popular appeal long after inferior works have disappeared; in the hard-boiled novel, literary and commercial success coincide.

Finally, the literary tradition which informs the American romance thriller nullifies the argument that such works serve merely trivial ends. With their American penchant for dissolution, alienation, and despair, the hard-boiled novels, however tough or exciting on the surface, cannot justly be called wish fulfilling. In fact, they do not even deserve to be termed escapist except in the sense that all art represents escape; as Chandler puts it, "All men who read escape from something else into what lies beyond the printed page; the quality of the dream may be argued, but its release has become a functional necessity." The quality of the American thriller's dream corresponds with the traditional visions of the national literature and life; not a fantasy of human gratification, but an hallucinated vision. The chronicles of the mean streets seem as true as, say, Dickens's murky portraits of London or Fitzgerald's and Hemingway's pictures of a decadent and corrupting society. And the private detective, a "man of honor in all things," seems as appropriate to his fiction as Natty Bumppo or the Arthurian knight. The hard-boiled detective novel, the romance thriller, clearly demonstrates a significant and meaningful relationship with some of the most important American literature; at its best, moreover, it possesses the thoughtfulness and artfulness of serious literary work. A valuable and interesting form, it presents a worthy alternative to the thriller of manners, and indicates the potency and durability of the national cultural vision, the American Dream, as it constantly metamorphoses into nightmare.

The Study of Literary Formulas

by John G. Cawelti

Formulas, Genres, and Archetypes

In general, a literary formula is a structure of narrative or dramatic conventions employed in a great number of individual works. There are two common usages of the term *formula* closely related to the conception I wish to set forth. In fact, if we put these two conceptions together, I think we will have an adequate definition of literary formulas. The first usage simply denotes a conventional way of treating some specific thing or person. Homer's epithets—swift-footed Achilles, cloud-gathering Zeus—are commonly referred to as formulas as are a number of his standard similes and metaphors—"his head fell speaking into the dust"—which are assumed to be conventional bardic formulas for filling a dactylic hexameter line. By extension, any form of cultural stereotype commonly found in literature— red-headed, hot-tempered Irishmen, brilliantly analytical and eccentric detectives, virginal blondes, and sexy brunettes—is frequently referred to as formulaic. The important thing to note about this usage is that it refers to patterns of convention which are usually quite specific to a particular culture and period and do not mean the same outside this specific context. Thus the nineteenth-century formulaic relation between blondness and sexual purity gave way in the twentieth century to a very different formula for blondes. The formula of the Irishman's hot temper was particularly characteristic of English and American culture at periods where the Irish were perceived as lower-class social intruders.

The second common literary usage of the term formula refers to larger plot types. This is the conception of formula commonly found in those manuals for aspiring writers that give the recipes for twenty-one sure-fire plots—boy meets girl, boy and girl have a misunderstanding, boy gets girl. These general plot patterns are not necessarily limited to a specific culture

John G. Cawelti, "The Study of Literary Formulas." From John G. Cawelti, *Adventure, Mystery, and Romance: Formula Stories as Art and Popular Culture* (Chicago: University of Chicago Press, 1976), pp. 5-9, 16-18, 20-33, 35-36. Reprinted with permission of John G. Cawelti and the University of Chicago Press. John Cawelti is Professor of English and Humanities at the University of Chicago.

or period. Instead, they seem to represent story types that, if not universal in their appeal, have certainly been popular in many different cultures at many different times. In fact, they are examples of what some scholars have called archetypes or patterns that appeal in many different cultures.

Actually, if we look at a popular story type such as the western, the detective story, or the spy adventure, we find that it combines these two sorts of literary phenomenon. These popular story patterns are embodiments of archetypal story forms in terms of specific cultural materials. To create a western involves not only some understanding of how to construct an exciting adventure story, but also how to use certain nineteenth- and twentieth-century images and symbols such as cowboys, pioneers, outlaws, frontier towns, and saloons along with appropriate cultural themes or myths—such as nature vs. civilization, the code of the West, or law and order vs. outlawry—to support and give significance to the action. Thus formulas are ways in which specific cultural themes and stereotypes become embodied in more universal story archetypes.

The reason why formulas are constructed in this way is, I think, fairly straightforward. Certain story archetypes particularly fulfill man's needs for enjoyment and escape. ... But in order for these patterns to work, they must be embodied in figures, settings, and situations that have appropriate meanings for the culture which produces them. One cannot write a successful adventure story about a social character type that the culture cannot conceive in heroic terms; this is why we have so few adventure stories about plumbers, janitors, or streetsweepers. It is, however, certainly not inconceivable that a culture might emerge which placed a different sort of valuation or interpretation on these tasks, in which case we might expect to see the evolution of adventure story formulas about them. Certainly one can see signs of such developments in the popular literature of Soviet Russia and Maoist China.

A formula is a combination or synthesis of a number of specific cultural conventions with a more universal story form or archetype. It is also similar in many ways to the traditional literary conception of a genre. There is bound to be a good deal of confusion about the terms "formula" and "genre" since they are occasionally used to designate the same thing. For example, many film scholars and critics use the term "popular genre" to denote literary types like the western or the detective story that are clearly the same as what I call formulas. On the other hand, the term is often used to describe the broadest sort of literary type such as drama, prose fiction, lyric poetry. This is clearly a very different sort of classification than that of western, detective story, spy story. Still another usage of genre involves concepts like tragedy, comedy, romance, and satire. Insofar as such concepts of genre imply particular sorts of story patterns and effects, they do bear some resemblance to the kind of classification involved in the definition of popular genres. Since such conceptions clearly imply universal or transcultural conceptions of literary structure, they are examples of what I have called archetypes. I don't think it makes a great deal of difference whether we refer to something as a formula or as a popular genre, if we are clear just what we are talking about and why. In the interests of such clarification let me offer one distinction I have found useful.

In defining literary classes, it seems to me that we commonly have two related but distinguishable purposes. First of all, we may be primarily interested in constructing effective generalizations about large groups of literary works for the purpose of tracing historical trends or relating literary production to other cultural patterns. In such cases we are not primarily interested in the artistic qualities of individual works but in the degree to which particular works share common characteristics that may be indicative of important cultural tendencies. On the other hand, we use literary classes as a means of defining and evaluating the unique qualities of individual works. In such instances we tend to think of genres not simply as generalized descriptions of a number of individual works but as a set of artistic limitations and potentials. With such a conception in mind, we can evaluate individual works in at least two different ways: (a) by the way in which they fulfill or fail to fulfill the ideal potentials inherent in the genre and thereby achieve or fail to achieve the full artistic effect of that particular type of construction. These are the terms in which Aristotle treats tragedy; (b) by the way in which the individual work deviates from the flat standard of the genre to accomplish some unique individual expression or effect. Popular genres are often treated in this fashion, as when a critic shows that a particular western transcends the limitations of the genre or how a film director achieves a distinctive individual statement. This is the approach implicit in much *"auteur"* criticism of the movies, where the personal qualities of individual directors are measured against some conception of the standard characteristics of popular genres.

The concept of a formula as I have defined it is a means of generalizing the characteristics of large groups of individual works from certain combinations of cultural materials and archetypal story patterns. It is useful primarily as a means of making historical and cultural inferences about the collective fantasies shared by large groups of people and of identifying differences in these fantasies from one culture or period to another. When we turn from the cultural or historical use of the concept of formula to a consideration of the artistic limitations and possibilities of particular formulaic patterns, we are treating these formulas as a basis for aesthetic judgments of various sorts. In these cases, we might say that our generalized definition of a formula has become a conception of a genre. Formula and genre might be best understood not as denoting two different things, but as reflecting two phases or aspects of a complex process of literary analysis. This way of looking at the relation between formula and genre reflects the way in which popular genres develop. In most cases, a formulaic pattern will be in existence for a considerable period of time before it is conceived of by its creators and audience as a genre. For example, the western formula was already clearly defined in the nineteenth century, yet it was not until the twentieth century that the western was consciously conceived of as a distinctive literary and cinematic genre. Similarly, though Poe created the formula for the detective story in the 1840s and many stories and novels made some use of this pattern throughout the later nineteenth century, it was probably not until after Conan Doyle that the detective story became widely understood as a specific genre with its own special limitations and potentialities. If we conceive of a genre as a literary class that views certain typical patterns in relation to their artistic limitations and potentials, it will help us in making a further useful clarification. Because the conception of genre involves an aesthetic approach to literary structures, it can be conceived either in terms of the specific formulas of a particular culture or in relation to larger, more universal literary archetypes: there are times when we might wish to evaluate a particular western in relation to other westerns. In this case we would be using a conception of a formula-genre, or what is sometimes more vaguely called a popular genre. We might also wish to relate this same western to some more universal generic conception such as tragedy or romance. Here we would be employing an archetype-genre. ...

The Artistic Characteristics of Formula Literature

Formula literature is, first of all, a kind of literary art. Therefore, it can be analyzed and evaluated like any other kind of literature. Two central aspects of formulaic structures have been generally condemned in the serious artistic thought of the last hundred years: their essential standardization and their primary relation to the needs of escape and relaxation. In order to consider formula literature in its own terms and not simply to condemn it out of hand, we must explore some of the aesthetic implications of these two basic characteristics.

While standardization is not highly valued in modern artistic ideologies, it is, in important ways, the essence of all literature. Standard conventions establish a common ground between writers and audiences. Without at least some form of standardization, artistic communication would not be possible. But well-established conventional structures are particularly essential to the creation of formula literature and reflect the interests of audiences, creators, and distributors.

Audiences find satisfaction and a basic emotional security in a familiar form; in addition, the audience's past experience with a formula gives it a sense of what to expect in new individual examples, thereby increasing its capacity for understanding and enjoying the details of a work. For creators, the formula provides a means for the rapid and efficient production of new

works. Once familiar with the outlines of the formula, the writer who devotes himself to this sort of creation does not have to make as many
difficult artistic decisions as a novelist working without a formula. Thus,
formulaic creators tend to be extremely prolific. Georges Simenon has
turned out an extraordinary number of first-rate detective novels, in addition to his less formulaic fiction. Others have an even more spectacular
record of quantity production: Frederick Faust and John Creasey each
turned out over five hundred novels under a variety of pseudonyms. For
publishers or film studios, the production of formulaic works is a highly
rationalized operation with a guaranteed minimal return as well as the possibility of large profits for particularly popular individual versions. I have
been told, for instance, that any paperback western novel is almost certain
to sell enough copies to cover expenses and make a small profit. Many
serious novels, on the other hand, fail to make expenses and some represent
substantial losses. There is an inevitable tendency toward standardization
implicit in the economy of modern publishing and film-making, if only
because one successful work will inspire a number of imitations by pro-
ducers hoping to share in the profits.

   If the production of formulas were only a matter of economics, we might
well turn the whole topic over to market researchers. Even if economic
considerations were the sole motive behind the production of formulas—
and I have already suggested that there are other important motives as well
—we would still need to explore the kind and level of artistic creation possible within the boundaries of a formula. . . . [We] seek escape from our
consciousness of the ultimate insecurities and ambiguities that afflict even
the most secure sort of life: death, the failure of love, our inability to accomplish all we had hoped for, the threat of atomic holocaust. Harry Berger
nicely described these two conflicting impulses in a recent essay:

> Man has two primal needs. First is a need for order, peace, and security,
> for protection against the terror or confusion of life, for a familiar and pre-
> dictable world, and for a life which is happily more of the same. . . . But the
> second primal impulse is contrary to the first: man positively needs anxiety
> and uncertainty, thrives on confusion and risk, wants trouble, tension,
> jeopardy, novelty, mystery, would be lost without enemies, is sometimes
> happiest when most miserable. Human spontaneity is eaten away by sameness:
> man is the animal most expert at being bored.[1]

In the ordinary course of experience, these two impulses or needs are
inevitably in conflict. If we seek order and security, the result is likely to
be boredom and sameness. But rejecting order for the sake of change and
novelty brings danger and uncertainty. As Berger suggests in his essay,
many central aspects of the history of culture can be interpreted as a dynamic

---

[1]Harry Berger, Jr., "Naive Consciousness and Culture Change: An Essay in Historical Struc-
turalism," *Bulletin of the Midwest Modern Language Association,* VI, no. 1 (Spring, 1973), 35.

tension between these two basic impulses, a tension that Berger believes has increased in modern cultures with their greater novelty and change. In such cultures, men are continually and uncomfortably torn between the quest for order and the flight from ennui. The essence of the experience of escape and the source of its ability to relax and please us is, I believe, that it temporarily synthesizes these two needs and resolves this tension. This may account for the curious paradox that characterizes most literary formulas, the fact that they are at once highly ordered and conventional and yet are permeated with the symbols of danger, uncertainty, violence, and sex. In reading or reviewing a formulaic work, we confront the ultimate excitements of love and death, but in such a way that our basic sense of security and order is intensified rather than disrupted, because, first of all, we know that this is an imaginary rather that a real experience, and, second, because the excitement and uncertainty are ultimately controlled and limited by the familiar world of the formulaic structure.

As we have seen, the world of a formula can be described as an archetypal story pattern embodied in the images, symbols, themes, and myths of a particular culture. As shaped by the imperatives of the experience of escape, these formulaic worlds are constructions that can be described as moral fantasies constituting an imaginary world in which the audience can encounter a maximum of excitement without being confronted with an overpowering sense of the insecurity and danger that accompany such forms of excitement in reality. Much of the artistry of formulaic literature involves the creator's ability to plunge us into a believable kind of excitement while, at the same time, confirming our confidence that in the formulaic world things always work out as we want them to. Three of the literary devices most often used by formulaic writers of all kinds can serve as an illustration of this sort of artistic skill: suspense, identification, and the creating of a slightly removed, imaginary world. Suspense is essentially the writer's ability to evoke in us a temporaty sense of fear and uncertainty that is always pointed toward a possible resolution. The simplest model of suspense is the cliff-hanger in which the protagonist's life is immediately threatened while the machinery of salvation is temporarily withheld from us. We know, however, that the hero or heroine will be saved in some way, because he always is. In its crudest form the cliff-hanger presents the combination of extreme excitement within a framework of certainty and security that characterizes formulaic literature. Of course, the cruder forms of suspense—however effective with the young and the unsophisticated—soon lose much of their power to excite more sophisticated audiences. Though there are degrees of skill in producing even the simpler forms of suspense, the better formulaic artists devise means of protracting and complicating suspense into larger, more believable structures. Good detective story writers are able to maintain a complex intellectual suspense centering on the possibility that a dangerous criminal might remain at large or that innocent people might be convicted of the crime. They sustain uncertainty until the final revelation, yet at the same time assure us that the detective has the qualities which will eventually enable him to reach the solution. Alfred Hitchcock is, at his best, the master of a still more complex form of suspense that works at the very edge of escapist fantasy. In a Hitchcock film like *Frenzy*, reassurance is kept to a minimum and our anxiety is increased to the point that we seriously begin to wonder whether we have been betrayed, whether evil will triumph and the innocent will suffer. After we have been toyed with in this way, it is a powerful experience when the hero is finally plucked from the abyss.

Complex as it is, the suspense in a work like Hitchcock's *Frenzy* is different from the kind of uncertainty characteristic of mimetic literature. The uncertainty in a mimetic work derives from the way in which it continually challenges our easy assumptions and presuppositions about life. This tends to reduce the intensity of suspense effects since, if we perceive the world of the story as an imitation of the ambiguous, uncertain, and limited world of reality we are emotionally prepared for difficulties to remain unresolved or for resolutions to be themselves the source of further uncertainties. But if we are encouraged to perceive the story world in terms of a well-known formula, the suspense effect will be more emotionally powerful because we are so sure that it must work out. One of the major sources of Hitchcock's effects is the way in which he not only creates suspense around particular episodes, but suggests from time to time that he may depart from the basic conventions of the formulaic narrative world. Of course, we don't really think he's going to, but the tension between our hope that things will be properly resolved and our suspicion that Hitchcock might suddenly dump us out of the moral fantasy in which mysteries are always solved and the guilty finally identified and captured can be a terrifying and complex experience of considerable artistic power. At the climactic moment of *Frenzy* the protagonist escapes from the prison to which he has been wrongfully condemned and sets out to murder the man who is truly guilty, but finds himself beating an already murdered victim in such a way that circumstantial evidence will certainly condemn him as the murderer. This is an extraordinary suspense effect because, in the few moments before the final appropriate resolution, we are suspended over the abyss of reality. Such a moment would be less powerful if we were not ultimately expecting and anticipating the formulaic resolution.

The pattern of expectations with which we approach an individual version of a formula results both from our previous experience of the type and from certain internal qualities that formulaic structures tend to have. One of the most important such characteristics is the kind of identification we are encouraged to have with the protagonists. All stories involve some kind of identification, for, unless we are able to relate our feelings and experiences to those of the characters in fiction, much of the emotional effect will be lost. In mimetic literature, identification is a complex phenomenon. Because mimetic fictions aim at the representation of actions that will confront us with reality, it is necessary for writers to make us recognize our involvement in characters whose fates reveal the uncertainties, limitations, and unresolvable mysteries of the real world. We must learn to recognize and accept our relationship to characters, motives, and situations we would not ordinarily choose to imagine ourselves as involved in or threatened by. "There but for the grace of God go I." Ordinarily I would prefer not to think of myself as a murderer, as a suicide, or as a middle-aged failure cuckolded by his wife. Yet in Dostoevsky's *Crime and Punishment,* Faulkner's *The Sound and the Fury,* and Joyce's *Ulysses* I am forced to recognize and come to terms with my participation in the fate of Raskolnikov, of Quentin Compson, and of Leopold Bloom. The process of identification in a mimetic fiction involves both my recognition of the differences between myself and the characters and my often reluctant but rather total involvement in their actions. I have at once a detached view and a disturbingly full sympathy and understanding. ...

Formulas and Culture

Formulas are cultural products and in turn presumably have some sort of influence on culture because they become conventional ways of representing and relating certain images, symbols, themes, and myths. The process through which formulas develop, change, and give way to other formulas is a kind of cultural evolution with survival through audience selection.

Many different sorts of stories are written about a great diversity of subjects, but only a few become clearly established as formulas. For instance, out of the vast number of potential story possibilities associated with the rise of urban industrialism in the nineteenth century, relatively few major formulaic structures have developed, such as the detective story, the gangster saga, the doctor drama, and various science-fiction formulas. Other story types have been repeated often enough to become partly formulaic, such as the story of the newspaper reporter and the scoop, or the story of the failure of success as represented in the figure of the great tycoon. But these two types have never had the sustained and widespread appeal of the western, the detective story, or the gangster saga. Still other potential story topics have never become popular at all. There is no formula for the story of the union leader—despite the best efforts of "proletarian" critics and novelists in the 1930s. There are no formulas with politicians or businessmen as protagonists, though they are social figures of major importance. Farmers, engineers, architects, teachers, have all been treated in a number of individual novels but have never become formulaic heroes.

What is the basis on which this process of cultural selection of formulas takes place? Why do some sorts of stories become widely popular formulas while others do not? How do we account for the pattern of change within formulas, or for the way one formula supersedes another in popularity? What does popularity itself mean? Can we infer from the popularity of a work that it reflects public attitudes and motives, or is it impossible to go beyond the circular observation that a story is successful with the public because the public finds it a good story?

First of all, we can distinguish, I think, between the problem of the popularity of an individual work and the popularity of a formula. Determining why a particular novel or film becomes a best-seller is problematic because it is difficult to be sure what elements or combination of elements the public is responding to. For example, in the case of the enormously successful novel *The Godfather,* is it the topic of crime and the portrayal of violence that made the book popular? Probably not, since there are many other novels dealing with crime in a violent way that have not been equally successful. Thus it must be something about the way in which crime and violence are treated. Only if we can find other books or films that treat the topic of crime in a similar way and also gain a considerable measure of popularity can we feel some confidence that we have come closer to isolating the aspects of *The Godfather* that are responsible for its public success. ... Clearly, we can only explain the success of individual works by means of analogy and comparison with other successful works, through the process of defining those elements or patterns that are common to a number of best-sellers.

A formula is one such pattern. When we have successfully defined a formula we have isolated at least one basis for the popularity of a large number of works. Of course, some formulaic writers are more successful than others, and their unique popularity remains a problem that must be explored in its own right. During his heyday, Mickey Spillane's hard-boiled detective stories sold far better than those of any other writer in the formula, and Spillane's success was certainly one main reason why other writers continued to create this type of story. Yet quite apart from Spillane's own personal popularity, the hard-boiled detective formula, in the hands of writers as diverse as Dashiell Hammett, Raymond Chandler, Carter Brown, Shell Scott, Brett Halliday, and many others, in hard-boiled detective films by directors like Howard Hawks, John Huston, Roman Polanski, and in TV series like "Cannon," "Mannix," and "Barnaby Jones," has been continually successful with the public since the late 1920s. When it becomes such a widely successful formula, a story pattern clearly has some special appeal and significance to many people in the culture. It becomes a matter of cultural behavior that calls for explanation along with other cultural patterns.

Unfortunately, to construct such an explanation requires us to have some notion of the relation between literature and other aspects of culture, an area which remains rather impenetrable. Are literary works to be treated primarily as causes or symptoms of other modes of behavior? Or is literature an integral and autonomous area of human experience without significant effects on political, economic, or other forms of social behavior? Do some works of literature become popular primarily because they contain a good story artistically told or because they embody values and attitudes that their audience wishes to see affirmed? Or does popularity imply some kind of psychological wish-fulfillment, the most popular works being those which most effectively help people to identify imaginatively with actions they would like to perform but cannot in the ordinary course of events? We certainly do not know at present which, if any, of these assumptions is correct. Persuasive arguments can be made for each one. Before attempting to develop a tentative method for exploring the cultural meaning of literary formulas, let us look briefly at what can be said for and against the principal methods that have been used to explore the relation between literature and other aspects of human behavior.

Three main approaches have been widely applied to explain the cultural functions or significance of literature. These may be loosely characterized as (1) impact or effect theories; (2) deterministic theories; and (3) symbolic or reflective theories.

1. Impact theories are the oldest, simplest, and most widespread way in which men have defined the cultural significance of literature. Such theories assume basically that literary forms and/ or contents have some direct influence on human behavior. Naturally, the tendency of this approach is to treat literature as a moral or political problem and to seek to determine which literary patterns have desirable effects on human conduct and which have bad effects, in order to support the former and suppress or censor the latter. Socrates suggested in *The Republic* that it might be necessary to escort the poet to the gates of the city since his works stimulate weakening and corrupting emotions in his audience. Over the centuries, men of varying religious and political commitments have followed this advice by seeking to censor literary expression on the ground that it would corrupt the people's morals or subvert the state. Today, many psychologists study what effects the representation of violence has on the behavior of children. Presumably if they are able to demonstrate some connection between represented violence and aggressive behavior, the widespread clamor against film and television violence will increase and laws will be passed regulating the content of these media.

The impact approach also dominated mass communications research in its earlier years, when sociologists were primarily interested in propaganda and its effects. Propaganda research sought to show just how and in what ways a literary message could have an effect on attitudes and behavior. This research discovered, for the most part, that insofar as any effect could be isolated, propaganda simply caused people to believe and act in ways they were already predisposed toward. It became evident to most researchers in this area that their original quest for a direct link between communication and behavior oversimplified a more complex social process. Much of the more interesting recent research has tended to focus on the process of communication rather than its impact, showing the ways in which mass communications are mediated by the social groups to which the recipient belongs, or by the different uses to which communications are put. But the more complex our view of the process of communication becomes, the less meaningful it is to speak of it in terms of cause and effect.

Another basic weakness of impact theories is that they tend to treat literary or artistic experience like any other kind of experience. Since most of our experience does have an immediate and direct effect on our behavior, however trivial, the impact theorists assume that the same must be true of literature. The difficulty with this view is that our experience of literature is not like any other form of behavior since it concerns events and characters that are imagined. Reading about something is obviously not the same thing as doing it. Nor are the very strong emotions generated in us by stories identical with those emotions in real life. A story about a monster can arouse fear and horror in me, but this is certainly a different emotion than the one I feel when confronted by some actual danger or threat, because I know that the monster exists only in the world of the story and cannot actually harm me. This does not mean that my emotion will necessarily be less strong than it would be in reality. Paradoxically, feelings experienced through literature may sometimes be stronger and deeper than those aroused by analogous life situations. For instance, I am inclined to believe that the fear and pity evoked by literature is more intense for many people than that generated in real-life experiences. That literature can give us such intensified emotions may be one of the reasons we need stories. Yet no matter how strong the feeling aroused by a work of literature, we do not generally confuse it with reality and therefore it does not affect us as such. There are probably some important exceptions to this generalization. Unsophisticated or disturbed people do apparently sometimes confuse art and reality. The same is apparently true of many younger children. There are many instances where people treat characters in a soap opera as if they were real people, sending them gifts on their birthdays, grieving when they are in difficulties, asking their advice and help. Some of this behavior is probably an unsophisticated way of expressing one's great pleasure and interest in a story, but some of it may well indicate that a person does not make our ordinary differentiation between imagination and reality. For such people literature may well have a direct and immediate behavioral impact. I suspect that this is particularly the case among relatively disturbed children. Not surprisingly, it is here that recent studies may indicate a causal connection between represented violence and violent behavior. Nonetheless, for most people in most situations, the impact approach assumes much too simple a relationship between literature and other behavior to provide a satisfactory basis for interpreting the cultural significance of any literary phenomenon.

If such reflections lead us to question the idea that literature has a direct causal effect on behavior, this does not mean that we must take the position that literature causes nothing and is only a reflection of reality without further consequence than the evocation of some temporary state of feeling. Such a view seems just as implausible as the notion that art directly and immediately changes attitudes and behavior. One of my colleagues has often remarked that all of us carry a collection of story plots around in our heads and that we tend to see and shape life according to these plots. Something like this seems to me to be the basic kernel of truth in the impact theory. Our artistic experiences over a period of time work on the structure of our imaginations and feelings and thereby have long-term effects on the way in which we understand and respond to reality. Unfortunately, no one has ever managed to demonstrate the existence of such long-term effects in a convincing way, in part because we have never been able to define with any precision just what are the most common and widespread patterns of literary experience. The analysis of formulas may be a promising method of beginning to study long-term effects, for formulas do shape the greater part of the literary experiences of a culture. If we can clearly define all the major formulas of a particular culture, we will at least know what patterns are being widely experienced. It may then be possible to construct empirical studies in the relation between these formulas and the attitudes and values that individuals and groups show in other forms of behavior. David McClelland and his associates managed to isolate a particular pattern of action in stories that they correlated with a basic cultural motive for achievement. In cross-cultural studies reported in *The Achieving Society,* McClelland suggests that the presence of this pattern of action in the stories of a particular culture or period is correlated with a definite emphasis on achievement in that culture or in a succeeding period. Some of the cases McClelland cites could be instances where the stories heard most often by children did have a long-term impact on their behavior as adults; it is, of course, difficult to determine the extent to which these story patterns were causes or symptoms, but this, I feel, is a problem that can never be solved. If we can establish correlations between literary patterns and other forms of behavior, we will have done all we can expect to do by way of establishing the long-term impact of literature. The reason for this can be best understood by turning to the second major approach that has been employed to explain the cultural significance of literature: the various theories of social or psychological determinism.

2. These deterministic theories — the most striking being various applications of Marxian or Freudian ideas to the explanation of literature — assume that art is essentially a contingent and dependent form of behavior that is generated and shaped by some underlying social or psychological dynamic. In effect, literature becomes a kind of stratagem to cope with the needs of a social group or of the psyche. These needs become the determinants of literary expression and the process of explanation consists in showing how literary forms and contents are derived from these other processes.

The deterministic approach has been widely applied to the interpretation of all sorts of literature with interesting if controversial results ranging from the Oedipal interpretation of *Hamlet* to interpretations of the novel as a literary reflection of the bourgeois world view. When used in conjunction with individual masterpieces, the deterministic approach has been widely rejected and criticized by literary scholars and historians for its tendencies toward oversimplification and reductionism. And yet the method has gained much wider acceptance as a means of dealing with formulaic structures like the western, the detective story, and the formula romance. Some scholars see the whole range of formulaic literature as an opiate for the masses, a ruling-class stratagem for keeping the majority of the people content with a daily ration of pleasant distractions. Others have interpreted particular formulas in deterministic terms: the detective story as a dramatization of the ideology of bourgeois rationalism or as an expression of the psychological need to resolve in fantasy the repressed childhood memories of the primal scene.

All such explanations have two fundamental weaknesses. (*a*) They depend on the a priori assumption that a particular social or psychological dynamic is the basic cause of human behavior. If it is the case that, for example, unresolved childhood sexual conflicts generate most adult behavior, then it does not really explain anything to show that the reading of detective stories is an instance of such behavior. The interpretation does not go beyond the original assumption, except to show how the form of the detective story can be interpreted in this way. But the only means of proving that the detective story *should* be interpreted in this way is through the original assumption. Because of this circular relationship between assumption and interpretation, neither can provide proof for the other, unless the assumption can be demonstrated by other means. Even then there remains the problem of showing that the experience of literature is the same as other kinds of human activity. (*b*) The second weakness of most deterministic approaches is their tendency to reduce literary experience to other forms of behavior. For example, most Freudian interpretations treat literary experience as if it could be analogized with free association or dream. Even if we grant that psychoanalysis has proved to be a successful approach to the explanation of dream symbolism, it does not follow that literature is the same or even analogous. Indeed, there seems to me to be as much reason to believe that the making and enjoying of art works is an autonomous mode of experience as to assume it is dependent, contingent, or a mere reflection of other more basic social or psychological processes. Certainly many people act as if watching television, going to the movies, or reading a book were one of the prime ends of life rather than a means to something else. There are even statistics that might suggest that people spend far more time telling and enjoying stories than they do in sexual activity. Of course, the psychological determinist would claim that listening to a story is in fact a form of sexual behavior, though stated in this way, the claim seems extreme.

Though there are many problems connected with the psychoanalytic interpretation of literature, it is difficult to dismiss the compelling idea that in literature as in dreams unconscious or latent impulses find some disguised form of expression. Formula stories may well be one important way in which the individuals in a culture act out unconscious or repressed needs, or express latent motives that they must give expression to but cannot face openly. Possibly one important difference between the mimetic and escapist impulses in literature is that mimetic literature tends toward the bringing of latent or hidden motives into the light of consciousness while escapist literature tends to construct new disguises or to confirm existing defenses against the confrontation of latent desires. Such a view might be substantiated by the contrast between Sophocles' play *Oedipus the King* and a detective story. In the play detection leads to a revelation of hidden guilts in the life of the protagonist, while in the detective story the inquirer-protagonist and the hidden guilt are conveniently split into two separate characters—the detective and the criminal—thereby enabling us to imagine terrible crimes without also having to recognize our own impulses toward them. It is easy to generate a great deal of pseudopsychoanalytic theorizing of this sort without being able to substantiate it convincingly. Nevertheless, I think we cannot ignore the possibility that this is one important factor that underlies the appeal of literary formulas.

Thus, though we may feel that most contemporary deterministic approaches oversimplify the significance of literary works by explaining them in terms of other modes of experience, I think we cannot deny that stories, like other forms of behavior, are determined in some fashion. Though artistic experience may have an autonomy that present theories of social and psychological determinism are not sufficiently complex to allow for, I presume that, as human behavior in general is more fully understood, we will also be better able to generalize about how social and psychological factors play a role in the process by which stories and other imaginative forms are created and enjoyed. In the present state of our knowledge, it seems more reasonable to treat social and psychological factors not as single determinant causes of literary expression but as elements in a complex process that limits in various ways the complete autonomy of art. In making cultural interpretations of literary patterns, we should consider them not as simple reflections of social ideologies or psychological needs but as instances of a relatively autonomous mode of behavior that is involved in a complex dialectic with other aspects of human life. It is reasonable to see collective attitudes entering into the artistic works created and enjoyed by a particular group as a limit on what is likely to be represented in a story and how it is likely to be treated. What we must avoid is an automatic reading into a story of what we take to be the prevailing cultural attitudes or psychological needs. This has been too often the path taken by the deterministic approach and in its circularity it tells us nothing about either the literary work or the culture.

3. A third approach to the cultural explanation of literary experience—symbolic or reflective theories—rejects the more extreme forms of reductive determinism by granting a special kind of autonomy to artistic expression. According to this approach, the work of art consists of a complex of symbols or myths that are imaginative orderings of experience. These symbols or myths are defined as images or patterns of images charged with a complex of feeling and meaning and they become, therefore, modes of perception as well as simple reflections of reality. According to this approach, symbols and myths are means by which a culture expresses the complex of feelings, values, and ideas it attaches to a thing or idea. Because of their power of ordering feelings and attitudes, symbols and myths shape the perceptions and motivations of those who share them. The flag is a relatively simple example of a symbol. Though nothing but a piece of cloth made in a certain pattern of colors and shapes, the flag has come to imply an attitude of love and dedication to the service of one's country that has even, in many instances, motivated individuals to die in an attempt to protect that piece of cloth from desecration. In recent years this symbol has in turn become a counter-symbol for some groups of an unreasoning and destructive patriotism, and this implication has motivated other individuals to risk danger and even imprisonment to desecrate the same piece of cloth. The first usage of the flag illustrates a class of symbolism that poses relatively few problems of analysis and interpretation since the meaning of the symbol is more or less established by some specific enactment, in this case laws designating a specific design as the national emblem. In this sense the flag has an official status with a designated set of meanings, as indicated by the fact that it is against the law to treat the flag in certain ways. But the second usage of the flag as counter-symbol of regressive or false patriotism is of a different sort altogether. This symbolism was not created by specific enactment and has

no official status. It emerged as one means of focusing and representing the rejection by certain groups of actions and attitudes taken in the name of the country and defended by traditional claims of patriotism. I don't know whether it is possible to determine who first conceived of using the flag as a symbol of this sort, but it is clear that throughout the 1960s, particularly in connection with the agitation against the Vietnam war, this new symbolism of the flag became a powerful force, generating strong feelings and even violent actions both in support of and in opposition to this new form of symbolism.

These two types of symbolism indicate the great significance that symbols have for culture and psychology. In fact, the concept of symbolism seems to resolve some of the problems we have noted in connection with the impact and deterministic approaches to explaining the cultural significance of literary experience. The symbolism of the flag suggests how it is possible for an image both to reflect culture and to have some role in shaping it. Not surprisingly, some of the most influential studies of American culture in the past two decades have been analyses of symbols and myths primarily as these are expressed in various forms of literature. And yet there remain a number of problems about this approach, many of which have been effectively articulated in a critique of the myth-symbol approach by Bruce Kuklick. ... Kuklick defines two kinds of objection: the first concerns certain confusions in the theoretical formulations of the leading myth-symbol interpreters, while the second involves a number of problems of definition and method. Since the formula approach that I am using...is essentially a variation of the myth-symbol method of interpretation, I feel we must examine the most important of Kuklick's objections to it.

Essentially, Kuklick argues that certain theoretical confusions in the myth-symbol approach prevent it from being a meaningful way of connecting literary expression with other forms of behavior. He points out that the myth-symbol critics assume the existence of a collective mind (in which the images, myths, and symbols exist) that is separated from an external reality (of which the images and symbols are some form of mental transmutation). This separation is necessary, he suggests, in order for the interpreter to determine which images are real and which are fantastic or distortions or value-laden. Unfortunately, this separation of internal mind from external reality leads the method right into the philosophical trap of the mind-body problem, as exemplified in what Kuklick calls crude Cartesianism. The result is as follows:

> A crude Cartesian has two options. First, he can maintain his dualism but then must give up any talk about the external world. How can he know that any image refers to the external world? Once he stipulates that they are on different planes, it is impossible to bring them into any meaningful relation; in fact, it is not even clear what a relationship could conceivably be

like. Descartes resorted to the pineal gland as the source and agent of mind-body interaction, but this does not appear to be an out for the [myth-symbol interpreters]. Second, the Cartesian can assimilate what we normally take to be facts about the external world—for example, my seeing the man on the corner—to entities like images, symbols and myths. ... Facts and images both become states of consciousness. If the Cartesian does this, he is committed to a form of idealism. Of course, this maneuver will never be open to ... Marxists, but it also provides problems for the [myth-symbol interpreters]: they have no immediate way of determining which states of consciousness are "imaginative" or "fantastic" or "distorted" or even "value-laden" for there is no standard to which the varying states of consciousness may be referred. On either of these two options some resort to platonism is not strange. A world of suprapersonal ideas which we all share and which we may use to order our experiences is a reasonable supposition under the circumstances. But this position, although by no means absurd, is not one to which we wish to be driven if we are setting out a straightforward theory to explain past American behavior.[2]

According to Kuklick, the only solution to this dilemma is to give up using symbols and myths to explain all kinds of behavior. Instead, he says, we should postulate mental constructs like images and symbols only as a means of describing a disposition to write in a certain way. In other words, a symbol or a myth is simply a generalizing concept for summarizing certain recurrent patterns in writing and other forms of expression. Insofar as it explains anything, the myth-symbol approach simply indicates that a group of persons has a tendency to express itself in certain patterns:

> Suppose we define an idea not as some entity existing "In the mind" but as a disposition to behave in a certain way under appropriate circumstances. Similarly, to say that an author has a particular image of the man on the corner (or uses the man on the corner as a symbol) is to say that in appropriate parts of his work, he writes of a man on the corner in a certain way. When he simply writes of the man to refer to him, let's say, as the chap wearing the blue coat, we can speak of the image of the man, although the use of "image" seems to obfuscate matters. If the man is glorified in poem and song as Lincolnesque, we might speak of the author as using the man as a symbol, and here the word "symbol" seems entirely appropriate. For images and symbols to become collective is simply for certain kinds of writing (or painting) to occur with relative frequency in the work of many authors.[3]

I think we must accept Kuklick's contention that insofar as the myth-symbol approach assumes a direct connection between literary symbols and other forms of behavior such as specific political or social actions, it is highly questionable. To explain the American course of action in Vietnam

---

[2]Bruce Kuklick, "Myth and Symbol in American Studies," *American Quarterly*, XXIV, no. 4 (October, 1972), 438.

[3]*Ibid.*, p. 440.

as the effect of the American western myth is to indulge in speculations about causal connections that can never be demonstrated or substantiated and that probably assume an oversimplified view of the relations between art and other kinds of experience. Yet, to take the further step of insisting that the myths and symbols found in written (and other forms of expressive) behavior can only be understood as a generalization about that specific kind of behavior seems contradictory to experience, for we can all think of many ways in which our lives have been shaped by the symbolic or mythical patterns we have encountered in various forms of literature. The problem is to arrive at some better and more complex understanding of the way in which literature interacts with other aspects of life, for I think we can grant that imaginative symbols do not have a direct and immediate causal effect on other forms of behavior. Otherwise the impact approach to interpreting the cultural significance of literature would long since have proved more fruitful.

The resolution of the problems posed by these criticisms of the myth-symbol approach lies, I think, in replacing the inevitably vague and ambiguous notion of myth with a conception of literary structures that can be more precisely defined and are consequently less dependent on such implicit metaphysical assumptions as that of a realm of superpersonal ideas, which Kuklick rightly objects to. One such conception is that of the conventional story pattern or formula. This notion has, in my view, two great advantages over the notion of myth. First of all, the concept of formula requires us to attend to the whole of a story rather than to any given element that is arbitrarily selected.[4] A myth can be almost anything—a particular type of character, one among many ideas, a certain kind of action—but a formula is essentially a set of generalizations about the way in which all the elements of a story have been put together. Thus it calls our attention to the whole experience of the story rather than to whatever parts may be germane to the myths we are pursuing. This feature of the concept leads to its second advantage: to connect a mythical pattern with the rest of human behavior requires tenuous and debatable assumptions, while the relation between formulas and other aspects of life can be explored more directly and empirically as a question of why certain groups of people enjoy certain stories. While the psychology of literary response is certainly not without its mysteries, it seems safe to assume that people choose to read certain stories because they enjoy them. This at least gives us a straightforward if not simple psychological connection between literature and the rest of life.

Beginning with the phenomenon of enjoyment, we can sketch out a tentative theory for the explanation of the emergence and evolution of literary

[4][See especially Robert Champigny, *What Will Have Happened: A Philosophical and Technical Essay on Mystery Stories* (Bloomington, Indiana, 1977) and Hanna Charney, *"This Mortal Coil": The Detective Novel of Manners* (forthcoming from Fairleigh Dickinson University Press), both of which use Roland Barthes to good advantage. Editor's note.]

formulas. The basic assumption of this theory is that conventional story patterns work because they bring into an effective conventional order a large variety of existing cultural and artistic interests and concerns. This approach is different from traditional forms of social or psychological determinism in that it rejects the concept of a single fundamental social or psychological dynamic in favor of viewing the appeal of a conventional literary pattern as the result of a variety of cultural, artistic, and psychological interests. Successful story patterns like the western persist, according to this view, not because they embody some particular ideology or psychological dynamic, but because they maximize a great many such dynamics. Thus, in analyzing the cultural significance of such a pattern, we cannot expect to arrive at a single key interpretation. Instead, we must show how a large number of interests and concerns are brought into an effective order or unity. One important way of looking at this process is through the dialectic of cultural and artistic interests. In order to create an effective story, certain archetypal patterns are essential, the nature of which can be determined by looking at many different sorts of stories. These story patterns must be embodied in specific images, themes, and symbols that are current in particular cultures and periods. To explain the way in which cultural imagery and conventional story patterns are fitted together constitutes a partial interpretation of the cultural significance of these formulaic combinations. This process of interpretation reveals both certain basic concerns that dominate a particular culture and also something about the way in which that culture is predisposed to order or deal with those concerns. We must remember, however, that since artistic experience has a certain degree of autonomy from other forms of behavior, we must always distinguish between the way symbols are ordered in stories and the way they may be ordered in other forms of behavior. To this extent, I think Kuklick is correct in suggesting that the existence of symbols and myths in art cannot be taken as a demonstration that these symbols are somehow directly related to other forms of behavior and belief. Yet there are certainly cultural limits on the way in which symbols can be manipulated for artistic purposes. Thus our examination of the dialectic between artistic forms and cultural materials should reveal something about the way in which people in a given culture are predisposed to think about their lives.

As an example of the complex relationship between literary symbols and attitudes and beliefs that motivate other forms of behavior, we might look at the role of political and social ideologies in the spy story. Because of its setting, the spy story almost inevitably brings political or social attitudes into play since conflicting political forces are an indispensable background for the antagonism between the spy-hero and his enemy. Thus, in the espionage adventures written by John Buchan and other popular writers of the period between World Wars I and II—"Sapper," Dornford Yates,

E. Phillips Oppenheim, and Saxe [sic] Rohmer, for instance—one dominant theme is that of the threat of racial subversion. The British Empire and its white, Christian civilization are constantly in danger of subversion by villains who represent other races or racial mixtures. Saxe Rohmer's Fu Manchu and his hordes of little yellow and brown conspirators against the safety and purity of English society are only an extreme example of the pervasive racial symbolism of this period. It is tempting to interpret these stories as reflections of a virulent racism on the part of the British and American public. There is no doubt some truth in this hypothesis, especially since we can find all kinds of other evidence revealing the power of racist assumptions in the political attitudes and actions of this public. Yet few readers who enjoyed the works of Buchan and Rohmer were actually motivated to embark on racist crusades, for it was in Germany rather than England and America that racism became a dominant political dogma. Even in Buchan's case, many of the attitudes expressed in his novels are far more extreme than those we find in his nonfiction and autobiographical works, or in his public life and statements. It is a little difficult to know just what to make of this. Was Buchan concealing his more extreme racist views behind the moderate stance of a politician? Or is the racial symbolism in his novels less a reflection of his actual views than a means of intensifying and dramatizing conflicts? Umberto Eco in a brilliant essay on the narrative structure of the James Bond novels suggests that something like this may well be the case with Ian Fleming's "racism."

> Fleming intends, with the cynicism of the disillusioned, to build an effective narrative apparatus. To do so he decides to rely upon the most secure and universal principles, and puts into play archetypal elements which are precisely those that have proved successful in traditional tales. . . . [Therefore] Fleming is a racialist in the sense that any artist is one, if, to represent the devil, he depicts him with oblique eyes; in the sense that a nurse is one who, wishing to frighten children with the bogey-man, suggests that he is black. . . . Fleming seeks elementary opposition: to personify primitive and universal forces he has recourse to popular opinion. . . . A man who chooses to write in this way is neither Fascist nor racialist; he is only a cynic, a deviser of tales for general consumption.[5]

As in the case of Fleming, many apparently ideological expressions in Buchan may arise more from dramatic than propagandistic aims. Therefore we must exercise some caution in our inferences about the social and political views that the author and audience of such stories actually believe in. Most audiences would appear to be capable of temporarily tolerating a wide range of political and social ideologies for the sake of enjoying a good yarn. As Raymond Durgnat has suggested, recent spy films with ideological implications ranging from reactionary to liberal have been highly success-

[5] Umberto Eco, ed., *The Bond Affair* (London: Macdonald, 1966), pp. 59-60.

ful. Or to take a different example of the same sort of phenomenon, a number of recent black detective films and westerns, which portray whites as predominantly evil, corrupt, or helpless, have been quite successful with substantial segments of the white as well as the black public.

But even if we grant that the melodramatic imperatives of formula stories tend to call forth more extreme expressions of political and moral values than either author or audience fully accept, there still remains a need for author and audience to share certain basic feelings about the world. If this sharing does not occur at some fundamental level, the audience's enjoyment of the story will be impeded by its inability to accept the structure of probability, to feel the appropriate emotional responses, and to be fascinated by the primary interests on which the author depends. An audience can enjoy two different stories that imply quite different political and social ideologies, so long as certain fundamental attitudes are invoked. Durgnat puts the point rather well in explaining why the same public might enjoy *Our Man Flint*, a spy film with very conservative political overtones, and *The Silencers*, which is far more liberal in its ideology:

> The political overtones of the movies appear only if you extrapolate from the personal sphere to the political, which most audiences don't. The distinct moral patterns would be more likely to become conscious, although neither film pushed itself to a crunch. In other words, the two moral patterns can co-exist; both films can be enjoyed by the same spectator, could have been written by the same writer. Both exploit the same network of assumptions.[6]

This "network of assumptions" is probably an expression, first, of the basic values of a culture, and on another level, of the dominant moods and concerns of a particular era, or of a particular subculture. That Buchan is still enjoyed with pleasure by some contemporary readers indicates that there are enough continuities between British culture at the time of World War I and the present day to make it possible for some persons to accept Buchan's system of probabilities and values at least temporarily for the sake of the story. That Buchan is no longer widely popular, however, is presumably an indication that much of the network of assumptions on which his stories rest is no longer shared.

These considerations suggest the importance of differentiating literary imperatives from the expression of cultural attitudes. In order to define the basic network of assumptions that reflect cultural values we cannot simply take individual symbols and myths at their face value but must uncover those basic patterns that recur in many different individual works and even in many different formulas. If we can isolate those patterns of symbol and theme that appear in a number of different formulas popular in a certain period, we will be on firmer ground in making a cultural interpretation, since those patterns characteristic of a number of different formulas pre-

[6]Raymond Durgnat, "Spies and Ideologies," *Cinema* (March, 1969), p. 8.

sumably reflect basic concerns and valuations that influence the way people of a particular period prefer to fantasize. In addition, the concept of the formula as a synthesis of cultural symbols, themes, and myths with more universal story archetypes should help us to see where a literary pattern has been shaped by the needs of a particular archetypal story form and to differentiate this from those elements that are expressions of the network of assumptions of a particular culture. Thus the spy story as a formula that depends on the archetype of heroic adventure requires a basic antagonism between hero and villain. The specific symbols or ideological themes used to dramatize this antagonism reflect the network of assumptions of a particular culture at a particular time. The creation of a truly intense antagonism may well involve pushing some of these cultural assumptions to extremes that would not be accepted b most people in areas of life other than fantasy. . . .

I would like to suggest four interrelated hypotheses about the dialectic between formulaic literature and the culture that produces and enjoys it:

1. Formula stories affirm existing interests and attitudes by presenting an imaginary world that is aligned with these interests and attitudes. Thus westerns and hard-boiled detective stories affirm the view that true justice depends on the individual rather than the law by showing the helplessness and inefficiency of the machinery of the·law when confronted with evil and lawless men. By confirming existing definitions of the world, literary formulas help to maintain a culture's ongoing consensus about the nature of reality and morality. We assume, therefore, that one aspect of the structure of a formula is this process of confirming some strongly held conventional view.

2. Formulas resolve tensions and ambiguities resulting from the conflicting interests of different groups within the culture or from ambiguous attitudes toward particular values. The action of a formula story will tend to move from an expression of tension of this sort to a harmonization of these conflicts. To use the example of the western again, the action of legitimated violence not only affirms the ideology of individualism but also resolves tensions between the anarchy of individualistic impulses and the communal ideals of law and order by making the individual's violent action an ultimate defense of the community against the threat of anarchy.

3. Formulas enable the audience to explore in fantasy the boundary between the permitted and the forbidden and to experience in a carefully controlled way the possibility of stepping across this boundary. This seems to be preeminently the function of villains in formulaic structures: to express, explore, and finally to reject those actions which are forbidden, but which, because of certain other cultural patterns, are strongly tempting. For example, nineteenth-century American culture generally treated racial mixtures as taboo, particularly between whites, Orientals, blacks, and In-

dians. There were even deep feelings against intermarriage between certain white groups. Yet, at the same time, there were many things that made such mixtures strongly tempting, not least the universal pleasure of forbidden fruit. We find a number of formulaic structures in which the villain embodies explicitly or implicitly the threat of racial mixture. Another favorite kind of villain, the grasping tycoon, suggests the temptation actually acceded to by many Americans to take forbidden and illicit routes to wealth. Certainly the twentieth-century American interest in the gangster suggests a similar temptation. Formula stories permit the individual to indulge his curiosity about these actions without endangering the cultural patterns that reject them.

4. Finally, literary formulas assist in the process of assimilating changes in values to traditional imaginative constructs. ... [The] western has undergone almost a reversal in values over the past fifty years with respect to the representation of Indians and pioneers, but much of the basic structure of the formula and its imaginative vision of the meaning of the West has remained substantially unchanged. By their capacity to assimilate new meanings like this, literary formulas ease the transition between old and new ways of expressing things and thus contribute to cultural continuity. ...

Detection and the Literary Art

by Jacques Barzun

I

...Because detective stories, short or long, are conventionally called cheap entertainment, and yet are read and written by talented people, absurd theories have been evolved about their significance and secret function. Some have said that the spectacle of crime and punishment purges the civilized man of fear and guilt; others, that it releases by a modern myth the animal instincts of the chase and the kill. Meanwhile, among those who perceive that all this is pretentious nonsense, many conclude that detective fiction can satisfy only a juvenile and unliterary taste. It rather adds to the confusion that the holders of these various views are thinking of different kinds of stories or of several kinds at once: they refer indiscriminately to "crime stories," "mystery stories," and "detective stories" as if they were all one.

What is morally worse—for it prevents the public from developing its own judgment—anthologists who understand the distinctions and who define the detective genre in their prefaces go on to fill their books with stories of crime and mystery absolutely devoid of detection. In the best of such books one is lucky to find four or five pieces out of fifteen or twenty that answer to the given description. No such insouciance would be tolerated elsewhere. An anthology of ghost stories is full of ghosts. A book labeled "westerns" does not include narratives of the mysterious East. A tale of love on Jones Beach would be deemed astray among sea stories.

You naturally ask, "What are the distinguishing marks of the true genre and what peculiar delights does it afford the person of literary tastes?" It is not enough that one of the characters in the story should be called a detective—nor is it necessary. What is required is that the main interest of the story should consist in finding out, from circumstances largely physical, the true order and meaning of events that have been part disclosed and part concealed. Crime is attractive but incidental. An excellent detective story

Jacques Barzun, "Detection and the Literary Art." From Barzun, *The Delights of Detection* (New York: Criterion Books, 1961), pp. 9-23. Reprinted with permission of Jacques Barzun.

could be written about the identification of an amnesia victim. The reason why murder animates most detective story-telling is that the gravity of the deed gives assured momentum. Crime, moreover, makes plausible the concealment that arouses curiosity.

Certain readers, of course, are impatient with any detection that busies itself with physical clues. They mutter against "mechanical puzzles" and say that they cannot be bothered with material facts: the mysteries of the soul are so much more—mysterious. And they conclude that detective fiction, being of the order of riddles, can have no connection with literature.

They may be right in their judgment of particular works that are dull through being mechanical, but the condemnation of riddles is unjust. Tradition itself speaks for the riddle as a compelling literary device. From the Bible and the Greek dramatists to Dickens and Henry James, the discovery of who is who and what his actions mean has been the mainspring of great narratives. The stories of Joseph and Oedipus, the plots of *Bleak House* and "In the Cage," pose questions of identification and work out puzzles in the most exact sense of these terms.

In the ancient stories a single physical fact—a ring or other object, a footprint, a lock of hair—usually suffices to disclose identity and set off the denouement. The object is symbolic and conventional rather than rationally convincing. What happens in modern detective fiction is that objects—and more than one in each tale—are taken literally and seriously. They are scanned for what they imply, studied as signs of past action and dark purpose. This search for history in things is anything but trivial. It reflects the way our civilization thinks about law and evidence, nature and knowledge. Our curiosity about objects has grown since the Greeks; we call the results science. By a parallel evolution of literature, the dominant kind of fiction is the prose narrative stuffed with material fact which we call the realistic novel. It blossomed a century and a half ago, with Scott and Balzac, and we are not surprised to find that the detective interest on the part of literary men dates from the same period of balanced rationalism and romanticism: detection is par excellence the romance of reason.

We see this new taste burgeoning in the eighteenth century in Voltaire's charming story of Zadig. We find it carried forward in a sketch by Beaumarchais about the identity of a lady at a ball. And when Balzac follows this fictional tradition he attaches to it more than passing importance, for in an actual murder case we see him attempting to defend the accused by a memoir in which he pleads that: "Criminal investigation must retrace the dead morally *and physically,* for the proofs for and against are everywhere *—in people, places, and things.*" The emphatic italicizing is Balzac's own. A few years earlier, across the Channel, Sydney Smith had attacked the custom of denying legal advice to those charged with felony, by arguing that if "a footmark, a word, a sound, a tool dropped…are all essential to the detection of guilt," then the "same closeness of reasoning is necessary for the establishment of innocence."   ,

From these and other examples it could be shown that the literary imagination of the first half of the nineteenth century was caught by what it understood of method in the new sciences (especially fossil reconstruction in geology) and by its sympathy with the new criminology, which called for the accurate use of physical evidence. At a time when [James] Marsh's test for arsenic was hailed as a triumph which would eliminate the Borgias from our midst while saving those falsely accused, Europe and America thrilled to the descriptions of Leatherstocking's primitive way of tracking down friends and enemies with the aid of physical clues. [William] Leggett's "The Rifle," published in 1830, shows how, in American fiction, crime was first brought home to a culprit by ballistics.

It remained for a genius to take this entrancing idea of detection and make it breed a distinctive literature by displaying it in an appropriate form. That genius was Edgar Allan Poe and the form was the short story, of which he was also the original theorist. "The Murders in the Rue Morgue," published in 1841, put an end to the episodic and casual use of detection. And when four years later Poe had written his three other detective tales, all the elements of the genre were in hand. What was to follow could only be elaboration, embellishment, and complication—most of it agreeable, some of it superior to the original in polish, but none of it transcending the first creation.

...I continue to think the short story the true medium of detection. Pleasant as it is to begin a novel that promises a crowd of actors and incidents, of clues and disquisitions upon clues, the pleasure is soon marred by the apparently unavoidable drawback of a subplot and its false leads. The poet C. Day Lewis, writing as Nicholas Blake the excellent *Minute for Murder*, apologizes for this fault by having his detective refer to "the monstrous red herring" that delayed the solution. Looking back over many a novel that is monster-ridden in this way, one cannot help thinking of the story as it was first conceived, without this artificial bustle and bulge which exists only to be deflated by a sentence or two near the end.

If this is true today, when a detective novel is also a slim volume, what are we to say of the earlier phase of expansion after Poe's sober contribution? When his idea was first stretched out to fill the dominant form, the novel meant a "tangled skein" of 150,000 words. The French *romans policiers* à la Gaboriau, the milder melodramas of Anna Katherine Green, and even the best novels of the 1920's from the hand of Agatha Christie or Dorothy Sayers were massive constructions in which a great many innocent people had to behave suspiciously if the main business was to be kept long enough out of the reader's sight. Conan Doyle himself went against sound instinct, though by another route, and concocted those intolerable middle sections which potbelly three out of four of his longer tales. The astute reader reads them once, at the age of twelve, and skips them forever after.

I grant that the short story also has its perils and defects, especially if for lack of invention it returns to the state of anecdote, that is, makes the dénouement hinge on one small point instead of on a chain of inferences drawn from several facts. Nothing is duller than the tale of the criminal who, having endured long questioning with aristocratic aplomb, turns green and claws the air because he is caught in a lie. The same holds true of the lost button, the spent match, the missing envelope—no matter how ingenious the situation or how skillfully built up the suspense, no solitary clue is good enough to satisfy the reader who knows what detection is and insists on getting it.

Ideally, the short detective story is a sequence of five parts, for which it is a pity that Greek names cannot at this late date be invented. First comes the preamble, philosophic in tone, and if possible paradoxical or otherwise arresting. It sets the mood by providing a sample of what Poe called ratiocination. However you pronounce it, ratiocination is a heart-warming prospect. The detective theorizes upon some aspect of life which the story will bear out, though he himself does not as yet know this. Next comes the predicament—mysterious, horrible, grotesque, or merely puzzling—the variation from the norm which invites inquiry. The commonplace mind, represented by the client or by some other embodiment of the *ewig-Watsonisches,* tries to assimilate the unusual and fails. But the superior mind, the detective intellect, seen through a cloud of smoke, discerns the true question and feels immortal inklings upon him—as may be gathered from the irritating silence which follows his voluble beginning.

Further events soon disconcert both the common and the superior minds, but, again, only the latter recovers. This is the signal for a little discourse on method, possibly given socratically, by questions and answers that dispose of the obvious hypothesis and leave everything in an engaging confusion. It is time for the detective to act on his still-hidden "deductions." He tests "places, people, and things." The sheep separate themselves from the goat, and the ensuing violence—confession, arrest, suicide—prepares the way for explanations.

These may of course be artfully distilled through the two or three closing sections of the tale, but if the end is not to be a wordy anticlimax, some provocation of sharp surprise must be kept to the last. We know that the culprit is the smooth solicitor with the pince-nez, but we still cannot see how he could have been in London and Buenos Aires at the same time. The final lecturette which leads up to this disclosure, far from being a rehash, is an illumination which is also an emotional peak, because it releases the tension of intelligent curiosity we have labored under from the beginning.

To be sure, "form" in narrative is rather a metaphorical guide than a commandment, and the combining of incident and ratiocination in the detective short story can be widely varied, as R. Austin Freeman proved in

The Singing Bone. In that volume he created the two-part invention, telling first the events in forward motion, as they occurred, then once again in reverse, as the detective reconstructs their sequence and meaning. To sustain interest in such a twice-told tale requires great generalship and a faultless choice of facts, for the repetition bares the machinery to the author's own practical criticism as well as the reader's. Unless the parts are solid and well-knit, what we accepted readily on a first recital will sound feeble or improbable when served up again to match a new pattern and a diminished suspense.

All that I have been saying about the genre could be summed up in one word: the detective story is a *tale.* The pleasure it affords is that of any narrative in which the ancient riddle of who is who unravels itself to an accompaniment of worldly wisdom. In the detective tale proper there is a double satisfaction answering a double curiosity—what can the solution be? and how was the solution arrived at? But to recapture this innocent pleasure one must be sophisticated enough to abdicate other sophistications.

II

The case for the detective story cannot of course stop on this dogmatic note, certain merits of the genre and certain objections to it are yet to be named. Among the objections is that of sameness—"read one and you have read them all." My description of the form could even be cited in support of the charge; it would be foolish to deny that detection in literature submits to very rigid canons. It is an art of symmetry, it seeks the appearance of logical necessity, like classical tragedy, and like tragedy it cherishes the unity of place—the locked room, the ship or train in motion. Its successes thus partake always of the tour de force. As Yeats rightly remarked, "The technique is *supairb.*"

But these very limitations, when appreciated, draw our eyes to the points of difference between one tale and another. Indeed, superficial sameness is a common attribute of tales, in contrast with the surface variety we expect of novels and novelistic short stories. If you read Boccaccio and Margaret of Navarre and Bandello and the *Cent Nouvelles Nouvelles* and the *Contes Drôlatiques,* you will find these tales as alike among themselves as any comparable number of detective stories. In the one group, lovers plot against husbands and are either successful or ridiculous. In the other, the detective is confronted by the inexplicable and he reasons his way to the explanation, with or without apprehending a culprit. Fairy tales also betray a strong family likeness. There is a task set and an ogre to be conquered before the princess' hand is available; and generally everything comes in threes. Still, one can distinguish the masterpieces from the dull imitations, whatever the genre, by the art with which the formula has been vivified.

What one seems to miss in the tale is the novel's lifelike looseness, the illusion of uncontrived actuality. One is conscious of *listening to a tale,* which is why I suggest that the enjoyment of detective stories requires a superior sophistication. Again, I concede that the reader who goes to novels in order to learn something new about human character will be disappointed in detection. The tale may teach nothing but its own neatness, and its effect then is to bring a smile to the lips rather than a commotion to the soul. These are two orders of pleasure, not necessarily two degrees of it.

But if what I say is true, what becomes of the connection we observed, at least historically, between detective fiction and the realistic novel? To perceive the connection one must turn from form to substance. The raw material of detection consists of the physical objects that surround action. These become literary substance when the detective imagination has chosen and arranged them so that some are clues while others produce atmosphere, verisimilitude, suspense. In detection details are numerous and must be instantly convincing. We are ready to swallow long descriptions of houses and their furnishings, we are greedy for the contents of posthumous pockets, we long to master time tables, speeds of vehicles, and procedures for collecting evidence, provided always that these records of matter moving through time and space conform to the common standards of credibility. That is the reason why many years ago Father Ronald Knox laid down as one of the laws of detective fiction: "There must be no Chinamen." For this cryptic rule, which its author said he could not explain, is in fact the principle of the realistic novel: the world of magic and mystery yields to a sense of reality based on the persuasiveness of things. To be sure, the great novels of the realistic school portray character even more painstakingly than things, whereas detection rightly keeps character subordinate. But detection makes up for this neglect by giving intelligence a place which it has in no other literary form. Only in the detective tale is the hero demonstrably as bright as the author says he is.

Some readers of course are by temperament impatient with small details. Trollope tells us that he did not like stories in which he had to remember what happened at a given hour on the Tuesday, or how many yards from the milestone the lady was abducted. But in so saying he is telling us about himself rather than criticizing the genre. His own work is full of little points to remember about people, church politics, and county snobbery. We follow him because, as we say, we gain an understanding of English life as well as of humankind. What do we gain from the details of detection? An understanding, first, of the silent life of things, and next, of the spectacle of mind at work. This is no doubt why detective feats have been, since Voltaire and Poe, the delight of intellectuals. The emotion called forth is that of seeing order grow out of confusion. This is no mean or despicable emotion: it can match in intensity the light of recognition which Aristotle declared the strongest effect of tragedy.

To experience this pleasure of discovery one must be willing to explore, as minutely and lovingly as the author desires, the nature and connections of the inanimate—including the corpse. One must be attentive to the inter-linked traces of human action upon the material world. No doubt this is an acquired taste, like the taste for reading the history of the earth in rocks and rivers. But a generation reared on Proust's crumb of cake in the teacup should readily concede that bits of matter matter.

To those who acknowledge this, the attempt to "improve" the detective story and make it "a real novel" seems a sign of bad judgment. Replacing clues with "psychology" and intelligible plot with dubious suspense is childish tinkering. Far from "maturing" detection and giving us genuine novels with "real" characters, the so-called stories of suspense have only obscured a true genre and further muddled the criticism of it. The name itself is meaningless. Any good tale is a "story of suspense." What we are in fact given in the new mongrel form is "stories of anxiety," which cater for the contemporary wish to feel vaguely disturbed. I do not question the pleasure derived from this sort of self-abuse. I merely decline to call it superior to another pleasure which is totally different. And I hope I need not add that I enjoy and admire, each in its own kind, a great many of the tales now confused with detection, from Dashiell Hammett's *Red Harvest* to Stanley Ellin's "Broker's Special" and from Agatha Christie's "Witness for the Prosecution" to Anthony Boucher's "Elsewhen." ...

Meanwhile, from the modern deviations one can reason backward to certain critical conclusions. If you ask the ordinary reader which of the Sherlock Holmes short stories he likes best, the chances are that he will say: "The Speckled Band." The vision of the snake coming down the bell pull is the utmost thrill he expects from detection. To the connoisseur, however, the tale is one of Doyle's weaker efforts. It stands far below, say, "The Six Napoleons." The point of the contrast is not that "sensationalism" is out of place because detection is "intellectual." Think of Ernest Bramah's "Brook-bend Cottage" and you will see how compatible detection can be with thrills and fireworks. The point is rather that in any combination of the detective interest with anything else, the something else must remain the junior partner.

By this principle we can see why it is so rare that a detective tale of French or German authorship is true to its name. The old *roman policier* tradition hangs over it and makes one groan. Fanciful "reconstructions" of the crime, inane accusations, a vicious love of coincidence, a smug acceptance of chance solutions—all this, saturated with the unhealthy flavor of the secret police, generally spoils the dish. Simenon's long-winded irrelevancies are the same thing modern style, that is, with morbid coloring added. What shall one say of the Oriental adaptation of our genre? To believe, among other things, that a criminal can for professional purposes conceal himself inside the upholstery of an armchair demands an effort of nonvisualization that few Western readers will be willing to make. The fact that the author of such inventions has taken the pseudonym of Edogawa Rampo only adds a touch of resentment to our dismay.[1]

Yet strict naturalism is not enough, either, as we see in the so-called novels of police routine. These works are a little too conscientiously instructive and sociological. They should be taken in moderation, unless one is a salesman and able to find a narcissistic pleasure in seeing other patient men ring doorbells. I repeat: nothing less than the play of the detective intelligence upon the physical world will give us a detective tale. It might seem at first sight as if Mr. [Harry] Kemelman's admirable "Nine-Mile Walk" destroyed the rule: what is his story but a few words overheard and analyzed? This is mere appearance. The detection is genuinely of the physical conditions surrounding the deed and implied by the one short sentence—an exemplary work as well as a tour de force.

III

But am I not still a good way from showing that detective fiction is a branch of literature in the honorific sense of belles-lettres? Is not detection perhaps a frivolous by-product of legal and scientific writing, a *jeu d'esprit* for tired professional men who lack the energy to tackle poetry? Behind these questions lurks a general suspicion about style. The literary conscience demands that anything called literature show mastery not only of structure but also of tone and diction. The manner of these is not prescribed, but the commonplace will degrade a narrative, however ingenious, to the rank of popular journalism.

Detective stories have been written, certainly, which show complete indifference to the felicities of feeling and expression. But this is true in equal measure of every type of story. Nick Carter has his counterparts in all genres, and we must judge detective fiction as we do other kinds, by the best examples. It is no concession to admit that there would be no genre to speak of and no art to criticize if detective stories gave us but stock situations

[1][Edogawa Rampo is a phonetic rendering of Edgar Allan Poe; it was thus the rather clever, not dismaying, pseudonym of Taro Hirai, the "father of the Japanese mystery." See Ellery Queen, ed., *Ellery Queen's Japanese Golden Dozen: The Detective Story World in Japan* (Rutland, Vt., 1978). Queen in this case is Frederic Dannay. Editor's note.]

interlarded with footprints and tobacco ash. It is the shuttling between the infinity of possible human actions and their equally varied physical setting that gives the detective story-teller the chance to be original, adroit, revelatory. And success here as elsewhere calls for the fundamental literary powers.

The supreme quality in our special genre is of course invention, which is to say imagination. Because the light shines on all the material circumstances, these must seem fresh, at least in function, and yet sufficiently common to be plausible—streets and moors and stairs and potting sheds must be recognizable and in no way fanciful. Incidents, likewise, must show a studious regard for the norms and conventions of life and yet avoid that predictability which is the mark of journalism in the derogatory sense. Only art, the art of words, will support a writer who tries to walk this narrow path. It is style that in the fictions of Dorothy Sayers or Rex Stout, of E. C. Bentley or G. K. Chesterton, makes their works at once worthy of belief and pleasurable to read. Here again, as in classical tragedy, the illusion works, artificiality disappears, thanks to a scrupulous attention to language. And as in Racine, a few clichés must be accepted as part of the convention: when "tangled skeins" are out of date we must tolerate the detective's happy thought that his work resembles "the fitting together of a jigsaw puzzle."

Nor is literature in abeyance because we consent to character drawing being in detective fiction a secondary concern. For in these tales characters must none the less move and talk agreeably to their role—and to ourselves. We must know them at least as well as we know the many people, not our intimates, with whom we deal in daily life. By a right use of the Jamesian "point of view" the writer of detection allows us to see into his actors far enough to recognize their type and judge their ostensible motives. Were we to go further we would see too much: the writer would have given away what it is his business to keep hidden until circumstances speak. In this half-concealment lies an art which is none other than literary.

The one exception to this deliberate superficiality is the portrait of the detective, and here too the literature can show some triumphs. Sherlock Holmes is as fully a character as Mr. Pickwick. And by virtue of Doyle's almost unique success in giving a soul to the detective's partner—the common man—we have in the two a companion pair to Don Quixote and Sancho Panza, a contrast and concert capable of occupying our imaginations apart from the tales in which the two figure. Similarly in Nero Wolfe and Archie Goodwin this old pattern of the knight and his squire, which is as old as the *Iliad*, is repeated with conspicuous success in the American idiom.

It does not of course take such a partnership to prove that writers of detective tales can animate their heroes with a picturesque variety. From Father Brown to Peter Wimsey the range is wide. There is in fact but one limit that must not be transgressed; the detective cannot be a fool. I have no use for those ineffectual little men who are always mislaying their belongings and nursing a head cold, yet manage to track down desperate murderers.[2] An all-embracing awareness of physical surroundings and great powers of ratiocination being the spectacle we look for, we are cheated when amiable bumblers hold the stage and succeed by accident at the last minute. They are as unconstitutional in their way as the "poison unknown to science" which kills before the cork is out of the bottle. And my objection to ineffectuality goes for the same paradox in any other form—the great Cointreau, let us say, who is always drinking and hiccuping, and who ends his cases snoring face down on the table while the prisoner is led away in a whiskey-scented haze. Poe decided once for all that the detective should be a man of independent mind, an eccentric possibly, something of an artist even in his "scientific" work, and in any case a creature of will and scope superior to the crowd. He is, in short, the last of the heroes. It follows that to produce him the author must be at least his equal in observation and vocabulary: wit, learning, and repartee constitute the hallmark of detective literature.

The final grace of the perfect tale is its ornamentation. I mean by this the small touches which, while they fit the working parts of the plot, give them a characteristic coloring. Beyond this, an exact measure of levity in detection shows the master's hand, for as Arthur Machen pointed out long ago, the true tone of the genre springs from the alliance of murder and mirth. The laughter is a touch sardonic and must never degenerate into hilarity. The joke of death is on us. Conan Doyle and Dorothy Sayers, among the classics, understood this better than anyone else. What finer-humored critique of detection itself, and at the same time what more brilliant invention, than the casual reference in the Holmes story to the case which hinged on "how far the parsley had sunk into the butter upon a hot day"?

A muffled irony is perhaps as much as our later sensibility will stand, but some such injection of butter and parsley is needed if we are to preserve our proper distance from what is after all ugly business. Murder and detection in real life can give pleasure to very few. The one evokes anger and misery, the other boredom. Only when transmuted into literature by the artificial light of reason and the arbitrary rearrangement of parts do these social and anti-social realities begin to afford delight: after a time, the horrors perpetrated by Burke and Hare become the stuff of DeQuincey's *Murder Considered as One of the Fine Arts*—the first model of still another genre. But since Poe's great feat, we need no longer depend on Burke and Hare and DeQuincey, nor on the four or five disciples of the last-named who have reshaped for us the incidents of actual crime. We have for our solace and edification the literary genre I have tried to describe...abundant, variegated, illustrious, classical—the detective story.

[2][The reference here is to Simenon's Maigret. Editor's note.]

The Short Story's Mutations

by Julian Symons

I *Decline*

In *Queen's Quorum*, the "History of the Detective-Crime Short Story as Revealed by the 106 Most Important Books Published in this Field since 1845," published in 1951, there is no hint of the short story's replacement by the novel as the dominant crime fiction form, nor of its decline in quality. There is instead a triumphal progress from the "Second Golden Era" to "The First Moderns," "The Second Moderns" and then "The Renaissance." Such conclusions do more credit to Ellery Queen's enthusiastic heart than to his analytical head. The Golden Age showed an immediate decline in the quality of short stories, and eventually in their number.

...The losses in circulation suffered by the kind of magazine that had nurtured the short detective story were slow but steady. The *Strand* clung for years to the formula that had brought success, which as its historian[1] has admitted involved ignoring during the Twenties "the new poor, the decline of the larger country houses, the General Strike," and anything else that readers might find uncomfortable. The last Doyle story appeared in April 1927, and although crime stories continued to appear they were with a few exceptions much inferior to those that had been published before World War I, or even to the Four Just Men tales that had been published during its course. The *Strand* relied upon the formula of frivolity that had served it so well in the Victorian and Edwardian years, and perhaps the magazine was not helped by the retention of an essentially Victorian editor, Greenhalgh Smith, until 1930. The circulation fell to 80,000 during World War II, and although its appearance was modernized, the paper that had grown up with Sherlock Holmes had no real reason for existence in the age of Philip Marlowe. By the time the last number appeared in March 1950, the flow of new short stories had almost stopped. It is typical of the maga-

Julian Symons, "The Short Story's Mutations." From Symons, *Bloody Murder: From the Detective Story to the Crime Novel: A History* (London: Faber and Faber, 1972), pp. 163-66, 168-72. Reprinted with permission of the author, Faber and Faber Ltd., and Harper & Row Pub., Inc.

[1][The reference here, surely, is to Reginald Pound, *Mirror of the Century: The Strand Magazine, 1891-1950* (New York, 1966). Editor's note].

zine's backward look that, long before the end, they used a Sherlock Holmes story written in imitation of the master by Ronald Knox, and illustrated in the manner of Sidney Paget.

In the United States the short story as a commercial article was replaced by serialized novels. The *Saturday Evening Post* had run the Thinking Machine and the Father Brown stories as series before World War I, but in 1927 the serialization of Frances Noyes Hart's *The Bellamy Trial* provided a signpost to the future. The *Post* went on to publish a great many serializations of crime novels by Rinehart, Christie, Stout and others during the inter-war years. In 1927 also, *Scribner's* managed temporarily to check a steady decline in circulation with publication of Van Dine's *The Canary Murder Case*. In the same years these and other magazines carried comparatively few short stories of the classic Holmes length.

To say that the serialized novel had become more important for magazines than the short story is not to say that short stories were no longer written or that they failed to find print, only that there was a decreasing demand for them. In America the pulp magazines which relied on short stories flourished in these years, and there was a considerable development also of the "short short story" of 2,000 words or less, which could easily be read in bus or train on the way home. Such a length gave no room for development of plot or character, or for anything more than the making of a single ingenious point, for instance that a man supposedly deaf has heard a casual remark made in another room, or that a man who claims to have been cut off from all communication during the past week knows the result of a football match that took place two days ago. Anecdotes of this kind can be entertaining both to write and to read, but a diet based on them soon becomes tiring.

Yet the short story's decline in these years was not only a matter of changes in editorial requirements. Crime fiction writers soon realized for themselves that the plot construction of a short story could be almost as demanding as that of a novel, and was far less rewarding. But again, one should not put too much stress on purely financial considerations. Allingham, Berkeley, Carr, Queen, Sayers, Van Dine (the names are taken almost at random) accustomed themselves to the leisurely pace of a novel, its accumulation of suspense and doubt, the final revelation and explanation that might take up some thirty pages. It is not surprising that some crime writers never attempted the short story, and that few between the Wars made it a major part of their work. The remarkable thing is that some of these stories were so good. Their merits are not those of Doyle in development of scene and character, or of Chesterton in revealing truths by paradox. The writers of short stories between the Wars attempted no more than the statement of a puzzle and its solution by decent detective work. Within these limits the short stories particularly of Queen, Sayers and Carr, give a great deal of pleasure.

Indeed, in some ways the short story is better suited than the novel to this kind of writing. That final snap of surprise can bring just as genuine a gasp of pleasure after a short period of suspense as after a long one.

This is notable especially in the case of Ellery Queen. The best of his short stories belong to the early intensely ratiocinative period, and both *The Adventures of Ellery Queen* (1934) and *The New Adventures* (1940) are as absolutely fair and totally puzzling as the most passionate devotee of orthodoxy could wish. At least one of the stories in the first book, "The Adventure of the Bearded Lady," is a perfect example of this kind of problem story, baffling in its components but simple when they are put in their right places. Half a dozen others are almost equally good, and every story in these books is composed with wonderful skill. Some of the later Queen stories are interesting, but generally they do not come up to those in the first two collections, because the structure is looser, and there is not much compensation in the way of greater depth. Most of Carr's stories are compressed versions of his locked-room novels, and at times they benefit from the compression. Probably the best of them are in the Carter Dickson book, *The Department of Queer Complaints* (1940), although this does not include the brilliantly clever Henry Merrivale story "The House in Goblin Wood" or a successful pastiche which introduces Edgar Allan Poe as detective.

Dorothy Sayers's short stories treat their subjects with an ease that most of the novels lack, and they are free from the worst excesses of Wimsey. Within the space of thirty pages there is mercifully no room for Wimsey-Bunter dialogue, although there is still some stuff that must seem strange to those who regard Sayers as a semi-realistic writer. "Go back to your War Office and say I will not give you the formula," cries a French Royalist Count to Wimsey. "If war should come between our countries—which may God avert!—I will be found on the side of France." This is from a preposterous but rather enjoyable story called "The Bibulous Business of a Matter of Taste," in which three Wimseys appear at a French chateau and have their credentials tested by a prolonged session of vintage and date naming. The collection that contains this story, *Lord Peter Views the Body* (1928), includes also the genuinely terrifying "The Man With The Copper Fingers" and "The Adventurous Exploit of the Cave of Ali Baba" which opens with a newspaper account of Wimsey's death, followed by his enlistment in some unspecified secret society. *Hangman's Holiday* (1933) includes the clever "The Image in the Mirror" and a funny, quite uncharacteristic Sayers (no detective appears in it) called "The Man Who Knew How." *In The Teeth of the Evidence* (1939) offers two good stories in which Wimsey appears rather mutedly, and several odds and ends, including the delightful "The Inspiration of Mr. Budd." Altogether, the short stories suggest that Dorothy Sayers might have been a better and livelier crime writer if she had not fallen in love with her detective. ...

II *Revival*

The short story's revival is linked directly with America, and partly with Hammett, Chandler, and their followers. Although the Continental Op stories were inferior to Hammett's novels, and although many of Chandler's stories are the work of a man learning his craft, they gave a lead in theme and language to other writers. Take the first line of a Hammett story, a line like "It was a wandering daughter job," or the evocation of the flavour of the desert town of Corkscrew in the story of that name, and you are in a world quite free from the gentility, and snobbery of the Golden Age. But even more important than the existence of Hammett and Chandler as examples from whom to learn, was the foundation in 1941 of *Ellery Queen's Mystery Magazine.* Here was a periodical which printed only short stories about crime and detection, and its influence upon the crime short story's development has been at least as great as that of the early *Strand.*

Ellery Queen, or at least half of him in the form of Frederic Dannay, has exercised an active editorial interest from the beginning, and from the beginning he recognized that the form of the crime story was changing and that a successful magazine had to accommodate the old and encourage the new. *E.Q.M.M.* was prepared to welcome equally a new story by Carr or Allingham, and the first short story of an unknown writer. They were ready to give the first prize in the yearly contest they inaugurated to stories which, as it seemed to some of their readers, were not detective stories at all, like H. F. Heard's "The President of the United States, Detective," or to a realistic story by an Italian-born writer. They gave special prizes for foreign stories, a gesture which produced in one year tales from Australia, Argentina (from Jorge Luis Borges), Portugal, the Philippines and South Africa. They have given at different times awards for the best first story, the best *tour-de-force,* the best piece of Sherlockiana, the best short short story, the best riddle story, and the best story by a college student. A full list of the prize stories in the yearly *Queen's Awards,* together with the new stories that have appeared in *E.Q.M.M.,* is a roll of honour of the crime short story in recent years. It is also, as Queen claims, a compendium of every possible kind of crime story. Some of the kinds are more important than others, not all of the stories are masterpieces, and some will madden anybody who has a fixed idea of what the crime short story should be like. The permanently excited editorial style will not be to everybody's taste. Yet the value of the magazine far transcends any criticisms that may be made of it. No doubt short stories would have been written if *E.Q.M.M.* had never existed, but they would have been much less various in style and interest, and almost certainly much poorer in quality. The editors have been directly responsible for encouraging the two most talented crime short story writers of the past thirty years.

In November 1946 the managing editor of the magazine told Ellery Queen

—in this case presumably Dannay—on the telephone that a remarkable new story had come in to the office. This was "The Specialty of the House," the first story published by Stanley Ellin. The story is now so famous that there can be no harm in revealing that it is about the delicious lamb Amirstan which is the speciality (to revert to English spelling) of an inconspicuous New York restaurant named Sbirro's, that the meat in the dish is human flesh, and that it is unwise for any diner to accept Sbirro's invitation to enter his kitchen. Stanley Ellin (1916-   ) was a steelworker before he became a full-time writer, and although he has said that his idea of an ideal workroom is Proust's cork-lined chamber plus a typewriter he is in most respects a strikingly unliterary character, interested in baseball, boxing and—surprisingly for an American—cricket. This earthy New Yorker from Brooklyn is, however, an exceptionally careful and easily dissatisfied writer who revises each page several times, and often tries out an opening sentence again and again until he "hits one that *feels* right." It was ten years before his first collection, *Mystery Stories* (1956), was published, and another eight before ten more stories were gathered between covers under the title *The Blessington Method.* His stories have been produced at an average rate of one a year.

Ellin has written several excellent novels, of which *The Eighth Circle* (1958) is the most notable, but his talent shows at its finest in his short stories. The great quality he has brought back to the crime short story is that of imagination. That concern with tricking the reader is all very well, but in the best crime stories it is subsidiary to the exercise of the imagination by which the writer becomes one with his subject. This is what makes us shiver a little when we read the Holmes stories. Ellin can be quite as ingenious as any Golden Age practitioner, but his ingenuity is turned to ends which produce the authentic shiver. The little final twist is a turn of the knife in the reader's sensibility. It is because he can imagine what might persuade a little man defeated by life to commit murder ("The Cat's-Paw") or the existence of a society to ease a way out of life for old people who are a nuisance to the young or middle-aged ("The Blessington Method") or what it is like to be a public executioner, that his work is a landmark in the history of the crime short story. His finest pieces go beyond the usual limits of the *genre* and turn into fables, occasionally tender but more often sharp, about the grotesque shapes of urban society and the dreams of the human beings who live in it.

The talent of Roy Vickers (1889-1965) was less remarkable than that of Stanley Ellin and was manifested late in his writing career, but it was wholly distinctive and operated particularly in the medium of the short story. Vickers wrote many crime novels from the Twenties onwards, but these books bear no mark of being produced by the same man who wrote the short stories which began with the invention of the Department of Dead

Ends, an imaginary branch of Scotland Yard in which the details of all unsolved murder mysteries are kept. Vickers began to write the Dead End stories in the Thirties, but found it hard to sell them, because their realistic tone was utterly incompatible with the requirements of magazines at the time. It was not until Ellery Queen discovered "The Rubber Trumpet" and one or two other stories in the dusty pages of *Pearson's* and asked if there was a series of these tales, that Vickers was moved to revive his highly original idea. "The Department does not grope for points missed in the investigation (but) keeps an eye open for any unusual occurrence to any of the persons who were once in the orbit of an unsolved murder," as Vickers himself put it. When at last a collection of stories appeared in hard covers, as *The Department of Dead Ends* (1946), the brilliance of the conception was at once appreciated. A rubber trumpet thrown out of a railway train provides a link with seventy-seven other rubber trumpets apparently sold over the counter of a chemist's shop, to bring George Muncey to justice, a begging letter which turns up in the Department two years after the apparently motiveless murder of Gerald Raffen leads directly to the murderer, and so on.

Vickers's method is generally to provide the setting for the crime, show it being carried out, and then go on to the accidental discovery that lays a trail to the criminal. He follows in this the pattern of the inverted story, but uses it with more flexibility and sophistication than its inventor. He also improves on the originals by giving almost every story a deadly probability. Many of the cases have a suburban setting, and the murderers are often respectable people, people like us. To quote Vickers again: "Together we must reach a moment in which we agree that a particular pressure of circumstance might well prove too much, not indeed for ourselves but perhaps for our neighbours." This might be a little dull but in fact it is not, because Vickers has his own, far from mechanical, ingenuity, exemplified in a story like "The Man Who Murdered In Public," where George Macartney is acquitted of forcibly drowning his wife because the two earlier "accidents" in which women have been drowned cannot be put in as evidence in relation to the third. George is eventually caught by one of those felicitous oddities that are the hallmark of the Dead End cases. The story obviously had its origin in the career of George Joseph Smith, the "Brides in the Bath" murderer, and a number of the other tales looked glancingly at real English murder cases.

Between the near-fables of Ellin and the near-documentation of Vickers, the modern crime story offers a great deal of entertainment, and some serious writing. The six stories in *Knight's Gambit* (1949), for instance, weigh lightly in the whole balance of William Faulkner's achievement, but they are undoubtedly more deeply conceived than most crime stories. One of them, "An Error in Chemistry," was submitted for the first Ellery Queen

Detective Short Story contest, and won second prize. The stories deal with the detective exploits of Gavin Stevens, county attorney, who is in these tales rather like Uncle Abner, although in the whole Faulkner saga (he appears in several novels) he is developed as a very different figure. Some of the stories were published long before they were gathered up in book form, and they show Faulkner's interest in the mystery story as a form. The detective stories about Johnson and Boswell of Lillian Bueno McCue (1902-   ), who used the name of Lillian de la Torre, collected in *Dr. Sam: Johnson, Detector* (1946), are perhaps the most successful pastiches in detective fiction. *E.Q.M.M.*, again, was responsible for their first publication. Miss de la Torre caught most happily the tone and weight of Johnson's conversation, and rightly made the puzzles almost incidental to the relationship between biographer and subject. One may dislike pastiche of any kind, but' here it is certainly done on a high level. No other collections of stories by individual writers come up to those already mentioned, but there are a great many which push the crime story into territory that had not been explored for a long time, like some of Jorge Luis Borges's extraordinary pieces, or one or two of the horrific tales in Roald Dahl's collections *Someone Like You* (1953) and *Kiss Kiss* (1960), and some of Patricia Highsmith's intensely imagined *pieces.* Dahl's story "Lamb to the Slaughter," is about the literally perfect disposition of a murder weapon.

...The short story has triumphantly revived....A continual flow of good crime stories presupposes magazines prepared to print them, and in Britain such magazines hardly exist. It is not too much to say that the continuation of the crime short story as we know it, like its development during the past twenty years, seems largely dependent upon *Ellery Queen's Mystery Magazine.*

The Case against the Detective Story

by Erik Routley

There are many kinds of people who have no use for detective stories, and there are several routes by which one can argue towards the conclusion that they, and the people who read them, are trivial. I am prepared here to examine three lines of argument—a moral line, a social line, and a philosophical line. And I get the moral line from an opinion expressed not long ago by the well known novelist L. P. Hartley.

In *The Novelist's Responsibility* (1967)—that is the title both of the book and the first essay in it, from which I am here quoting—Hartley is, towards the end of an argument against irresponsible and nihilistic novel-writing, led into a discussion of the disappearance of a sense of justice from common life. Compassion, he notes, has come to mean something very different from what it used to mean, and the change of significance he finds sinister.[1]

> Compassion is the order of the day. The highest praise that a reviewer can give a novelist is to say that he writes with compassion. I had a letter from a stranger the other day in which he said he was sure my books came from an unusually compassionate heart. Well, I have nothing against compassion, far from it: if one considered only a millionth of the sufferings of mankind, not to mention one's own, one's tears would never be dry. But the reviewers mean another sort of compassion, compassion for men's misdeeds, and with that I'm not sure I am altogether in sympathy. What becomes of justice? Is it to be completely drowned in compassion?

So far the argument is very clear. Compassion without justice becomes sentimentality, and sentimentality becomes cruelty: so compassion defeats itself if it is not subordinate to justice, which says that a crime must be punished, not that compassion may condone it. He goes on to give a specific example of the moral error he is exposing.

Erik Routley, "The Case Against the Detective Story" and "On Being Serious-minded." From Routley, *The Puritan Pleasures of the Detective Story: From Sherlock Holmes to Van der Valk* (London: Victor Gollancz, 1972), pp. 201-21, 223-26, 228-29. Copyright © 1972 by Erik Routley. Reprinted with permission of Erik Routley.

[1]L. P. Hartley. *The Novelist's Responsibility* (Hamish Hamilton, 1967), pp. 15-16.

A little while ago there was a case of a young woman who was telephoning from a public call-box...and two youths who had possessed themselves of some firearms and were crawling about on the roofs nearby, shot her. I don't know how seriously she was injured, but some of the comments, I was told, ran like this: "Why did she choose that moment to be telephoning, when two high-spirited lads were crawling about the roofs, armed with guns? What more natural than that they should shoot her? It was a provocative act on her part...." In their eyes the boys were to be pitied much more than the girl. There are a great many people, and some very good people, who are more shocked by punishment than by crime.

Now between the statement about the corruption of justice and that narrative, so placed that it forms a direct link between them and completes a continuous paragraph, there is this sentence:

Detective stories have helped to bring this about, and the convention that the murderee is always an unpleasant person, better out of the way.

Detective stories have helped to produce a society in which justice abdicates and compassion goes sour: that society has produced incidents like the story of the girl in the telephone box.

I find that fascinating. It is, on the face of it...an argument from moral premises against detective stories. It is a little less crude than the argument that detective fiction causes people to accept violence without protest: but it is of much the same kind. It is an argument one often hears.

My question is, what does Mr. Hartley think a detective story is? At least, that's my first question, but I have others. The notion that what he calls the "murderee" (if that's all right for a good novelist it should be all right for me, but I still find it a bit gritty) is an unpleasant person who is rightly got out of the way is a very unsafe induction from the various fields of detective fiction. One of the Sherlock Holmes short stories could be described in that way—"Charles Augustus Milverton." I suppose it was E. C. Bentley who made the "justifiable homicide" aspect of the detective story fashionable: but we recall that his historic contribution was by way of being a detective story to end all detective stories.

It is indeed very strange that people should so often say that the detective story is immoral. It is necessarily proper to distinguish between detective stories that are authentic and those that are in one way or another degenerate. Not only is it proper so to distinguish: it is affected and stupid to pretend that the distinction isn't perfectly easy to draw. And the detective story which conforms to the basic design of the form is the most moral kind of literature there is. It precisely doesn't commend a society in which crime gets more compassion than suffering. Indeed, it can't live in such a society as that—and it is dying before our eyes in a society which Mr. Hartley quite rightly describes as sick of that disease. Its whole assumption is that of "law and order," and if law and order is a moral notion, then detective fiction is a very soundly moral form of fiction.

The fact is that Mr. Hartley is hanging a respectable argument on the wrong peg and supporting it with a very tendentious illustration. It was naughty of him to produce so emotive a story with so little collateral evidence. Who says that the story is true? It is so vague as to be unverifiable. We don't know even whether the guns were popguns or twelve-bores, whether the girl was frightened or killed, whether the police were involved and the culprits apprehended; above all, we don't know who said those unsurprising things about the incident. We can guess; we can guess so easily that it's tempting to believe that Mr. Hartley simply made them up and attributed them to public opinion in general in the style of a Greek chorus or a speech in Thucydides. Indeed, the whole thing has an oddly Greek flavour — it reminds me of the epigram in the Greek Anthology about a character who was so polite that when somebody stepped on his toe he invariably apologised for putting his toe in the way of the other man's foot. I needn't believe Mr. Hartley's story, and the fact that he's so ready to produce it without any facilities for the reader's verifying it tends to indicate that the point he is making is an emotionally loaded one. It is indeed: the previous paragraphs prove that. He is one of those people upon whom the fashionable asperities of society are bearing very heavily; like any traditional western artist he is an individual who is worried about the increasing difficulty of being an individual in a crowded society. Fair enough. Anything that looks like contributing to that difficulty will be condemned. So he has a side-swipe at the detective story. But the proposition is derived from the wrong premises.

The moral argument that will stand up is this: that the detective story is the product and the weapon of a middle class puritan society whose morality makes claims that have no foundation. The point of attack is that at which the detective story makes the criminal (not the "murderee") the undesirable person. It encourages us to be too sure who is wicked, and too little hesitant about who is disposable. It throws too much weight into the scale-pan marked "justice," too little into "compassion."

That is the direction the argument ought to take. It can, I think, be refuted by repeating the distinction between true detective stories and imitation ones which fail to show understanding of what the form is really for. It is all the bastards and hybrids that do the damage, or at least make it possible for the analysts to represent them as falsifying morality.

The person who should attack the morals of detective fiction is not the tory first-culture novelist but the situation-ethics avant-garde philosopher. Where morality is re-stated in terms of situation instead of in terms of prevenient dogma, then the detective story is bound to suffer revision. The situation-ethics man will not want any novel to reinforce *a priori* assumptions about morals ("This is always and everywhere wrong"); he will only want to uncover truth. He will be prepared to assume that deceit is wrong—for the condoning of deceit and lies will make communication impossible. He is less interested in advertising the opinion that murder, or theft, or fruad are always and everywhere wrong. In practice he will never defend a blackmailer, not often a forger, fairly often a thief, and very often indeed a murderer. But he will never consider defending a writer who himself falsifies evidence, and he will be content with a detective story that simply detects.

Now the argument against dogmatic morals will succeed provided it really admits that it is a social argument—an argument against social attitudes disguised as moralities. It is no argument against a detective story to say that it accepts basic *a priori* moralities, because in a totally amoral society there is no chance for its survival at all: indeed there is no chance for the survival of anybody who is weaker than anybody else. And in practice it will be found...that decent detective writing preserves a nice balance between moral dogmatism and the compassion which Mr. Hartley wants. It was inevitable that in the end detective writing should become detection of character; and where a novelist really knows how to depict character, the very last thing he or she will allow is the forcing of character into a preconceived moral mould. The good novelist doesn't even tell the reader what a character is: he leaves it to the reader to gather that, paying the reader the compliment, by what is left unsaid, of assuming his capacity for receiving the message, and making sure, by what he does say, that the reader is in no danger of being misled.

It is this overstatement and oversimplification of background assumptions that the detective novelist has to guard against. Incautious technique at this point leads to the kind of error that makes the modern sociologist and anthropologist react at once. But for all that there has to be a minimal background assumption that what is metaphysically or morally self-contradictory is wrong and inadmissible. Loosen that assurance, and no kind of pattern can be built up at all.

There is a social argument against the detective story which would be closely allied to what we have just been representing as the moral argument. This would be to say that detective stories perpetuate and celebrate a set of social assumptions which are undesirable and ought to be discouraged. To put it less precisely, detective stories are reactionary. They rely on the acceptance of assumptions about law and order, about the rights of property, about the sanctity of human life, and about the propriety of the punishment of wrongdoers, which should be allowed to change, or perhaps should at once be changed.

That is, anyhow, the argument. And naturally it comes from those who do not regard an established social order as self-evidently beneficial. The question is how far detective fiction does rely on an unchangeable social order, and it can at once be seen that any who would defend the detective story against the charge of incorrigible political illiteracy will have to take a long journey round some forbidding obstacles.

The exceptions are sufficiently rare to prove the general rule that the detective story is socially smug. We are not now speaking of morals: I should contend that in assuming that murder is wrong a detective writer is within his rights. The more awkward question is whether the social assumptions are healthy. In building up the case against the detective story, the prosecutor would be likely to mention the preoccupation of detective writers with the affluent and the literate, and their assumption that what happens to such people is interesting, whereas what happens to people in the lower ranges of society would not be worth writing about. If it be answered that the detective writers only took over where the Victorian novelists left off, and that it certainly was the assumption of Trollope and Wilkie Collins and many other popular Victorians that affluence made a better story than poverty, the prosecutor can then reply that the detective writers kept the fantasies of affluence and heroism going much longer than other novelists did.

One thing one notices in detective stories that indicates how far a detective writer seems to have to limit his social apprehensions is in the manner in which children are treated in them. The obvious assumption is that children have no place in these incidents at all. What on earth (saving only the Baker Street Irregulars) have children to do with the Sherlock Holmes world? Or that of Thorndyke? Or of Father Brown? We have already seen how difficult detective writers find children when they are writing straight detective novels, and although there were some conspicuous exceptions— one or two pleasant and intelligent children, one or two terrible ones—and although Mr. Fortune had that peculiar horror of cruelty to children which appears in a number of his adventures, the detective world is obviously a world in which children count for no more than they counted for with Trollope. Since so many novels of middle class life from 1940 onwards handled children very well and calmly, it is clear that here again the detective story was socially laggard. But the reason is that the detective story is not really a middle class story in its essence—which is why it made such clamorous appeal to the middle classes. Those things which are especially middle class have become material for novelists only since life became difficult for the middle classes, and since the middle class became the object of scorn and hatred. In the world in which Holmes moved, as in that in which Poirot was at home, children were about somewhere but simply didn't bother adults. When that world disappeared and even tolerably affluent professional fathers were taking quite a new attitude to the kitchen and the nursery, the novelists seized on it and made a meal of it; but not the detective writers, because unless they were very careful the introduction of all this would bring a disturbing element into the story which they did not want.

That is it: the detective story has to maintain a nice poise or it will collapse. It simply won't do what it is designed to do. It will gather to itself a seriousness, a message, a mission, and in the end a conscience; and the result of all that will be that no problem will be solved at all.

What we have just said has really introduced our third point, which I call a philosophical one, although it is really made most often by men of letters.

I here bring in evidence two passages from the recent work of literary critics: the first is from Frank Kermode's *The Sense of an Ending* (New York, Oxford University Press, 1967), who quotes Sartre.

> Novels, says Sartre, are not life, but they owe their power upon us, as upon himself as an infant, to the fact that they are somehow like life. In life, he once remarked, 'all ways are barred and nevertheless we must act. So we try to change the world: that is, to live as if the relations between things and their potentialities were governed not by deterministic processes but by magic'. The *as if* of a novel consists in a similar negation of determinism, the establishment of an accepted freedom by magic.   [p. 135]

Sartre, that pervasive pessimist, reveals the "make-believe" of all fiction. To him all life, all human existence, is to some extent fiction. Kermode is content to apply his pessimism to the novel. Later he says, "The novel has to lie. Words, thought, patterns of words and thought, are enemies of truth." The whole chapter (indeed the whole book) deserves careful attention on the part of anyone who would investigate the truth content in literature. But the reader will by now have grasped the point that is relevant here. It is that if any novel is artificial, a detective novel is more artificial than the rest: more subject to imposed pattern. Holmes must not only work a minor miracle in reading Watson's thoughts: he must be right. His rightness strains the reader's credulity. A more subtle and sophisticated detective story may by-pass the reader's critical faculties and therefore arouse no anxiety. But what about the anxiety he would have felt had he been wide-awake, or not taken in by the author's dexterity? There can be no planning of a plot without contrivance and artificiality and an assumption that the reader will leave certain questions unasked. The chief question he may not ask is, "Who are you, the author, to say that? By what right did you make your character like that?" Kermode...mentions a remark of Sartre's about his own inventive processes. "Sartre," he summarises, "determines...that Lola shall possess the money Mathieu needs for Marcelle's abortion." So does Dorothy Sayers determine that Wimsey shall have independent means, and Doyle that Holmes shall be free to build up as well as pursue a practice, and Bailey that Mr. Fortune shall not have too busy a consultancy, and Ngaio Marsh that Roderick Alleyn shall be physically compelling. Exactly. It depends where the particular reader is sensitive; but in one way or another he says "Hey! By what right did you do that?" It isn't precisely the clay asking the potter by what right he made that jug or that basin (as in Paul's argument in Romans 9), but it is the tourist visiting the pottery at Barnstaple and asking what he shouldn't ask of the patient potter, who would be happy to tell him anything about his craft but that. It is a matter of evaluating the conflict between the author's and the reader's right to take decisions; and the detective form of literature seems to move within a set of conventions that admits the author's right to take a number of decisions concerning the plot—rather more than the normal number: and rather less than the normal number of decisions about morality.

The decision that lies furthest away from the author's choice, however, is that there shall be a solution, a revelation, a restoration of a broken pattern. The object of detection is to detect, not to document failure. This brings the detective author into conflict with those who hold that the greatest of all literature is tragic. On this subject an essay by D. D. Raphael entitled *The Paradox of Tragedy* (Allen & Unwin, 1960) makes an important and disturbing point concerning tragedy and religion. To summarise a fascinating argument, Mr. Raphael shows us the difference between the values of tragedy and the values of orthodox Christianity. Every statement about human destiny in the Scriptures, he shows, presupposes some kind of "happy ending": the redress at last of injustice, the special certainty of the faithful that God will, however improbable human experience makes it appear, bring things in the end to a righteous solution. Job, he says, after a great spiritual struggle, submits: that is a happy ending. The Psalmist's agnosticism about human perfectibility is absorbed in his faith in the power of God to overrule human misfortune and injustice for good purposes. All the way from there to the Resurrection, "the religion of the Bible is inimical to tragedy." And of all tragedians he goes on to show, Shakespeare is the most ruthless. He contrasts the story of *Lear* or of *Romeo and Juliet* with the Biblical stories of Jephthah and Samson (referring explicitly to Milton's retelling of that second story and to the well-known parallel, and contrast, between Jephthah and Iphigenia), showing that whereas a Shakespeare tragedy brings grief and death upon its central figures, with no thought of justice and very little suggestion that the consummation of this evil or sorrowful episode left the way clear for a good or happy chapter to open (a touch of it in *Romeo;* none in *Lear)*, the Biblical stories always lead directly to either a vindication of the moral law or the demonstration of a good which the tragedy made possible (in the Old Testament, usually another step in the preservation and maturing of the people of Israel).

We cannot here pass judgement on the dispute whether tragedy is incomplete religion, or whether religion, lacking tragedy, is illiterate. But any religion, as Raphael points out, is an escape from tragedy, and certain religions, notably that of Christians, are a denial that tragedy has the last word. Tragedy, says the Christian religion, is that which brings people to repentance, which reminds us of the overwhelming weight of evil, error and nonsense in the world that we know: tragedy is a General Confession which is answered by an Absolution. The Absolution is not in the tragedy—tragedy can't provide it, doesn't seek to provide it, doesn't even need to admit its possibility.

That could be a philosophical point against the detective novel, which cannot ever allow the open-ended style that many novels nowadays affect. Once again it's a Victorian novel that hasn't grown up, or moved with the times. Trollope must provide some sort of tying-up of loose ends in his last chapter even when the actual crisis of his story (as in *The Eustace Diamonds* or *Orley Farm)* is strictly tragic. The worst of his characters is never wholly condemned—not even Sir Felix Carbury, to whom in the end the worst Trollope can do is send him to Germany with a hired clergyman as mentor. In more protesting and dissenting fiction than that—much of Dickens, of course—the tragedy in the foreground is set against a background of comedy in which righteousness (though not the righteous people in the book) does by implication triumph. A nihilistic novel was unthinkable in the age when detection entered fiction, even though a tragic novel wasn't. So it could be said, and indeed often is said, that about the detective novel there is necessarily something immature.

It could also be said that the detective novel could not have emerged otherwise than from an age which was to a quite unusual extent explicitly religious. ...

I think, however, that these three charges, the moral, the social and the philosophical, can be quite successfully made against the detective story. There are few enough such stories which offer any serious attempt at refutation. *The Tiger in the Smoke*[2] is inevitably one: it comes as near tragedy as such a story possibly can. I can recall in a few others being left with that sense of something profoundly unsolved lying just behind the foreground solution of that particular crime. And that makes me feel that the way to put the Raphael point about tragedy and religion is really this: that tragedy and religion (anyhow, Christianity) are fundamentally opposed: religion does talk of a victory. But it is vitally important to insist that before the solution, or absolution, or resurrection can be understood and appropriated, before anyone has any shadow or right to claim that he can answer tragedy, tragedy must be allowed to run its full course. ...

The case against the detective story, then, would not rest so much on its being impervious to tragedy: it doesn't have to be although it often is. The case rests more firmly on the extent to which detective stories can trivialise

2[By Margery Allingham. Editor's note.]

the conflict. They can be like a false religion in which everything comes right at cut rate. They can appeal to people who are in that sense trivial-minded, and encourage and nourish trivial-mindedness. That, anyhow, is a serious charge.

ON BEING SERIOUS-MINDED

Why then do serious people read detective stories? Researchers whose purposes are far different from mine have admitted that the reading of detective stories can be something more significant than a mere aberration or self-indulgence. The reader of these pages will have gathered already what kind of explanation I propose in the end to offer, but I must first comment on two explanations which I don't personally believe to be primary.

The first is the very obvious critical comment, very frequently made and treated as almost axiomatic, that it is the puzzle that attracts the reader. Clearly this can't be denied, simply because so many people believe it that it can't be entirely untrue. But I am equally convinced that it is not more than a part of the truth. To speak personally, I have never myself been particularly held by a story whose only attribute is that it is a good puzzle. I should feel short-changed if the author didn't in the end tell me whodunit; but that would be a resentment comparable with which I should hear a piece of music—or, come to that, a piece of prose—which didn't make sense. I certainly don't want the author to leave that undone; but if that is all he does, he leaves much else undone which I most certainly do want done.

There are many people who would state their experience differently. It is almost certainly true that some readers find the same satisfaction in detection that they find in doing a demanding crossword puzzle, or in answering those depressing questions and brain-teasers in the Sunday newspapers. This is an intellectual satisfaction and altogether without emotional associations. You are competing with an adversary who cannot possibly cheat you, and need never outwit you, because his statement is frozen on the paper and he cannot, as he would in, say, a game of chess, adjust his strategy to yours. If you know enough, or have noticed enough, or are alert enough or retentive enough of memory, you can beat him. This naturally gives great satisfaction. It's good for the ego. ...

But quite apart from my own personal testimony that I read detective stories for the people rather than the plot, and that I go back to those whose people interest me even when I know the answer to the "puzzle" perfectly well, I find a more public and convincing proof of the inadequacy of the mere intellectual puzzle argument in the extraordinary literature that has grown up around the Sherlock Holmes tales. Not only is this literature of interest to those who know the plots perfectly well; it specialises in people and situations and para-history, and says very little (and then indulgently) about the intellectual content of the puzzles. ... [T]he intellectual content of the Holmes stories is well below what one who placed a high value on "puzzle content" would be bound to regard as a normal level.

And once you have arrived at the detective novel proper, why, the "puzzle" aspect is never more important than it is in any other novel. *The Tiger in the Smoke* isn't a "puzzle" novel at all, but it's a great novel. In my own view, when a detective story or novel springs a surprise at the end the writer's purpose is much less to evoke in the reader admiration for the cleverness of the plot than to produce a moment of self-criticism in which the reader says "Now, I ought to have seen that." This "ought" may have only the lightest moral content — or, as in late Allingham, in Fortune and in Father Brown, it may have a quite weighty moral content.

I should distinguish, anyhow, between those detective novels which detect moral truth as well as the specific truth about the murder or theft or suicide from those which are primarily designed to puzzle the reader. And I should further assert that whatever the "puzzle" content, whatever the moral weight, the reader's satisfaction in what he calls a good detective story has much more to do with his need for moral and psychological security than with his superficial pleasure in solving puzzles. Moreover, I suspect that the later Allingham has a better chance of surviving the permissive blizzard which is engulfing so much detective fiction at present than, say, the more stilted and contrived puzzles of John Dickson Carr. The "puzzle" is part of something larger and deeper.

This is usefully confirmed in the following passage from a detective story published in 1935 by G. D. H. and Margaret Cole. The Coles were in their time the most celebrated husband-and-wife pair in the detective field, and they were also pioneers in "academic" detective writing. They record the following conversation between two of their characters:

> "You do like detecting?" she returned to the question she had put before.
>
> "Why, I'm not sure," Everard said with some hesitation. "I suppose I do."
>
> "The chase? The exciting hunting? To catch your criminal hot, and hang his brush round your neck?" Felice suggested.
>
> "No! It's not that at all. I am not in the least anxious to 'catch anybody hot,' as you put it," Everard said. "Or to hang scalps round my neck. I don't think I desire anybody's death, for which reason I should probably make a very bad policeman — not that I mind particularly when criminals are hanged. I think most of them probably deserve it, and I've no strong feelings about the sacredness of human life; most human lives seem to be extraordinarily expensive and tiresome to keep going, and on any showing not worth the trouble. But if I eat meat, that doesn't make me want to be a head-hunting member of the Worshipful Guild of Butchers."
>
> "Then it is the puzzle, the chess, you like? You like to pursue the clue to its

last lurking-place and say, 'There, I have you! This smut, that fell sideways on Allister Quentin's nose, is tied to a long, long, winding string and it leads me through thousands of calculations to the criminal at the other end.' "

"It's not quite that, either, though I suppose it must be partly that. At least when I find a mystery, even a small one, I do want to know what the answer to it is, and I do, of course, sometimes mess around with what one would call chess. But what interests me more is looking at what people are like, what they do and why they do it, and it always seems to me that when there are crimes about, the working of people's minds gets much more easy to trace. They seem to become undressed, to come out into the open, if you see what I mean. And you can see much more how they can become thieves and murderers, even if they don't."[3]

Note there how the romantic style denies vengeance and discovery as motives for detection and concentrates on mastery of another person's psychology; note also a puritan detachment from the notions of "the sanctity of human life" when they collide with the claims of justice. What Everard Blatchington there claims for himself may well be attributed to many readers of such stories.

But secondly I venture to introduce and comment on a psychological assessment of detective reading which, first uttered in 1956, was made current in a recent book. It will strike some readers as being just about as esoteric as the "puzzle theory" is ubiquitous. In Dr. Charles Rycroft's *Imagination and Reality*[4] there is an essay entitled "Analysis of a Detective Story," and its opening sentences are these:

> Of the various psycho-analysts who have discussed the psychology of the detective story only one, Geraldine Pedersen-Krag, has put forward a specific hypothesis to account for their popularity. In her article "Detective Stories and the Primal Scene" (1949) she suggests that it arises from their ability to reawaken the interest and curiosity originally aroused by the primal scene. According to her the murder is a symbolic representation of parental intercourse, and "the victim is the parent for whom the reader (the child) has negative oedipal feelings. The clues in the story, disconnected, inexplicable and trifling, represent the child's growing awareness of details it had never understood, such as the family sleeping arrangements, nocturnal sounds. …The reader addicted to mystery stories tries actively to relive and master traumatic infantile experiences he once had to endure passively. Becoming the detective, he gratifies his infantile curiosity with impunity, redressing completely the helpless inadequacy and anxious guilt unconsciously remembered from childhood."

Thus far Rycroft takes over the argument set in motion by Pedersen-Krag; but the rest of his essay is devoted to a confirmation, or illustration, of this analysis by reference to Wilkie Collins's story *The Moonstone*.

[3]*Scandal at School* by G. D. H. and M. Cole, 1935 (paperback ed., Collins), pp. 198-99.
[4]Hogarth Press, International Psycho-analytical Library, no. 75 (London, 1968).

This story is exposed by the Pedersen-Krag line of argument as "an un-conscious representation of the sexual act." Very briefly, the symbolic correspondences by which Rycroft illustrates this suggestion are these:

1. the theft of the Moonstone is a defiance of the prohibited intercourse be-tween Franklin Blake and Rachel Verinder;

2. the Moonstone itself, with its central flaw and lunar changes in lustre, is a female symbol;

3. the theft is also the dream of a man in sexual conflict, and therefore it is significant that the theft is found to have taken place during a sleep-walk;

4. the hiddenness of the Moonstone, its unavailability, is the traditional convention that upper middle class women in 1850 knew nothing at all about sex;

5. Rachel's denial that the stone has been stolen at all is her conventional ignorance of sex: that insincerity of the denial symbolises the hollowness of the convention;

6. Rosanna Spearman, in love with Franklin Blake, is Rachel's suppressed sexuality: Godfrey Ablewhite, betrothed to Rachel but not in love with her, is Blake's repressed sexuality.

Many smaller details fit in with this system of interpretation. And while from some points of view the whole structure of the argument looks bizarre, it is, to put it at its lowest, a possible interpretation of what one finds in the text of *The Moonstone*.

Dr. Rycroft brings in evidence one other story by the same author, a far less famous one called *Basil;* and after showing many points of resemblance between the two stories he reminds the reader that while *Basil* was published in 1852 as a contemporary tale, *The Moonstone* was published in 1868 but gives its narrated events the date 1850. *Basil* is found to be a cruder and less convincing performance than the later book: and indeed it is. Is not the later book, then, argues Dr. Rycroft, to be related to the earlier as Rachel to Rosanna, or Blake to Ablewhite?

Collins, anyhow, is shown to have a peculiar obsession with "the primal scene." Now I have no means of knowing how much of Wilkie Collins Dr. Rycroft read in preparing his paper. It happens that many years ago I had, and took, the opportunity of reading more than half his novels in a very old edition (and in eerie circumstances which I must not pause here to recount), and I formed the impression that Collins was indeed an obsessed author; but I saw it at that time not in terms of sex but more naively in terms of [a] mental abnormality or imbecility and [b] his violent hatred of the Roman Catholic Church. The atmosphere of Trollope's *The Way We Live Now* re-peats itself often when Collins mentions the Catholics, and there are few of his stories which don't make some sort of play either with idiocy or with an attempt to derange the mind of another. I am quite ready to be told that there is a sexual association with what to Collins is the exotic and baneful power of the Church of Rome. This was the period immediately after Emancipation and leading up to the Establishment of the Hierarchy (1850). The encounter with Catholicism—an encounter from which since 1688 puritan Englishmen had been able to regard themselves as immune—aroused all sorts of strange rumours and evoked many irrational fears. That is all quite understandable, especially when Collins's own puritan background is remembered. And the puritan's approach to the spooky and sinister would most naturally be through the corruption (accidental or deliberate) of the intellectual faculties of people—for to a puritan those were his most precious possession and their corruption the greatest grief.

What I should say by way of criticising the Rycroft approach to detective stories is what he brings in evidence does not by any means justify his statement, which he makes at the beginning of his article, that "the detective story writer connives with the reader's need to deny his guilt by providing him with ready-made fantasies in which the compulsive question 'whodunit' is always answered by a self-exonerating, 'Not I.'"

For, in the first place, it was unwise to take *The Moonstone*, as it would have been unwise to take any work of Collins, as evidence for propositions about detective fiction: and in the second, the "It wasn't I, anyhow" reaction to detective fiction needs much more delicate handling than it gets at the hands of the psychologists; it's the beginning, not the end, of an argument.

It was unwise to base the argument on *The Moonstone* precisely because that is such a sensational and romantic story. When Eliot gave it that accolade which has become so famous he did it no service and confused the whole issue. *The Moonstone* isn't a detective story: it is a love-story. (By the same token *The Woman in White* isn't a detective story but a romantic thriller.) The police interest is negligible. The whole point of the story is that the police retire baffled. Later the central crime is found not to have been committed at all; the guilt which the reader hoped to see fixed on an identifiable individual was not there. The whole business was accident, not crime, and the criminal intentions and devices are confined to the sub-plot. It's a story about the relations between Franklin Blake and Rachel Verinder, with just about the same detective content (and in both the detective content is perfectly sound and agreeable provided it is not asked to carry any weight) as you find in Trollope's *John Caldigate*. If *The Moonstone* is "the first, the longest and the best detective story in the English language," then *Bleak House* is a detective story, and so are *Is He Popenjoy?* and *Orley Farm*. . . . .

The argument would stand up better, and have the advantage of somewhat lighter construction, if for "guilt" we read "anxiety." The reader of detective stories probably does read them partly because of the curious property they have of providing relaxation from anxiety. If the reader identifies himself with the successful detective, and to some extent with the forces of law and order, he gets some satisfaction from seeing crime brought home to the right culprit, honesty vindicated, and the law protecting society, including himself, from the consequences that would come if the crime were allowed to run free. He gets satisfaction from this precisely because he is worried by the extent to which, in real life, crime does run free.

Yes: but until that statement is modified it goes far beyond the evidence. Two things must be said at once. The first is that the typical detective story reader is not a person who is in fact involved in the situations that free-running crime produces; and the other, associated with that proposition, is that the amount of anxiety which the detective story can allay is very narrowly limited.

Nobody will turn to a detective story if he is really in deep trouble. I can't believe that detective stories are read in concentration camps, or in countries subject to natural disasters just after earthquakes or volcanic eruptions, or in times of violent political revolution. Nor do I believe that they are primarily read by people who are governed by violent passions (whether benevolently or antisocially directed). They are not the characteristic relaxation, I believe, of social reformers, and I should be surprised to learn that they formed any considerable part of the luggage of a pioneering missionary.

The suggestions of Dr. Rycroft were subjected to a penetrating comment in a review of this chapter of his book by Dr. John Wren-Lewis.[5] This review expresses dissent from Dr. Rycroft's analysis, but goes on to make a much more damaging point in the case against the detective story. Dr. Wren-Lewis wants to associate detective stories not with the "primal scene" but with a psychological interpretation of the Fall itself: in other words, with something that has gone wrong, and always tends to go wrong, with human nature. The Fall...he takes to be a distortion of man's view of the nature and role of goodness in the world:...

> The Adam and Eve story unmasks the least likely character as the real cause of all the trouble. Adam and Eve's basic alienation of themselves from each other and from the creative power which operates in their relationship is induced by *eating of the tree of the knowledge of good and evil* — in other words by moralising. Just as it is the policeman in *The Mousetrap* who is really the murderer all along, so it is the activity which normally represents itself as the only hope of rescuing human life *from* inhumanity which turns out, in the final analysis, to be the root cause of man's inability to pull himself out of inhumanity.

And the concluding words are these:

---

[5]"Adam, Eve, and Agatha Christie" by J. Wren-Lewis, in *New Christian*, April 16, 1970, pp. 9-10.

> The world's deepest need is precisely for a new morality—a morality in which people respond to God in creativity and love but recognise that the tendency to try to be as gods themselves, judging good and evil, is the fundamental perversion of human freedom against itself.

I think that Dr. Wren-Lewis is saying, in the first of the above quotations, that the real villain of the Fall story is God himself as there represented. Theologically this is, I believe, quite right. But the point about moralising is the point to concentrate on here. If the detective story really did come of age at two cardinal points where it transcended itself—in Father Brown and in *The Tiger in the Smoke*—then Dr. Wren-Lewis is abundantly vindicated: for, as I have tried to show, both these moments were moments when a detective-story author found it possible to show awareness of the futility of moralising. Father Brown does not moralise, although his statements are unequivocally moral. The Jack Havoc situation is shown to be far beyond moralising.

This is the right ground on which to build the case against the detective story. There is a real danger that readers of detective stories, if they become addicts, will be persuaded that moralism—judging right and wrong in others with no doubts about one's own rightness—is a legitimate and sufficient way of life. It may well be possible to show that addiction to detective stories nourishes mental philistinism. If it is possible to show that…then we have yet another point of meeting between detective literature and the puritan tradition: for it is the occupational disease of puritanism to become facilely and blindly moralistic.

I believe that the ideal client of the detective story writer is the man or woman who is near enough to the moral workshop of society to know what the problems and necessities are, but is not actually either so close to a position of ultimate command as to be able to take radical decisions, nor profoundly concerned with repairing, replacing or updating the machinery. The detective writer will sell nothing to a reader below a certain level of intellectual attainment who cannot attend to a rational plot; but neither will he have any success with a person who lives very close to that moral machinery, for such a person will repudiate the fantasy of detection as an insulting comment on the problems he is handling. …

I think, then, that detective stories are strictly literature for amusement, accidentally swerving now and again towards more serious fields, and perhaps accidentally slipping on other occasions towards the underworld. But they served an age in which increasing numbers of literate people were becoming conscious of the need for honouring the notion of moral and social stability. These things were no longer to be counted on as human rights; but people were secure enough to look steadily and unshockably at the crimes which brought into play the genius of the detective and the strength of the law. To many they provided release from a nagging feeling of helplessness, and a confirmation of their faith in the rightness of orderly and peaceable societies. Had they been confused by such clamorous feelings of guilt as the psychologists attribute to them, would the posture of guilt in the very conventional fashion of the ordinary detective story have helped them? Had they been looking for a release from those oedipal complexes which link sex and violence, would the discipline which the best detective fiction observes concerning violence have provided a better response than the Gothic thriller that they had had for two or three generations?

The detective story reader is not a lover of violence but a lover of order. I do not say that a lover of order must needs be more moral than a lover of violence: obviously a fascist can approve violence for the sake of keeping what he takes to be order. I only say that the detective story reader, who is often (I should say always, if he is a real *aficionado)* left cold or repelled by thrillers, spy-stories and science fiction, does not love violence, and is not even primarily interested in what is bizarre. He can take "The Speckled Band," but it isn't the snake that makes it a great story for him but "dummy bell-ropes and ventilators which do not ventilate." What he gets from Dr. Priestley, Reginald Fortune, Roderick Alleyn at their best is entirely different from what he gets from the deliverance of the hero, tied to the railway line, from the oncoming express with seconds to spare. It's not a matter of fear or guilt, but of assurance: it's not being held over hell and drawn back at the last moment, but being allowed for a space to go in out of the draught of doubt—that's what the detective story reader thanks his author for.

And this feeling of surprising comfort is achieved not merely by the drawing of a satisfying rational diagram (though this in itself gave some pleasure when the draughtsman was Austin Freeman), but most of all by the disciplined dance of character which detection calls for and makes possible. Time and again we have said that detective stories often deal in pale and unconvincing characters. When they do they fall short. There are enough stories in this form which introduce really credible and dynamic characters without trivialising their intellectual content to show not only that the counterpoint between reason and emotion can be achieved, but also how pleasant and satisfying it is when it is achieved.

...I must now return to that point which I have intermittently made, and with the deliberate intention of tantalising the reader, in the course of this essay. I must now say what I mean by my suggestion that detective literature is a puritan form of fiction.

...I have associated [the English puritan tradition] with [1] commerce and the values of the city, [2] rationalism and a suspicion of the super-natural..., [3] the assumption that work is a virtue and idleness a vice..., [4] the cult of masculinity..., [5] the relegation of sex to a subordinate place in the scheme of human values, exemplified not least in the commen-dation of late marriage for men...and [6] a special love of good conversation. ...

...Among certain other attributes of puritanism...are xenophobia, Englishness, a suspicion of artists, and a profound fear of the young. All these are qualities which appear strongly enough in all English literature in the period under review, but which are brought together in a unique combination in detective literature. Detective literature, we have shown, accepts these values and retains them long after other literature, reflecting movements of social thought, has reacted against them.

In two particulars we find this thesis confirmed. Two subjects on which you will always get a positive reaction from the puritan tradition are sex and money. Sex in detective literature is handled on strictly puritan lines. The novelist may be somebody who would be horrified to be called a puritan—but if we were right about the effect of mixing the detective up with sexual tensions, then there are enough examples to demonstrate that detective writers have in the end been thankful to rely on the puritan pattern that makes sex secondary to intellect and muscle and work. Nobody but a fool pretends sex doesn't exist, but we don't have to talk about it and there are other things to write novels about—that is, broadly speaking, the Doyle maxim. As for money, its lack is a stock situation that produces anxiety and greed; but for the rest, everybody on the "right" side is pretty comfortable. The police take the advice of John the Baptist in not complaining about their wages (and it was my guess that Lomas and Alleyn don't live on them either). Even the artists, if they aren't actually in dubious situations, are tolerably pecunious in Innes. Debt is a major vice in the puritan culture, but the puritan never exalts poverty.

Detective fiction, then, I repeat, is entertainment for puritans. It cannot withstand the assaults of "respectable" critics nowadays simply because it does not attempt, in the style of serious novels, to react to life. Here again it is conservative—so conservative, say its detractors, as to be infantile. Here on the one hand is D. H. Lawrence pouring out his soul concerning the monstrous and loathsome evangelical culture of those sordid little South Derbyshire industrial towns—and there is Agatha Christie posturing in drawing rooms at places where bodies are found in libraries by butlers. Very well. On the assumption that literature must react to life, detection stands no chance. Neither does Trollope, nor do most novelists before Dickens. You can defend the detective story only if you admit sabbaticals for the serious-minded. And you are bound to admit that detective fiction can do harm to people who abuse it and treat all life as a sabbatical. They can be used to give assurance and respectability to trivial and irresponsible attitudes. Or I suppose they can, though if pressed I'd have to admit that I never actually saw one doing it. ...

In a perfect world there will be no need for detective stories: but then there will be nothing to detect. Their disappearance at this moment, however, will not bring the world any nearer to perfection. The high-minded would say that the removal of this form of relaxation would free the energies of the literate for the contemplation of real mysteries and the over-coming of real evils. I see no reason to count on that. If we are constantly told that there is no morality, no justice, no trustworthiness, and therefore no human society at all: if we are taught with unrelieved assiduity that there is no distinction of character to be admired, no integrity of personality to be corrected by, I see no reason why we should be more likely than we were thirty years ago to exercise such admiration, submit to such correction, and pursue such ideals in real life. What is more, I am quite clear that men who are too serious ever to appreciate any art provided for amusement or even to admit their need of relaxation are neither men whose advice I would cross the road to get nor men by whom I wish to be governed.

Indeed, I don't mind too much if I am wrong about my modestly serious deductions concerning the social standing of the detective story. What means much more to me is to be able to say that without it I should have found the world a less agreeable place. I would rather be ruled by contented men than by discontented men, and I am not sorry to be surrounded by ex-amples of credible goodness. What harm did they ever do? I think that one admirable phrase from a contemporary critic sums up with complete justice and precision what I believe about these things. Writing of detective fiction, with its admixture of science and morals, with its touch of occasional pas-sion and anger, with its modest openings towards greater issues which greater prophets are left to explore, Colin Wilson says that detective stories are "imaginings with a certain authority."[6]

[6]Colin Wilson, *The Strength to Dream* (Gollancz, 1962), p. 108.

PART FOUR

A Closer Look at Specific Authors

The Writer As Detective Hero

by Ross Macdonald

A producer who last year was toying with the idea of making a television series featuring my private detective Lew Archer asked me over lunch at Perino's if Archer was based on any actual person. "Yes," I said. "Myself." He gave me a semi-pitying Hollywood look. I tried to explain that while I had known some excellent detectives and watched them work, Archer was created from the inside out. I wasn't Archer, exactly, but Archer was me.

The conversation went downhill from there, as if I had made a damaging admission. But I believe most detective-story writers would give the same answer. A close paternal or fraternal relationship between writer and detective is a marked peculiarity of the form. Throughout its history, from Poe to Chandler and beyond, the detective hero has represented his creator and carried his values into action in society.

Poe, who invented the modern detective story, and his detective Dupin, are good examples. Poe's was a first-rate but guilt-haunted mind painfully at odds with the realities of pre-Civil-War America. Dupin is a declassed aristocrat, as Poe's heroes tend to be, an obvious equivalent for the artist-intellectual who has lost his place in society and his foothold in tradition. Dupin has no social life, only one friend. He is set apart from other people by his superiority of mind.

In his creation of Dupin, Poe was surely compensating for his failure to become what his extraordinary mental powers seemed to fit him for. He had dreamed of an intellectual hierarchy governing the cultural life of the nation, himself at its head. Dupin's outwitting of an unscrupulous politician in "The Purloined Letter," his "solution" of an actual New York case in "Marie Roget," his repeated trumping of the cards held by the Prefect of Police, are Poe's vicarious demonstrations of superiority to an indifferent society and its officials.

Ross Macdonald, "The Writer as Detective Hero." From Macdonald, *On Crime Writing* (Santa Barbara, Calif.: Capra Press, 1973), no. 11 in Yes! Capra Chapbook Series, pp. 9-24; the last four paragraphs are from Macdonald's, "Down These Streets a Mean Man Must Go," printed in *Antaeus,* nos. 25-26 (Spring/Summer, 1977), pp. 215-16. Reprinted by permission of Kenneth Millar and (for the last four paragraphs) *Antaeus,* New York, New York.

Of course Poe's detective stories gave the writer, and give the reader, something deeper than such obvious satisfactions. He devised them as a means of exorcising or controlling guilt and horror. The late William Carlos Williams, in a profound essay, related Poe's sense of guilt and horror to the terrible awareness of a hyperconscious man standing naked and shivering on a new continent. The guilt was doubled by Poe's anguished insight into the unconscious mind. It had to be controlled by some rational pattern, and the detective story, "the tale of ratiocination," provided such a pattern.

The tale of the bloody murders in the Rue Morgue, Poe's first detective story (1841), is a very hymn to analytic reason intended, as Poe wrote later, "to depict some very remarkable features in the mental character of my friend, the Chevalier C. Auguste Dupin." Dupin clearly represents the reason, which was Poe's mainstay against the nightmare forces of the mind. These latter are acted out by the murderous ape: "Gnashing its teeth, and flashing fire from its eyes, it flew upon the body of the girl and embedded its fearful talons in her throat, retaining its grasp until she expired."

Dupin's reason masters the ape and explains the inexplicable—the wrecked apartment behind the locked door, the corpse of a young woman thrust up the chimney—but not without leaving a residue of horror. The nightmare can't quite be explained away, and persists in the teeth of reason. An unstable balance between reason and more primitive human qualities is characteristic of the detective story. For both writer and reader it is an imaginative arena where such conflicts can be worked out safely, under artistic controls.

The first detective story has other archetypal features, particularly in the way it is told. The "I" who narrates it is not the detective Dupin. The splitting of the protagonist into a narrator and a detective has certain advantages: it helps to eliminate the inessential, and to postpone the solution. More important, the author can present his self-hero, the detective, without undue embarrassment, and can handle dangerous emotional material at two or more removes from himself, as Poe does in "Rue Morgue."

The disadvantages of the split protagonist emerge more clearly in the saga of Dupin's successor Sherlock Holmes. One projection of the author, the narrator, is made to assume a posture of rather blind admiration before another projection of the author, the detective hero, and the reader is invited to share Dr. Watson's adoration of the great man. An element of narcissistic fantasy, impatient with the limits of the self, seems to be built into this traditional form of the detective story.

I'm not forgetting that Holmes' *modus operandi* was based on that of an actual man, Conan Doyle's friend and teacher, Dr. Joseph Bell. Although his "science" usually boils down to careful observation, which was Dr. Bell's forte, Holmes is very much the scientific criminologist. This hero of scientism may be in fact the dominant culture hero of our technological society.

Though Holmes is a physical scientist specializing in chemistry and anatomy, and Dupin went in for literary and psychological analysis, Holmes can easily be recognized as Dupin's direct descendant. His most conspicuous feature, his ability to read thoughts on the basis of associative clues, is a direct borrowing from Dupin. And like Dupin, he is a projection of the author, who at the time of Holmes' creation was a not very busy young doctor. According to his son Adrian, Conan Doyle admitted when he was dying: "If anyone is Sherlock Holmes, then I confess it is myself."

Holmes had other ancestors and collateral relations which reinforce the idea that he was a portrait of the artist as a great detective. His drugs, his secrecy and solitude, his moods of depression (which he shared with Dupin) are earmarks of the Romantic rebel then and now. Behind Holmes lurk the figures of nineteenth-century poets, Byron certainly, probably Baudelaire, who translated Poe and pressed Poe's guilty knowledge to new limits. I once made a case for the theory (and Anthony Boucher didn't disagree) that much of the modern development of the detective story stems from Baudelaire, his "dandyism" and his vision of the city as inferno. Conan Doyle's London, which influenced Eliot's "Wasteland," has something of this quality.

But Holmes' Romantic excesses aren't central to his character. His Baudelairean spleen and drug addiction are merely the idiosyncrasies of genius. Holmes is given the best of both worlds, and remains an English gentleman, accepted on the highest social levels. Permeating the thought and language of Conan Doyle's stories is an air of blithe satisfaction with a social system based on privilege.

This obvious characteristic is worth mentioning because it was frozen into one branch of the form. Nostalgia for a privileged society accounts for one of the prime attractions of the traditional English detective story and its innumerable American counterparts. Neither wars nor the dissolution of governments and societies interrupt that long weekend in the country house which is often, with more or less unconscious symbolism, cut off by a failure in communications from the outside world.

The contemporary world is the special province of the American hard-boiled detective story. Dashiell Hammett, Raymond Chandler, and the other writers for *Black Mask* who developed it, were in conscious reaction against the Anglo-American school which, in the work of S. S. Van Dine for example, had lost contact with contemporary life and language. Chandler's dedication, to the editor of *Black Mask*, of a collection of his early stories (1944), describes the kind of fiction they had been trying to supplant: "For Joseph Thompson Shaw with affection and respect, and in memory of the time when we were trying to get murder away from the upper classes, the weekend house party and the vicar's rose-garden, and back to the people who are really good at it." While Chandler's novels swarm with plutocrats as well as criminals, and even with what pass in Southern California for aristocrats, the *Black Mask* revolution was a real one. From it emerged a new kind of detective hero, the classless, restless man of American democracy, who spoke the language of the street.

Hammett, who created the most powerful of these new heroes in Sam Spade, had been a private detective and knew the corrupt inner workings of American cities. But Sam Spade was a less obvious projection of Hammett than detective heroes usually are of their authors. Hammett had got his early romanticism under strict ironic control. He could see Spade from outside, without affection, perhaps with some bleak compassion. In this as in other respects Spade marks a sharp break with the Holmes tradition. He possesses the virtues and follows the code of a frontier male. Thrust for his sins into the urban inferno, he pits his courage and cunning against its denizens, plays for the highest stakes available, love and money, and loses nearly everything in the end. His lover is guilty of murder; his narrow, bitter code forces Spade to turn her over to the police. The Maltese falcon has been stripped of jewels.

Perhaps the stakes and implied losses are higher than I have suggested. The worthless falcon may symbolize a lost tradition, the great cultures of the Mediterranean past which have become inaccessible to Spade and his generation. Perhaps the bird stands for the Holy Ghost itself, or for its absence.

The ferocious intensity of the work, the rigorous spelling-out of Sam Spade's deprivation of his full human heritage, seem to me to make his story tragedy, if there is such a thing as dead-pan tragedy. Hammett was the first American writer to use the detective-story for the purposes of a major novelist, to present a vision, blazing if disenchanted, of our lives. Sam Spade was the product and reflection of a mind which was not at home in Zion, or in Zenith.

Chandler's vision is disenchanted, too, but in spite of its hallucinated brilliance of detail it lacks the tragic unity of Hammett's. In his essay on "The Simple Art of Murder," an excitingly written piece of not very illuminating criticism, Chandler offers a prescription for the detective hero which suggests a central weakness in his vision:

> In everything that can be called art there is a quality of redemption. ... But down these mean streets a man must go who is not himself mean, who is neither tarnished nor afraid. ... The detective in this kind of story must be such a man. He is the hero, he is everything. ... He must be the best man in his world and a good enough man for any world.

While there may be "a quality of redemption" in a good novel, it belongs to the whole work and is not the private property of one of the characters.

No hero of serious fiction could act within a moral straitjacket requiring him to be consistently virtuous and unafraid. Sam Spade was submerged and struggling in tragic life. The detective-as-redeemer is a backward step in the direction of sentimental romance, and an over-simplified world of good guys and bad guys. The people of Chandler's early novels, though they include chivalrous gangsters and gangsters' molls with hearts of gold, are divided into two groups by an angry puritanical morality. The goats are usually separated from the sheep by sexual promiscuity or perversion. Such a strong and overt moralistic bias actually interferes with the broader moral effects a novelist aims at.

Fortunately in the writing of his books Chandler toned down his Watsonian enthusiasm for his detective's moral superiority. The detective Marlowe, who tells his own stories in the first person, and sometimes admits to being afraid, has a self-deflating wit which takes the curse off his knight-errantry:

> I wasn't wearing a gun...I doubted if it would do me any good. The big man would probably take it away from me and eat it.
>
> (*Farewell, My Lovely*, 1940)

The Chandler-Marlowe prose is a highly charged blend of laconic wit and imagistic poetry set to breakneck rhythms. Its strong colloquial vein reaffirms the fact that the *Black Mask* revolution was a revolution in language as well as subject matter. It is worth noticing that H. L. Mencken, the great lexicographer of our vernacular, was an early editor of *Black Mask*. His protegé James M. Cain once said that his discovery of the western roughneck made it possible for him to write fiction. Marlowe and his predecessors performed a similar function for Chandler, whose English education put a special edge on his passion for our new language, and a special edge on his feelings against privilege. Socially mobile and essentially classless (he went to college but has a working-class bias), Marlowe liberated his author's imagination into an overheard democratic prose which is one of the most effective narrative instruments in our recent literature.

Under the obligatory "tough" surface of the writing, Marlowe is interestingly different from the standard hardboiled hero who came out of *Black Mask*. Chandler's novels focus in his hero's sensibility, and could almost be described as novels of sensibility. Their constant theme is big-city loneliness, and the wry pain of a sensitive man coping with the roughest elements of a corrupt society.

It is Marlowe's doubleness that makes him interesting: the hard-boiled mask half-concealing Chandler's poetic and satiric mind. Part of our pleasure derives from the interplay between the mind of Chandler and the voice of Marlowe. The recognized difference between them is part of the dynamics of the narrative, setting up bipolar tensions in the prose. The marvellous opening paragraph of *The Big Sleep* (1939) will illustrate some of this:

> It was about eleven o'clock in the morning, mid October, with the sun not shining and a look of hard wet rain in the clearness of the foothills. I was wearing my powder-blue suit, with dark blue shirt, tie and display handkerchief, black brogues, black wool socks with dark blue clocks on them. I was neat, clean, shaved and sober, and I didn't care who knew it. I was everything the well-dressed private detective ought to be. I was calling on four million dollars.

Marlowe is making fun of himself, and of Chandler in the role of brash young detective. There is pathos, too, in the idea that a man who can write like a fallen angel should be a mere private eye; and Socratic irony. The gifted writer conceals himself behind Marlowe's cheerful mindlessness. At the same time the retiring, middle-aged, scholarly author acquires a durable mask, forever 38, which allows him to face the dangers of society high and low.

Chandler's conception of Marlowe, and his relationship with his character, deepened as his mind penetrated the romantic fantasy, and the overbright self-consciousness, that limited his vision. At the end of *The Long Goodbye* (1953) there is a significant confrontation between Marlowe and a friend who had betrayed him and apparently gone homosexual. In place of the righteous anger which Marlowe would have indulged in in one of the earlier novels he now feels grief and disquiet, as if the confrontation might be with a part of himself.

The friend, the ex-friend, tries to explain his moral breakdown: "I was in the commandos, bud. They don't take you if you're just a piece of fluff. I got badly hurt and it wasn't any fun with those Nazi doctors. It did something to me." This is all we are told. At the roaring heart of Chandler's maze there is a horror which even at the end of his least evasive novel remains unspeakable. Whatever its hidden meaning, this scene was written by a man of tender and romantic sensibility who had been injured. Chandler used Marlowe to shield while half-expressing his sensibility, and to act out the mild paranoia which often goes with this kind of sensibility and its private hurts, and which seems to be virtually endemic among contemporary writers.

I can make this judgment with some assurance because it applies with a vengeance to some of my earlier books, particularly *Blue City* (1947). A decade later, in *The Doomsters,* I made my detective Archer criticize himself as "a slightly earthbound Tarzan in a slightly paranoid jungle." This novel marked a fairly clean break with the Chandler tradition, which it had taken me some years to digest, and freed me to make my own approach to the crimes and sorrows of life.

I learned a great deal from Chandler—any writer can—but there had always been basic differences between us. One was in our attitude to plot. Chandler described a good plot as one that made for good scenes, as if the parts were greater than the whole. I see plot as a vehicle of meaning. It should be as complex as contemporary life, but balanced enough to say true things about it. The surprise with which a detective novel concludes should set up tragic vibrations which run backward through the entire structure. Which means that the structure must be single, and *intended*.

Another difference between Chandler and me is in our use of language. My narrator Archer's wider and less rigidly stylized range of expression, at least in more recent novels, is related to a central difference between him and Marlowe. Marlowe's voice is limited by his role as the hardboiled hero. He must speak within his limits as a character, and these limits are quite narrowly conceived. Chandler tried to relax them in *The Long Goodbye*, but he was old and the language failed to respond. He was trapped like the late Hemingway in an unnecessarily limiting idea of self, hero, and language.

I could never write of Archer: "He is the hero, he is everything." It is true that his actions carry the story, his comments on it reflect my attitudes (but deeper attitudes remain implicit), and Archer or a narrator like him is indispensable to the kind of books I write. But he is not their emotional center. And in spite of what I said at the beginning, Archer has developed away from his early status as a fantasy projection of myself and my personal needs. Cool, I think, is the word for our mature relationship. Archer himself has what New Englanders call "weaned affections."

An author's heavy emotional investment in a narrator-hero can get in the way of the story and blur its meanings, as some of Chandler's books demonstrate. A less encumbered narrator permits greater flexibility, and fidelity to the intricate truths of life. I don't have to celebrate Archer's physical or sexual prowess, or work at making him consistently funny and charming. He can be self-forgetful, almost transparent at times, and concentrate as good detectives (and good writers) do, on the people whose problems he is investigating. These other people are for me the main thing: they are often more intimately related to me and my life than Lew Archer is. He is the obvious self-projection which holds the eye (my eye as well as the reader's) while more secret selves creep out of the woodwork behind the locked door. Remember how the reassuring presence of Dupin permitted Poe's mind to face the nightmare of the homicidal ape and the two dead women.

Archer is a hero who sometimes verges on being an anti-hero. While he is a man of action, his actions are largely directed to putting together the stories of other people's lives and discovering their significance. He is less a doer than a questioner, a consciousness in which the meanings of other lives emerge. This gradually developed conception of the detective hero as the mind of the novel is not wholly new, but it is probably my main contribution to this special branch of fiction. Some such refinement of the conception of the detective hero was needed to bring this kind of novel closer to the purpose and range of the mainstream novel.

It may be that internal realism, a quality of mind, is one of the most convincing attributes a character can have. Policemen and lawyers have surprised me with the opinion that Archer is quite true to life. The two best private detectives I personally know resemble him in their internal qualities: their intelligent humaneness, an interest in other people transcending their interest in themselves, and a toughness of mind which enables them to face human weaknesses, including their own, with open eyes. Both of them dearly love to tell a story.

I believe that popular culture is not and need not be at odds with high culture, any more than the rhythms of walking are at odds with the dance. Popular writers learn what they can from the masters; and even the masters may depend on the rather sophisticated audience and the vocabulary of shapes and symbols which popular fiction provides. Without the traditional Gothic novel and its safety net of readers, even Henry James could not have achieved the wire-walking assurance with which he wrote *The Turn of the Screw*. The work which T.S. Eliot considered the next step taken after James by the Anglo-American novel, *The Great Gatsby*, has obvious connections with American crime fiction and the revolution effected in that fiction during the twenties. The skeleton of Fitzgerald's great work, if not its nervous system, is that of a mystery novel.

A functioning popular literature appears to be very useful if not essential to the growth of a higher literature. Chandler's debt to Fitzgerald suggests that the reverse is also true. There is a two-way connection between the very greatest work and the anonymous imaginings of a people.

I don't intend to suggest that popular literature is primarily a matrix for higher forms. Popular fiction, popular art in general, is the very air a civilization breathes. (Air itself is 80 percent nitrogen.) Popular art is the form in which a culture comes to be known by most of its members. It is the carrier and guardian of the spoken language. A book which can be read by everyone, a convention which is widely used and understood in all its variations, holds a civilization together as nothing else can.

It reaffirms our values as they change, and dramatizes the conflicts of those values. It absorbs and domesticates the spoken language, placing it in meaningful context with traditional language, forming new linguistic synapses in the brain and body of the culture. It describes new modes of behavior, new versions of human character, new shades and varieties of good and evil, and implicitly criticizes them. It holds us still and contemplative for a moment, caught like potential shoplifters who see their own furtive images in a scanning mirror, and wonder if the store detective is looking.

Artistic Failures and Successes:
Christie and Sayers

by John G. Cawelti

Agatha Christie has deservedly earned the title of Queen of the Detective Story, not only through her sustained productivity over six decades,
but through the remarkable ingenuity of her structures of detection and
mystification. Because many of her tales employ nearly identical structures
of this sort it is possible to get a better appreciation of the various aspects
of art within the classical formula by comparing instances where the same
basic strategy of mystification has been developed with greater or lesser
success. Here is one such structure:

> A rich and powerful man has secured his great position in life by commit-
> ting a crime at an earlier period. With the aid of a female accomplice he has
> been able to prevent this crime from becoming known and has risen to a
> situation of great responsibility and influence. His accomplice has con-
> tinued to be faithful to him and together they have been able to deceive all
> their present acquaintances about their past crime and their actual relation
> to each other. The mystery plot commences when a person who knew the
> culprit or his accomplice at an earlier period comes into the present situation
> and endangers it by the threat of exposure. This witness from the past ac-
> cidentally or purposely reveals the situation to an unscrupulous blackmailer
> who threatens the culprit and his accomplice. They determine to murder the
> witness and the blackmailer, constructing an ingenious scheme that makes
> full use of the female accomplice's capacity for impersonation. To insure that
> they will not be caught for the murder the culprit and his accomplice not only
> skillfully frame an innocent scapegoat, but do their best to make it appear
> that one of them is among the intended victims of the murderer. In addition,
> because of the culprit's important position there are hints that the situation
> involves some form of espionage or international politics. The murders are
> skillfully accomplished without the slightest suspicion falling on the cul-
> prits. The scapegoat is nearly convicted of the crime before Poirot finally
> arrives at the proper solution.

John G. Cawelti, "The Art of the Classical Detective Story," From Cawelti, *Adventure, Mystery, and Romance* (Chicago: University of Chicago Press, 1976), pp. 111-16, 119-25. Reprinted
with permission of John G. Cawelti and the University of Chicago Press.

The ingenuity of this structure is considerable, for it not only provides a suitable machinery for the crime (impersonation) and a lavish possibility of red herrings, it also, even more importantly, allows for the kind of basic reversal in assumption so important to a truly effective scheme of mystification. We are not simply confronted with the question of which suspect nipped into the bedroom and slipped the prussic acid to dear old Aunt Penelope but are led from the beginning to make the wrong assumptions about just who was murdered and why. This well-constructed set of false assumptions is a more elaborate analogy to what Poe accomplished so brilliantly in "The Purloined Letter" with his revelation that one can hide most effectively by not concealing. If well handled, this structure makes possible not only one big reversal of expectations when the guilty person is unmasked but a progression of incidents through which the reader continually faces a new series of deductions from the basic clues only to find himself mystified once more. Agatha Christie's ability to work out stratagems of this sort is preeminent.

But, as we have seen, the ingenious scheme of detection and mystification is only one aspect of the art of the classical detective story. The selection or invention of a good detective stratagem does not guarantee that it will be effectively deployed in a story. Here, Christie's own example is illuminating for she employed the same structure of detection and mystification in two works, one of which is her finest and the other one of her biggest failures. The novels I refer to are *An Overdose of Death* (originally *The Patriotic Murders* [1940]) and *Third Girl* (1967). What accounts for the enormous difference in effectiveness between these two embodiments of the same stratagem of mystification?

Essentially, in one novel Christie finds specific embodiments for her ingenious system of crime and inquiry that establish an effective balance between the major elements held by the detective formula in tension, while, in the other, some of the elements get out of control and destroy the delicate formal equilibrium so essential to the genre. Let us look first at the basic balance between detection and mystification. This depends on the relationship the writer establishes between the crime, the detective's pattern of inquiry, and the way in which the inquiry is presented to the reader. The crime is essentially the same in both *An Overdose of Death* and *Third Girl*. But when we come to the two related patterns of detective and reader inquiry we find a very different treatment in the two books. In *Overdose* a crime at the beginning of the story draws both Poirot and the reader into the inquiry. From that point on, the reader is present with Poirot at every significant event, interview, or examination of clues. Throughout most of the first two-thirds of the book the reader shares to a considerable extent in Poirot's perception of things and is thus able to follow the course of events with clarity and interest. Only at the end of chapter 6 (out of a total of ten) does it become evident that Poirot has been able to draw major deductions about the case, a fact that Christie carefully announces to the reader, thus indicating quite clearly the terms on which the reader's and the detective's structure of inquiry must either significantly change or diverge. This announcement is a striking one. It is set off by a biblical quotation and ends up with a clearly formulated challenge to the reader's powers of deduction:

> Hercule Poirot essayed a hesitant baritone.
> "The proud have laid a snare for me,'" he sang "'and spread a net with cords: yea, and set traps in my way.'"
> His mouth remained open.
> *He saw it*—saw clearly the trap into which he has so nearly fallen!...
> He was in a daze—a glorious daze where isolated facts spun wildly round before settling neatly into their appointed places. It was like a kaleidoscope—shoe buckles, size nine stockings, a damaged face, the low tastes in literature of Alfred the page boy, the activities of Mr. Amberiotis, and the part played by the late Mr. Morley, all rose up and whirled and settled themselves down into a coherent pattern.
> For the first time, Hercule Poirot was looking at the case *the right way up*.[1]

This is the moment at which Poirot grasps the basic structure of the crime, namely that the man who had been assumed to be the victim was actually the culprit and that all the prime suspects heretofore presented to the reader and Poirot have actually been victims. In fact, all the clues mentioned in the quoted passage do play an important part in the deduction as one recognizes in retrospect after Poirot explains it all. Even the dullest reader is probably able to make some kind of inference from one or more of these clues. Yet it seems to me that the important thing from an artistic point of view is not Christie's vaunted fairness to the reader—of which this is an unusually full example—but her successful accomplishment of the effect of combined rationality and mystification. The striking clarity of this announcement of the solution assures us that these seemingly unconnected fragments have a perfectly rational relation if we can understand the meaning of "looking at the case *the right way up*." For most readers, however, the crimes and the characters have been skillfully enough presented that the right set of deductions is impossible. The end result is a more suspenseful mystification that enables Christie to develop another narrative interest in the remainder of the tale. Now, in addition to the attempt to figure out the crime, we are also confronted with the puzzle of the detective's activity. Since Poirot has come to understand what is going on, his actions in testing his hypothesis and entrapping the criminal become further clues for the reader to chew on. In the final phase of the story all three lines of the structure of detection and mystification become separated as the reader tries to figure out not only who the culprit is but the logic behind Poirot's actions. This tension between the activity of the criminal, the detective, and the

[1]Agatha Christie, *An Overdose of Death* (New York: Dell Publishing Co., 1967), pp. 140-41.

reader leads to a very satisfying climax when the explanation finally arrives.

Before turning to the confusions of *Third Girl*, let us look more fully at two of the ways in which Christie makes it nearly impossible for the reader to break through the pattern of mystification while at the same time she keeps him deeply interested in the effort to do so. Characterization in *An Overdose of Death* is well calculated to perform its necessary function in the structure of mystification. The culprit is a fine example of the least likely person in both senses of the term. First of all, he is presented to us throughout the story not as a suspect but as a victim. Moreover, despite his importance as a possible motive for the crimes, the culprit remains a rather marginal figure in the inquiry until he is unmasked at the very end. Other characters talk a good deal about him, but he himself appears only briefly in a couple of scenes. In the most important of these, he actually urges Poirot on to discover the missing Miss Sainsbury Seale and insists that the idea of a plot against him cannot be true, two items that further suggest his innocence, unless of course we are familiar with Christie's habit of making her culprits play this kind of role in the inquiry. But even the reader's wariness of such devious narrative practices tends to be lulled by a nicely imagined stroke of character. The culprit is made a prime exponent of reason, order, and responsibility in a social universe that seems dangerously on the verge of chaos. The most likely suspects presented to us, on the other hand, are embodiments of loutishness, irrationality, and anarchy. Thus Christie makes the deeper emotional structure of the classical formula, with its emphasis on the restoration of order, function as a means of distracting the reader's attention from the true culprit.

The crime in *An Overdose of Death* is also designed with remarkable ingenuity, not only in the sense that it is complex and difficult, but also in the way it establishes a balance of inquiry and action throughout the story. In general, there seem to be six main ways in which a reader can be effectively misled about a fictional crime: he can be deceived as to the person, the motive, the means of the crime, the time at which it is committed, the place where it occurs, and, finally, whether it is a crime or not. In this case, Christie manages to work all these modes of mystification into her pattern. The first crime is the apparent suicide of Poirot's dentist. Actually, this is a murder, the key to which lies in the fact that its motive is hidden and that it takes place at an earlier time than the evidence leads one to believe. The handling of this crime is a nice example of how to involve the reader effectively in attempts at detection that lead only to further mystification. Though Morley's, the dentist's, death is officially accounted a suicide by the police, Christie makes it clear to the reader that this cannot be true by both logical and narrative means. One of the most unshakable conventions

²*Ibid.,* p. 16.

of the classical detective story is that every crime must have a rationally comprehensible motive, and there appears to be no such motive for Morley's suicide. Then, in her presentation of the brief conversation between Poirot and his dentist, not long before Morley's mysterious suicide, Christie carefully inserts a tantalizing remark. Morley says: "'I don't remember names, but it's remarkable the way I never forget a face. One of my patients the other day, for instance—I've seen that patient before.'"[2] Actually this remark is not simply a narrative trick; it later turns out to be a significant clue. At this point, it serves primarily to warn the reader that some kind of plot is afoot. On both the grounds of physical evidence and this bit of dialogue the reader cannot accept the conclusion that Morley's death is suicide. In fact, this situation is so firmly based on formulaic conventions that one of the most striking possible solutions at the end of the tale would have been a demonstration that Morley had in fact committed suicide.

Christie does not choose to develop things in this way. Instead, she introduces a second murder, which is first thought to be an accidental death. This is the mysterious Amberiotis who dies of an overdose of dental anesthetic after a visit to Morley. The police theory is the obvious deduction: having recognized that he had accidentally given his client a lethal dose of anesthetic, Morley commits suicide in despair. Again the reader is challenged and drawn further into the tale by a conclusion that is patently superficial and inconclusive. The reader is certain that this explanation is unsatisfactory when a second dental client mysteriously disappears. Here, as throughout the story, a phase of inquiry leads to an action that stimulates further deductions. Because of the ingenious structure of the crime, however, these deductions can only produce further mystification. After rejecting the superficial inference offered by the police, the reader is first led to seek out some explanation for the murder of Morley on the assumption that his death is the primary crime. This is, of course, the reverse of the truth. In fact, Morley's death is secondary; the real targets of the culprit are Amberiotis and Miss Sainsbury Seale. In addition, we are skillfully misled as to the order of the murders (Miss Seale's death actually occurs first; the person we see in the dentist's office is one of the culprits dressed as Miss Seale) and to their time (the dentist is killed almost an hour earlier than we have been made to believe).

Christie seems to be well aware that most readers confronted by a fruitless detection situation such as that just outlined will soon lose interest. Thus another red herring appears and we are offered another possible line of inquiry with the introduction of Alastair Blunt—the actual culprit—as the most logical intended victim. Blunt, too, had been a patient of Morley on that crowded morning. A further complication is added when the corpse of the real Miss Sainsbury Seale turns up and is identified by her teeth as Mrs. Chapman, wife of a mysterious secret agent, thus adding force to the hypothesis that Alastair Blunt is the victim of some international plot.

By this time the reader is more mystified than when he began, drowned in a mass of tantalizing clues, none of which seem to fit with the possible explanations that have been offered. Then, in still another twist of the story, a young man who has been sullenly lurking around the edges of the story is caught in what appears to be an attempt on Alastair Blunt's life. This actually is the scapegoat that the culprits have cunningly prepared. The reader, of course, is encouraged to suspect that something is wrong here. As she often does, Christie plays one of the unwritten conventions of the detective story against what appears to be a palpable fact. We seemingly see Frank Carter attempt to murder Alastair Blunt, but we know that he cannot be the real culprit because he has been such an obvious suspect all along. Moreover, a moment's reflection shows that this character could not have planned a crime so elaborate and ingenious as we have come to understand this sequence of deaths to be.

It is just at this point that the story takes another twist. Poirot announces that he has finally seen the crime the right side up. We enter the final phase of the story in which our mystification about Poirot's doings is added to our bewilderment about the crime itself. The climax when Poirot unmasks Blunt and his mistress and explains the incredibly elaborate motive and method of the crime becomes a fully satisfying reversal and release from the cognitive and emotional tension.

Thus, as this ingenious and artful narrative structure unrolls itself before us, we are confronted at each moment with a new twist that at first seems to lead to a more likely possibility of solution but that in fact drives us deeper and deeper into mystification. It is important to note that this is not the mystification of the thriller or the ghost story, because we never lose our certainty that the right chain of reasoning will explain everything. *An Overdose of Death* illustrates the classical detective formula in its most concentrated and purest form. Character and atmosphere are reduced to the barest minimum and function only as necessary embodiments to the structure of detection and mystification. Actions have little interest in their own right; they exist solely to enable the introduction of a new line of inquiry. ...

Sayers is not as skillful as Christie in constructing a cast of characters and a situation that will effectively dramatize the twists and turns of the detection-mystification structure. A work like *Five Red Herrings,* perhaps the most complicated and ingenious of Sayers's crime plots, is finally boring to read because it bogs down in the interminable examination of clues and schedules without Christie's little touches of character and changing situations to dramatize the process of inquiry. When Sayers involves the presentation of mystery with the evocation of a set of characters and a social atmosphere, she is in my opinion a far richer and more complex artist than Christie.

Sayers's best work, *The Nine Tailors,* uses the classical detective story structure to embody a vision of the mysteries of divine providence. This

moral and religious aspect of the story by no means prevents it from having
an effective and complex structure of detection and mystification, but this
structure relates to the other interests of character, atmosphere, and theme
in a very different way than is typical of Christie. For one thing, to a considerable extent we experience the inquiry as Lord Peter Wimsey does.
Indeed, he remains mystified about the central crime in much the same way
that we do and the way in which he finally arrives at the true solution is
shown to us in much the same light as it appears to him. In other words, the
detective and the reader do not part company two-thirds of the way through
the tale but share in the process of discovery throughout. Character, also,
assumes a kind of prominence in the story that is almost unknown to
Christie. While the cast of characters is much the same as one would expect
to find in a Christie story and has a decided stereotypical quality, they are
not simply functional adjuncts of the detection-mystification structure. For
instance, there are a number of characters who are never presented to us as
possible suspects and who yet play important parts in the story. This is
almost never the case with Christie, except in her less successful tales. Finally, there is a great deal of material that characterizes or explains important
aspects of the social setting without significantly contributing to the development of the mystery. The most notorious instance of this is Sayers's
elaborate treatment of the art and ritual of change-ringing. While the bells
do have an important role in the mystery, it was obviously not necessary to
present a treatise on campanology in order to account for that circumstance.

Thus *Nine Tailors* is an example of a classical detective tale in which
alternative narrative interests in character, social setting, and thematic
significance have been interwoven into the structure of a mystery. At this
point one might reasonably ask why bother with the mystery structure at
all? If Sayers really wanted to write a novel about English rural society
combining piquant touches of local color with traditional religious themes,
why did she not simply do so? In fact, some critics of Sayers have argued
that these other elements in *The Nine Tailors* interfere with the effectiveness of the detection-mystification structure just as the necessities of mystification limit and weaken the development of character and theme. I would
like to argue, however, that in this case these various aspects of the tale are
successfully integrated, that the nature of this particular mystery required
this kind of treatment, and that Sayers's religious and social vision was perhaps most effectively expressed through the format of a classical detective
story.

The background of the mystery is as follows:

> About fifteen years before the story opens a very expensive emerald neck-
> lace belonging to a guest at the Thorpe mansion in Fenchurch St. Paul was
> stolen. Though the thief, Jeff Deacon, a servant in the Thorpe house, was
> identified by his London confederate, one Nobby Cranton, the emeralds

were never found because they had been hidden in a church by Deacon who had kept a paper in cipher to remind himself of the location. Deacon and Cranton were both given extensive prison sentences, while the Thorpe family was reduced to considerably straitened circumstances by Sir Henry Thorpe's insistence on paying his guest for the missing emeralds. After serving four years of his term, Deacon escaped from prison and was thought to have been killed while fleeing the police, though in fact he escaped to France during the confusion of the First World War. There he had taken up a new identity while waiting for a chance to return and secure the hidden emeralds. In the meantime, back at Fenchurch St. Paul, Deacon's former wife had remarried a local man named Will Thoday.

Shortly before the opening of the book, Deacon returns to Fenchurch St. Paul where he is found prowling around the church by Will Thoday. Deacon threatens to reveal Mary Thoday's bigamy. Will agrees to hide him and to give him money to get out of the country. Will ties Deacon up in the bell chamber of the church until he can arrange for the money, but before he can do so, Will falls deliriously ill of the flu, barely managing to confide his problem to his visiting brother Jim. It happens that the very evening Deacon is tied in the bell chamber, the local rector has arranged for an all night change-ringing. The terrible noise of the bells kills Deacon, and the next morning he is found by Jim Thoday. Jim concludes that Will has killed Deacon and hides the body in a newly dug grave, which happens to be that of Lady Thorpe. He then returns to his ship and leaves the country.

Looked at in this way, the mystery of *The Nine Tailors* is an incredible tissue of improbability, coincidence, and turgid sensationalism. Compared to the relative clarity and plausibility of the Christie mystery plot outlined above, this tale of dark doings and complex betrayals in deepest rural England sounds like a fiction by some demented follower of Thomas Hardy. Indeed, *The Nine Tailors* with its atmospheric treatment of the Fen country, its climactic natural catastrophe, and its theme of the tragic reappearance of a former villager bears more than a little resemblance to *The Return of the Native*. What is most striking, however, is the transformation of this garish melodrama by its integration into the inquiry structure of the classical detective story. By doing so, Sayers transforms the incredible tissue of coincidence into a ritual allegory of providential action with the detective as priest, uncovering and expounding the mysterious ways of God to the bewildered participants in the action. With the actual structure of the crime in mind, let us now briefly summarize the pattern of the inquiry:

The story begins with an accident. Lord Peter Wimsey has been driving through the Fen country on a dark New Year's Eve when his car runs into a ditch near Fenchurch St. Paul. Going to the nearby vicarage for help, Lord Peter discovers the rector, Mr. Venables, in a considerable state. He has scheduled an epic ring of changes to celebrate the New Year, but one of his ringers, Will Thoday, has become prostrated with illness. Lord Peter agrees to take his place, and the change-ringing goes on as scheduled. As he leaves the next day, Lord Peter encounters on the road a suspicious looking older man who asks the way to Fenchurch St. Paul.

Some months later, at Easter time, Lord Peter receives a letter from Rector Venables inviting him to inquire into the mysterious appearance of a corpse in the graveyard, discovered when Lady Thorpe's grave was opened to bury the recently deceased Sir Henry Thorpe. Wimsey is intrigued with the situation, and, having heard of the earlier theft of emeralds from the Thorpe mansion, assumes there is some connection between the mysterious body and the earlier crime. Of course, at this stage Wimsey (and the reader) believe that Deacon is dead; therefore, the proper inferences about the body cannot be arrived at. After inquiries based on clues connected with the body, Wimsey does succeed in tracing the dead man to France where he has been living for several years under what is obviously an assumed name.

At this point attention shifts from the dead man to a strange paper which had been found at Easter time by Miss Hilary Thorpe, the attractive daughter of the unfortunate Thorpes. The paper, which reads like the apocalyptic vision of a lunatic, turns out on examination by Wimsey to be a cipher revealing the hiding place of the missing necklace. Lord Peter retrieves the necklace from its place of concealment among the gilded angels in the church ceiling. The discovery of the emeralds only leaves the mystery of the dead body still more in the dark.

It is at this point of complete mystification that Lord Peter has the insight which seems to unravel most of the mystery; by inferring that the dead body is actually the long-dead Jeff Deacon he is able to understand and explain the role of Will Thoday and his brother. When confronted, the two brothers explain everything, but claim in a plausible way that neither one has actually killed Deacon. In fact, neither Wimsey nor the police are able to establish with any certainty the manner of Deacon's death. Thus, though we seem to know every person involved and understand the whys and wherefores of Deacon's movements, the cause of his death remains still more mysterious than ever.

More time passes. Wimsey decides to spend Christmas at Fenchurch St. Paul. As he drives toward the village on Christmas Eve he notices the waters ominously rising in the canals and sluices. A few days later the sluice gates break and a flood spreads over the land forcing all the inhabitants to cluster at the high ground of the church for safety. While the alarm bell is ringing to warn the people around, Lord Peter happens to climb into the bell tower and narrowly escapes being killed himself by the sound. Finally he realizes how and in what manner Jeff Deacon has met with his death: that Deacon has been investigated, tried, and given judgment by a higher power. Will Thoday drowns trying to save a friend, and the whole area is, one might say, purged and cleaned out by the rising and receding flood waters.

Miss Sayers's powers of invention, organization, mystification, and style seem to have reached a peak in *The Nine Tailors* perhaps because this story embodied more deeply than most not only some of her own deepest social and religious feelings, but also her sense of what was most basic about the detective story. In the introduction to her *Omnibus of Crime* published just six years before *The Nine Tailors* Sayers offered her own speculations about the fundamental human appeal of puzzles and mysteries:

> It may be that in them [man] finds a sort of catharsis or purging of his fears and self-questionings. These mysteries made only to be solved, these horrors which he knows to be mere figments of the creative brain, comfort him by subtly persuading that life is a mystery which death will solve, and whose horrors will pass away a tale that is told.[3]

Whether or not this statement fully explains the detective story genre, it is a rich insight into the special vision of *The Nine Tailors,* for in that work Sayers does work with a kind of catharsis both with the developing events of her story and with the kind of mystery that they reveal. This special kind of feeling is enhanced by the ritual and ceremonial symbolism that Sayers employs in so many ways throughout the book. The entire story is wrapped in the formal symbolism of change-ringing, each chapter title being derived from some aspect of campanology; the action takes place around a church, and its major events occur at the main points of the ritual year: New Year's, Easter, and Christmas; biblical rhetoric and symbology are encountered at every point, and the climax arrives with a flood that does unto the microcosmic village of Fenchurch St. Paul what Noah's Flood did to the world.

While some readers may find something mildly blasphemous or perhaps even comically incongruous in this deployment of the great tradition of the Church of England in order to enliven the rhetoric of a detective story, a more sympathetic reader might think of all this as rather "metaphysical" in homage to the great seventeenth-century poets whose love of puzzles, wit, and incongruous stretched-out metaphors did not seem to conflict with their sincere religious feeling or their high artistry. The process of the inquiry in *The Nine Tailors* is carefully organized in such a way that human reason resolves minor mysteries, but only realization of the hand of God can solve the ultimate mystery of life and death. The sense of providential action is built up most skillfully and consistently throughout the story. Wimsey enters the inquiry through an accident, which turns out to be providential in the sense that only he has the capacity to explain the mystery. Deacon's death has the same pattern, though of larger magnitude. He dies because coincidentally with his temporary incarceration in the bell chamber the saintly Rector Venables had decided to ring a record peal of Kent Treble Bob to celebrate the New Year, and because the one man aware of Deacon's situation was helplessly ill and delirious. The emeralds are discovered only because the piece of paper accidentally dropped by Deacon is picked

---

[3]See that essay, quoted *supra,* p. 53.

up by Hilary Thorpe, whose parents' lives had been ruined by the original theft. Throughout the text references to providence, humorous and serious, abound and serve as clues in the structure of detection and mystification that confronts the reader. These seemingly random comments have a clearly articulated order of development. Early in the story, even before the Eastertide resurrection of Deacon's corpse, the following colloquy occurs between Rector Venables and one of his parishioners:

> "We mustn't question the ways of Providence," said the Rector.
> "Providence?" said the old woman. "Don't yew talk to me about Providence. First he took my husband, and then he took my 'taters, but there's one above as'll teach him to mind his manners, if he don't look out."[4]

Though one first reads this as a bit of colorful local humor, it turns out in the light of later events to have more than one serious implication. The frequent presence of passages like this makes *The Nine Tailors* unusually rewarding on rereading. Later, after the discovery of Deacon's body, the sexton suggests that the ironically appropriate hymn "God moves in a mysterious way" be sung at the graveside. Finally, when the truth of Deacon's death is accidentally revealed during the flood, Rector Venables makes explicit in a serious statement the theme of providential agency:

> "There have always been," he said, "legends about Batty Thomas [one of the bells]. She has slain two other men in times past, and Hezekiah will tell you that the bells are said to be jealous of the presence of evil. Perhaps God speaks through those mouths of inarticulate metal. He is a righteous judge, strong and patient and is provoked every day."[5]

Thus, in *The Nine Tailors*, Dorothy Sayers effectively integrates the formulaic structure of the classical detective story with the additional narrative interests of religious theme and social setting. The mixture works effectively in this case without breaking the bounds of the formula because the mystery and the structure of inquiry through which it is presented are unified with the central theme of the mystery of God's providential action. Though this is a high accomplishment in the art of the classical detective story, some of its limitations become immediately apparent if we place *The Nine Tailors* in comparison with some of the great novels that deal with the religious aspects of murder, such as *Crime and Punishment* or *The Brothers Karamazov*. In *The Nine Tailors* God's will rather too comfortably aligns itself with a noticeably limited vision of English class justice. Compared with Dostoevsky's treatment of the purging and redemption of Raskolnikov one becomes too easily aware that in Sayers's English village evil seems to be defined more in terms of nasty, aggressive members of the lower classes trying to punch their way up the social scale than as the more uni-

---

[4]Dorothy Sayers, *The Nine Tailors* (New York: Harcourt, Brace and World, 1962), p. 68.
[5]*Ibid.*, p. 310.

versally meaningful sense of mystery and evil that Dostoevsky so powerfully delineates. To enjoy fully and be moved by *The Nine Tailors* one must be able temporarily to accept the snobbish, class-ridden, provincial world of Fenchurch St. Paul as a microcosm of the world; otherwise one will inevitably agree with those readers who find the religious symbolism of the book pretentious and inappropriate. Whether these limitations of vision represent the attitudes of Miss Sayers or the formulaic boundaries of the classical detective story—and they are probably a combination of both— does not greatly matter. The fact that Sayers was able to work comfortably within the basic patterns of the classical formula suggests that her own religious commitments made sense in this way. Nonetheless, those who are willing to accept the stringent limitations of this fictional universe for the sake of such curious pleasures as the final twist by which it becomes apparent that God is the least likely person, are grateful to Dorothy Sayers for this embodiment of her art.

A Detective Story Decalogue

By Ronald A. Knox

I. *The criminal must be someone mentioned in the early part of the story, but must not be anyone whose thoughts the reader has been allowed to follow.*

The mysterious stranger who turns up from nowhere in particular, from a ship as often as not, whose existence the reader had no means of suspecting from the outset, spoils the play altogether. The second half of the rule is more difficult to state precisely, especially in view of some remarkable performances by Mrs. Christie. It would be more exact to say that the author must not imply an attitude of mystification in the character who turns out to be the criminal.

II. *All supernatural or preternatural agencies are ruled out as a matter of course.*

To solve a detective problem by such means would be like winning a race on the river by the use of a concealed motor-engine. And here I venture to think there is a limitation about Mr. Chesterton's Father Brown stories. He nearly always tries to put us off the scent by suggesting that the crime must have been done by magic; and we know that he is too good a sportsman to fall back upon such a solution. Consequently, although we seldom guess the answer to his riddles, we usually miss the thrill of having suspected the wrong person.

III. *Not more than one secret room or passage is allowable.*

I would add that a secret passage should not be brought in at all unless the action takes place in the kind of house where such devices might be expected. When I introduced one into a book myself, I was careful to point out beforehand that the house had belonged to Catholics in penal times. Mr. Milne's secret passage in *The Red House Mystery* is hardly fair; if a modern house were so equipped — and it would be villainously expensive — all the country-side would be quite certain to know about it.

IV. *No hitherto undiscovered poisons may be used, nor any appliance which will need a long scientific explanation at the end.*

Ronald A. Knox, "A Detective Story Decalogue." From Knox, Introduction to *The Best Detective Stories of 1928* (London: Faber and Faber, 1929). Reprinted by permission of Faber and Faber Ltd.

There may be undiscovered poisons with quite unexpected reactions on the human system, but they have not been discovered yet, and until they are they must not be utilized in fiction; it is not cricket. Nearly all the cases of Dr. Thorndyke, as recorded by Mr. Austin Freeman, have the minor medical blemish; you have to go through a long science lecture at the end of the story in order to understand how clever the mystery was.

V. *No Chinaman must figure in the story.*

Why this should be so I do not know, unless we can find a reason for it in our western habit of assuming that the Celestial is over-equipped in the matter of brains, and under-equipped in the matter of morals. I only offer it as a fact of observation that, if you are turning over the pages of a book and come across some mention of 'the slit-like eyes of Chin Loo,' you had best put it down at once; it is bad. The only exception which occurs in my mind—there are probably others—is Lord Ernest Hamilton's *Four Tragedies of Memworth.*

VI. *No accident must ever help the detective, nor must he ever have an unaccountable intuition which proves to be right.*

This is perhaps too strongly stated; it is legitimate for the detective to have inspirations which he afterwards verifies, before he acts on them, by genuine investigation. And again, he will naturally have moments of clear vision, in which the bearings of the observations hitherto made will become evident to him. But he must not be allowed, for example, to look for the lost will in the works of the grandfather clock because an unaccountable instinct tells him that that is the right place to search. He must look there because he realizes that that is where he would have hidden it himself if he had been in the criminal's place. And in general it should be observed that every detail of his thought-process, not merely the main outline of it, should be conscientiously audited when the explanation comes along at the end.

VII. *The detective must not himself commit the crime.*

This applies only where the author personally vouches for the statement that the detective *is* a detective; a criminal may legitimately dress up as a detective, as in *The Secret of Chimneys,* and delude the other actors in the story with forged references.

VIII. *The detective must not light on any clues which are not instantly produced for the inspection of the reader.*

Any writer can make a mystery by telling us that at this point the great Picklock Holes suddenly bent down and picked up from the ground an object which he refused to let his friend see. He whispers 'Ha!' and his face grows grave—all that is illegitimate mystery-making. The skill of the detective author consists in being able to produce his clues and flourish them defiantly in our faces: 'There!' he says, 'what do you make of that?' and we make nothing.

IX. *The stupid friend of the detective, the Watson, must not conceal any thoughts which pass through his mind; his intelligence must be slightly, but very slightly, below that of the average reader.*

This is a rule of perfection; it is not of the *esse* of the detective story to have a Watson at all. But if he does exist, he exists for the purpose of letting the reader have a sparring partner, as it were, against whom he can pit his brains. 'I may have been a fool,' he says to himself as he puts the book down, 'but at least I wasn't such a doddering fool as poor old Watson.'

X. *Twin brothers, and doubles generally, must not appear unless we have been duly prepared for them.*

The dodge is too easy, and the supposition too improbable. I would add as a rider, that no criminal should be credited with exceptional powers of disguise unless we have had fair warning that he or she was accustomed to making up for the stage. How admirably is this indicated, for example, in *Trent's Last Case!*

PART FIVE

Epilogue: An Eye to the Future

The Criticism of Detective Fiction

by George N. Dove

Although it has been in existence for less than a century and a half, the detective story has already generated a body of criticism that is quite respectable in quantity, quality, and diversity. My purpose here is to offer two suggestions for future development in the criticism of detective fiction, but first, by way of background, I should like to identify five critical modes that have developed in this field and discuss one or two of the best-known exponents of each.

In the early years of the twentieth century, the criticism of detective fiction tended to be apologetic in tone and intent in defense against an attitude that held detective stories to be sensational and sub-literary. Beyond question the best apologia was delivered by G. K. Chesterton in "A Defense of Detective Stories" (1902),[1] and it is one of the anomalies of detective story criticism that this perceptive essay appeared so early in the development of the genre. Chesterton was apparently the first writer to gain insight into the mythic nature and the basic paradox of detective fiction and certainly the first to see in it the poetry of modern urban life.

One of the most frequent arguments of the apologists was that detective fiction should be judged by the best examples of the craft, not the worst, and the natural next step was to define the "good" story, as Carolyn Wells did in *The Technique of the Mystery Story* (1913).[2] Thus developed the second critical mode, legitimization, which ultimately took the form of "rules" for the detective story, such as Ronald A. Knox's "Ten Commandments of Detection" and S. S. Van Dine's "Twenty Rules for Writing Detective Stories" (both 1928),[3] each so dogmatic as to have value now chiefly as a quaint curiosity.

The third mode is what might be called form-and-function or means-and-

---

George N. Dove, "The Criticism of Detective Fiction." From *The Popular Culture Scholar,* I (Winter, 1977), 1-7. Reprinted with permission of the author, Frostburg State College (Frostburg, Md.), and Pearl G. Aldrich.

[1]In Howard Haycraft, ed., *The Art of the Mystery Story: A Collection of Critical Essays* (New York: Simon and Schuster, 1946), pp. 3-6.

[2](Springfield, Massachusetts: The Home Correspondence School, 1913).

[3]In Haycraft, pp. 189-93, 194-96. [Knox was actually published in 1929.]

ends criticism because it deals with basic purposes and legitimate boundaries. Dorothy Sayers, in her introduction to *Great Stories of Detection, Mystery, and Horror* (1928),[4] laid down the classic definition of the detective story as an exercise of limited scope, governed by rules that were well defined, although somewhat more flexible than the dogmas of Knox and Van Dine. Detective fiction, she wrote, is part of the literature of escape and not of expression, and she drew the limits tight by saying that "it does not, and by hypothesis never can, attain the loftiest level of literary achievement."[5] Not so, replied Raymond Chandler in "The Simple Art of Murder" (1944)[6]: the detective story as defined by Sayers was an "arid formula which could not even satisfy its own implications."[7] The concept of escape literature is a meaningless abstraction; a good detective story, according to Chandler's definition, is movement, intrigue, cross-purposes, and gradual elucidation of character, which is not "by hypothesis" incapable of anything.[8] It is, of course, not surprising that the hypothesis was accepted by Dorothy Sayers, one of the best writers of the classic formal-problem school, and rejected by Raymond Chandler, a master of the "hard-boiled" private eye story.

The best-known example of mythic criticism, the fourth mode, is W. H. Auden's "The Guilty Vicarage" (1948),[9] which was intended in part as a reply to Chandler's "The Simple Art of Murder." Although his central image is the Christian concept of Grace and the Law, Auden takes a mythological approach in his development of the dialectic of innocence and guilt in the detective story as a parallel to the Aristotelian description of tragedy in terms of Concealment and Manifestation, which is by extension the Garden of Eden myth.[10] Auden's point of reference· is the classic "whodunit," in which the story proceeds from the innocent society in a state of grace to the restoration of innocence and withdrawal of the necessity for the law.

Two other studies are so close to the mythic mode that they should be mentioned at this point: Robert K. Edenbaum's "The Poetics of the Private Eye" (1968)[11] and George Grella's "Murder and the Mean Streets" (1970).[12]

[4]Published in the United States as *The Omnibus of Crime* (Garden City: Garden City Publishing Company, 1929). References are to this edition.

[5]Sayers, p. 37.

[6]*The Atlantic Monthly,* Dec. 1944, pp. 53-59.

[7]Chandler, p. 57.

[8]Chandler, p. 58.

[9]*The Dyer's Hand and Other Essays* (New York: Random House, 1948), pp. 146-58.

[10]Auden, p. 148.

[11]In David Madden, ed., *Tough Guy Writers of the Thirties* (Carbondale: Southern Illinois University Press, 1968), pp. 80-103.

[12]In Dick Allen and David Chacko, eds., *Detective Fiction: Crime and Compromise* (New York: Harcourt Brace Jovanovich, 1974), pp. 411-29.

Edenbaum's essay is a treatment of the allegorical elements in the novels of Dashiell Hammett, with emphasis on the daemonic and god-like quality in Hammett's protagonists. Grella's thesis is closer to myth: he proposes Cooper's Leatherstocking as the archetype of the fictional private eye, physically able, honest, and compassionate.

A number of writers (including Sayers, Chandler, Auden, and Jacques Barzun) have commented on the prevalence of formula in detective fiction, but as a result of the publication of John Cawelti's *Adventure, Mystery, and Romance* (1976),[13] formulaic criticism of detective fiction must now be recognized as a major mode. Cawelti devotes two full chapters to the classic deductive story and two to the hard-boiled story, showing among other things how the two basic formulas evolved and how they differ from each other.

I realize that this hasty summary has made it necessary to pass over a large body of social-cultural, historical, and biographical criticism, much of which is interesting and some of which has merit, but most does not contribute anything to critical theory beyond the five modes I have named.

Most of the old critical issues regarding the detective story are by now pretty well settled. I doubt if it is now necessary to apologize for detective fiction, although Jacques Barzun seemed compelled to do so as late as 1961.[14] Neither is it necessary to formulate "rules" beyond a few flexible admonitions to aspiring writers. Even the debate over form and function, as exemplified by the statements of Sayers and Chandler, seems to be resolved. There just isn't that much difference between the classic formal problem and the hard-boiled private eye story. Both are mysteries, both are stories about detectives and the act of discovery, and both must have some kind of satisfying resolution. The formal problem and the hard-boiled element can even be combined in the same story, as Rex Stout has done in the Nero Wolfe stories and Francis Nevins in *Publish and Perish*. Analysis of mythic elements in the detective story will undoubtedly persist, but hopefully the limitations of the myth methodology will be kept in mind. The same, I think, can be said for formula analysis, which is useful in the criticism of all popular literature with respect to cultural themes and traditions.

The question may be raised, then: What kinds of developments seem to be appropriate at this point? I should like to suggest two lines of critical inquiry that could be profitable, and I base these proposals on the recognition of the detective story as a mature and reputable class of popular fiction.

The first would be some studies of the special relationship between the

---

[13](Chicago: The University of Chicago Press, 1976).
[14]"Detection and the Literary Art," introduction to *The Delights of Detection* (New York: Criterion Books, 1961) pp. 9-10.

detective fiction writer and his reader. There *is* a special relationship not found in any other kind of writing and reading of fiction, and it has never been satisfactorily defined. The writer of detective stories is not just a formulator of clever puzzles and a fabricator of baffling clues; neither is he only a tough opportunist who knows how to bring in a man with a blazing gun or a blonde with blazing eyes whenever the suspense begins to lag. The writer's role is rather to lead the reader through a mythos of life and death, violence and redemption, without the reader's suffering hurt or distress.

Two critics have touched at least indirectly upon this special relationship. W. H. Auden postulates an audience of professional people, scientists, and artists for the classic deductive story and suggests that such people feel guilty only about the subjective existence of a sense of guilt. "I suspect," he says, "that the typical reader of detective stories is, like myself, a person who suffers from a sense of sin."[15] Such people do not read detective fiction to sublimate their own murderous desires, but rather to gain "the illusion of being dissociated from the murderer."[16]

John Cawelti approaches the problem from a more strictly mechanical viewpoint when he states that it is the task of the writer to establish a satisfying relationship between the crime, the detective's pattern of inquiry, and the way in which this inquiry is presented to the reader; and a few pages farther along he says that the detective story formula, which transforms innately horrible situations into problems perceived from a detached point of view "makes it possible for writer and reader to confront and try to understand aspects of life that may be too painful or disturbing to confront without this mediating structure."[17] It is in passages like these, I think, that critics begin to approach the essential relationship between the detective fiction writer and his reader. The subject needs much broader development.

Possibly the critic best qualified to do this kind of thing is the successful writer of detective fiction, as Ross Macdonald came close to doing in his two essays, "The Writer as Detective Hero" and "Writing *The Galton Case*."[18] In the second of these pieces, Macdonald tells about watching his small grandson hood himself with a towel, announce himself to be a monster, laughingly cast off his disguise to become a little boy again, and fall pleasantly asleep. The author sees a connection between this little charade and his own fiction, both of which draw directly on life and feed back into it; both are something the artist does for his own sake, but both need an audience to fulfill the public and the private function.[19] The key image is the small boy's towel, which, like the writer's fictional disguise, enables the

[15]Auden, p. 157.
[16]Auden, p. 158.
[17]Cawelti, p. 131.
[18]*On Crime Writing* (Santa Barbara: Capra Press, 1973).
[19]Macdonald, pp. 25-27.

work to be both private and public. Elsewhere in this essay Macdonald compares the writer's use of a literary detective to "a kind of welder's mask enabling us to handle dangerously hot material."[20]

It may be, then, that the detective writer and reader are essentially participants in a ritual, with the writer as celebrant and the reader as communicant. If my metaphor is valid, part of its truth derives from the rapport between writer and reader and part from the fact that in ritual the normal conceptions of reality do not apply.

My second suggestion would be development of a body of theory of the special sense of reality in detective fiction. In suggesting such a line of inquiry, I certainly do not propose any more discussions of "realism" in the detective story, most of which are old hat and substantively fruitless. Consider for example Sutherland Scott's observation on the Philo Vance stories:

> S. S. Van Dyne [*sic*] was also responsible for a comparable attempt at so-called realism—the pretense that the story, as evidenced by the author's nom de plume, was written by someone actually associated with the case.[21]

Now, if there is one detective of the old classical school who is considered unrealistic by most historians, it is Van Dine's Philo Vance, with his effete English accent and his erudition in such subjects as Renaissance façades,[22] yet Scott has put his finger upon the special ability of the detective story to create its own illusion of reality. John Cawelti, speaking of formula fiction generally, points out that "the formula creates its own world with which we become familiar by repetition...without continually comparing it with our own experience."[23] An extension of that statement beyond its formulaic bounds could bring us much closer to an understanding of the whole ontology of the detective story.

This special quality in detective fiction lies, to some extent, in the fact that we are not to read it with the same sense of seriousness as we read, for example, most historical novels. In the detective story, says Northrop Frye, "the protecting wall of play is still there,"[24] and Jacques Barzun reminds us that the tone of the story springs from "the alliance of murder and mirth."[25]

I think Erik Routley has come closest to isolating the element of the special reality in the detective story. Following a discussion of the romantic element in the Sherlock Holmes stories, Routley goes on to add,

---

[20]Macdonald, p. 25.

[21]*Blood in Their Ink: The March of the Modern Mystery Novel* (London: Stanley Paul, 1953), p. 39.

[22]Julian Symons, *Mortal Consequences* (New York: Harper and Row, 1972), p. 112.

[23]Cawelti, p. 10.

[24]*Anatomy of Criticism* (Princeton: Princeton University Press, 1957), p. 47.

[25]Barzun, p. 23.

[26]*The Puritan Pleasures of the Detective Story: A Personal Monograph* (London: Victor Gollancz, 1972), p. 52.

> There is a certain amount of gentle humbug about all this. Those who defend the detective tale and those who attack it go equally astray if they do not correctly assess the humbug-content of this kind of literature.[26]

To fail to recognize this "humbug element" is to miss the unique sense of reality in the detective story because it is pervasive in the craft. There is certainly a strong taste of it in Philo Vance's being repeatedly called away from his translation of the Menander fragments in order to solve a case that has baffled the New York City police. Nor is it confined to the fantasies of the classic formal-problem school: there is a certain amount of the "humbug element" in Travis McGee's winning an expensive houseboat as the result of a busted flush, or Philip Marlowe's throwing both of the Sternwood sisters out of his bed (Vivian figuratively, Carmen literally) within the space of one hour. We accept the humbug and we love it, but we must recognize it as part of Frye's "protecting wall of play."

Realization of the unique relationship between the detective story writer and reader and of the special sense of reality in detective fiction could save otherwise competent critics from overstating their cases, as W. H. Auden does when he says that detectives of the hard-boiled school "are motivated by avarice or ambition and might just as well be murderers,"[27] or as Jacques Barzun does when he excludes Hammett's *Red Harvest* from the canon of detective fiction,[28] or as George Grella does when he says that "Nero Wolfe's massive misanthropy and misogyny seem more psychopathic than endearing."[29] To be carried away to this extent is surely to have missed something basic in the detective story.

I base these two suggestions on the assumption that nothing which has been created can be adequately or accurately criticized without an understanding of the special purpose of its creation. To interpret the detective story, we must first understand why detective stories are written, in what tradition, and for what audience.

[27]Auden, p. 154.
[28]Barzun, p. 18.
[29]Grella, p. 411.

The Sordid Truth: Four Cases

by Robin W. Winks

DONALD HAMILTON

Publish only in paperback and you'll never make it big. This used to be a writer's kind of truth, for steady sales year in and year out depend upon cloth publication and library sales. John D. MacDonald has put Travis McGee between boards twice now, and the annual Christie always appears as a hardbound book first. Of course making it big is pretty relative, and Donald Hamilton is a case in point: with over 17 million of his books in print, with five of his books made into movies, he hardly needs to worry about sales. Even so, his books seldom show up on library shelves (a quick check of two local public libraries reveals 47 Christies, eight MacDonalds, not one Hamilton) and while more and more people know that Travis McGee drinks Plymouth gin (or even, after only two books, that Jonathan Hemlock drinks Laphroig when not stealing art treasures or climbing the Eiger) no one can tell you what Matt Helm drinks.

Matt Helm is Donald Hamilton's series figure—for the loyal audiences are best kept on the string by a series hero, as Conan Doyle discovered long ago with Sherlock Holmes—and he is so credible a character and so busy keeping himself alive while defending his country's interests, he hasn't time to insist that his Martini be shaken and not stirred. Indeed one learns relatively little about Matt Helm that is explicit, although a great deal by indirection, and this is one of his attractions. He grows on one, as his actions reveal his attitudes. A fair amount of philosophy—conservative, hard-nosed, clear-eyed—is slipped in here and there but Hamilton does not permit Helm any windy discourses on the state of the economy. On fishing, guns, travel and women, yes; but most of the time is spent on sheer compulsive storytelling.

Although Matt Helm is not as widely known as James Bond, Hercule Poirot, Sam Spade, Phillip Marlowe or Lew Archer, he has not been ignored

Robin W. Winks, "The Sordid Truth," from *The New Republic* (July 26, 1975), pp. 21-24; "Murder and Dying," *ibid.* (July 31, 1976), pp. 31-32; "Murder without Blood," *ibid.*, (July 30, 1977), pp. 30-33; and "Murder by Holocaust," *ibid.*, (July 22, 1978), pp. 31-33. Reprinted by permission of the author and *The New Republic,* Inc.

by the critics. While there is a *JDM Bibliophile* which has reached its 19th issue and while every number of *The Armchair Detective* appears to comment on Father Brown or Nero Wolfe and virtually never on Matt Helm, the tall silent Swede has had his admirers, including the late Anthony Boucher of *The New York Times*. Boucher never let a new Helm book pass without comment, usually highly favorable; he found Hamilton a master of indirect exposition, a "harsh and sometimes shocking" writer in the tradition of Peter Cheyney's "Dark" series, "sternly logical," "the Hammett of espionage," filled with "resolute hardness," "hard-bitten objectivity," and "sheer storytelling compulsion." High praise this. Low praise that Boucher also once linked Donald Hamilton's creation with Sam Durell, the Cajun agent, and Chet Drumm, both manifestly inferior.

Boucher was right the first time. If one wants a summer read, a new Donald Hamilton is to be put in the bag with the new Gavin Lyall, Berkley Mather, Desmond Bagley, and Francis Clifford, for taking away to the beach. It is no accident that the company here is all British, for although resolutely American in his attitudes and loyalties, a Donald Hamilton book is nonetheless written to the model of the master of them all, John Buchan. Every once in a while some reviewer hails a new thriller as "in the Buchan vein"—Robert Harling and William Haggard (Richard Clayton) have both received this encomium more than once—when it clearly is not, missing the Hamiltons the while.

John Buchan wrote the classic thriller in *The Thirty-Nine Steps* in 1915 and ever since, British writers in particular—those above and others like Lionel Davidson—have been improving upon him. The model is clean and simple: take an attractive hero with a hint of danger and untold experience in his background (Richard Hannay's South African years, Matt Helm's introduction in 1960 as a quiet and married writer living in Santa Fe, who 15 years earlier was a professional killer for his country). Make these figures fallible but stubborn, resourceful and unwilling to be pushed around or to see others pushed around. Give them an unexpected task to perform, which involves being chased across an exotic landscape, and set obstacles in their way, some predicted and some unpredicted. If the hero is in pursuit, be certain that he also is being pursued, so that he may not come into the open or draw upon the customary resources of society. Better yet have him pursued by both the police and the other side. In a world made up of ever more city-bound readers, have the chase take place in a desert, a wilderness or in the sea, so that hero and evildoers alike must contend with nature and turn nature to their advantage. This last gambit also offers an opportunity for using a variety of knowledge those chair-bound readers will think esoteric, from being able to render a man unconscious by pressing behind his ear just so (an old native trick learned by Hannay while in Africa) to recognizing the "characteristic dimple" a bullet makes when hitting water to know that one is being shot at even before the report is heard (as Helm does in *The Intriguers*). Finally add a woman to the scene, attractive but not too attractive, and see to it that reader and hero do not know whether she is friend or foe.

Allowing for the changes that 60 years have brought to the world, Donald Hamilton is a direct descendant of John Buchan and a master at the craft. The violence is more explicit now, the decisions more cruel, and while Hannay married the girl before sleeping with her, Helm does what he needs to do in the line of duty and good mental health (although he is no womanizer, really preferring a solitary day of hunting or fishing). Above all, the moral ambivalence of the hero's actions bring him, as Boucher noted, "close to the sordid truth of espionage."

The truth is Hamilton tells it pretty much like it is or is proving to have been. Hannay would not have shot anyone in the back; neither will Helm if he can avoid it, but if he must he does. When *The Ambushers* appeared in 1963, its plot about a stray atomic missile and an effort to exterminate a Castro-in-the-making may have seemed a bit fantastic, but it seems less so now. Allowing for the natural excesses of the genre, Hamilton's Helm is about as credible a figure as one can find.

If one doubts that Hamilton is a lineal descendant of Buchan, read *The Ravagers*, the eighth Matt Helm escapade, issued in 1964, the same year John D. MacDonald introduced us to McGee in *The Deep Blue Goodbye*. (The working pace, incidentally, is interesting—there have been 16 McGees in 11 years, and 16 Helms in 16 years. By my reckoning McGee now has to be at least 40, Helm 52. Neither acts like it.) *The Ravagers* is a suspense story made all the tighter by its healthy dose of protagonist and reader ambivalence. The plot turns upon a set of papers that must be allowed to reach the Russians, while Helm makes every effort to appear to stop them in order to give them credibility. The scene is Canada and most of the action focuses on a transcontinental chase from Regina to Brandon to Montreal. I have driven that route more than once and I can testify that Hamilton has too. He has as good an eye and ear for landscape as Buchan had and his Canada (used again in *The Interlopers* in 1969) is a vivid, well-realized place. Just to show he could do it on Buchan's own ground, Hamilton puts Helm into northern Scotland in *The Devastators* (1965), and his Ullapool countryside is authentic (I can attest from having traveled the same road) even though his Kinnochrue does not exist. If you'll settle for the Gaelic Kinloch ("at the head of the lake") Row (originally *rue,* pronounced "roo," and meaning "a cape or point") you'll have a description of the place to which Helm then makes his way.

Hamilton obviously combines his pleasures with his work. He likes to hunt and fish, as all of the books show (and his collection of rather slight stories, *On Guns and Hunting,* drawn together in 1970 from pieces published between 1955 and 1969 in *Outdoor Life, Gun World* and *Gun Digest* attests). One can imagine his deciding on which stream or range he would like to fish or hunt next, taking himself there and using the scene later in one of his books. He has brought his readers to Norway, Sweden, Labrador, Mexico, Hawaii and pretty well all over the American Southwest this way and Baja California is promised next.

That trip to Sweden also gave some of the game away, for the book reflects a bit too lovingly on the Swedish landscape and a bit too sternly on Swedish society not to represent a return to a lost love. Hamilton was, in fact, born in Uppsala and oddly enough he apparently is a Swedish count, at least by title. Still the Southwest is his first love as his writing shows. It is arguable that his best written book is one of the earliest, now in print as *Assassins Have Starry Eyes,* but originally published in 1956 under the unhappy title *Assignment: Murder.* Lurking behind its trite cover is one of the very best books of its kind, set (it seems to me) somewhere north of Jemez and east of Espanola in the New Mexico high country, land of piñon forest, scrub and pine, the odor of which permeates the opening scene. And the opening is typical Hamilton, direct and to the point in appearances, ironically mis-directive in content: a research boffin from Los Alamos, James Gregory, Ph.D., out alone hunting for deer, is shot in the back on the fifth page, vic-tim he thinks of a city-bred hunter who can't tell human from antler, and he shoots back. There is a good sense for the undeveloped subplot of a mar-riage that is OK but nothing to base marriage counsellors' success records on, and a subtle awareness of where the Spanish-speaking population of New Mexico fits into the local scene. The book is tough minded from the start; only once does it lapse into the kind of sentimentalism one finds in Raymond Chandler (and that Chandler tried to cover up with hard words), and the solution to the mystery is quite satisfying, thank you.

The point is the book *is* a mystery and so are most of the others. That is unless one demands snowed-in mountain cabins, locked railway coaches, hidden maps and messages (Rache?) scrawled in blood to recognize a mys-tery. For Hamilton's books are not merely derring-do, all chase and no ratiocination (as the critics of the "classical period" had it). One is given the same clues as Helm is given, and can reach the same urgent decisions he reaches as to the ultimate source of danger if one wants. One mustn't be misled by the notion that Hamilton writes "spy fiction" or "thrillers" and that such books do not qualify for the hammock reserved only for the genuine mystery addict. Hamilton has learned, one would guess, from Ross Macdonald back in the days when he was John Ross Macdonald and per-haps even Kenneth Millar, that one can honestly misdirect the reader while setting all the evidence before him. Perhaps *The Shadowers,* in 1964, comes the closest to the "pure" puzzle but all pay proper homage to the Chandler school.

For my money Hamilton has come closer to avoiding the major pitfall of the series figure than Ross Macdonald has done. Obviously if one creates a series character, one presumes his survival through a number of the books, eliminating an element of suspense, but increasing the shock when ready to do a Van der Valk or push one's creation off the Reichenbach Falls. Less obviously perhaps, but more limitingly, the author of books that depend upon a series figure may stunt his growth, for he cannot allow his style (or his character) to depart too far from that which proves that it sells. Not if the writer is a professional and in it for the money, that is. So the writer creates a winning figure and must then repeat at least the major elements of the successful formula thereafter if he is to retain that audience. Ross Macdonald is caught up in this net badly now, each story reading as though it were taken from a textbook co-authored by Freud, Kraft-Ebbing and the Biblical prophets. I find that one can pretty well guess whodunit with Macdonald—it will be the daughter of the cousin who is really the illegitimate brother of the nephew's youngest uncle twice removed—and one can't yet with Hamilton.

This is not to say that Donald Hamilton has overcome the problems of formula fiction. The last two Matt Helms, *The Intimidators* (1974) and *The Terminators* (1975), are off the standard set by most of the earlier ones (although *The Interlopers*, in 1969, falls off into some pretty unconvincing moments too). The books have grown longer, and their spacing has moved from about nine months to 14 months apart in publication, both signs that the lean and hungry look may be gone. Still one suspects that it has just been set aside for the moment and that Matt Helm will return to form with adventure number 17.

For there have been 16 Helm books to date. A quick summary of their plots shows where we (and Hamilton) have travelled; all are clear descendants of *Assignment: Murder*, so that in many ways it too should be included in the series. Helm was launched (before, I might add, Richard Helms had come much to public notice, so scotch that idea) with *Death of a Citizen* early in 1960, drawing Helm back to the work he had left 15 years before. Not surprisingly his marriage doesn't survive his renaissance, so there is an opportunity to explore the attitudes of men and women toward violence. Later the same year Helm is in Sweden in *The Wrecking Crew*, his wife behind him, and in 1961, in *The Removers*, one finds that his ex-wife still depends upon him and is attracted to him despite her remarriage. This ambivalence is integral to the plot that involves a foreign secret agent who has spent seven years as a sleeper. In 1962, in *The Silencers*, Helm is involved with underground atomic tests and later that year he is charged with rescuing (if he can) and killing (if he must) an American scientist who must be denied to the Russians. This book, *Murderers' Row*, is a departure from its predecessors and rather less good for that. Helm returns to form with *The Ambushers* (1963), that book about the straying atomic missile. At the same time the earlier Helms were reprinted, an indication that the series figure had now caught on.

From this point Hamilton may have had less room to let Helm change. Even so the plots remain complex and convincing and the prose remains taut in the way an old navy hand means when he talks about a tight ship. *The Shadowers* (1964) leads Helm into marriage with a space scientist in order to be able to protect her; *The Ravagers* (the same year) provides that chase across Canada; *The Devastators* (1965) turns on bacteriological warfare; and *The Betrayers* (1966) gives Helm the task of removing his agency's local top man in Hawaii, since he has been doubled. In 1968 we get *The Menacers*, which turns on UFO sightings in Mexico, and which is so much better than Martin Caidin's effort with a similar subject (although in Nebraska) as to be a case study of sheer professional competence. *The Interlopers* followed in 1969: Helm replaces an enemy agent and pursues his delivery route to see what he can unearth. *The Poisoners* (1971) has Helm trying to find out why an agent who was not on assignment has been eliminated; *The Intriguers* (1972) introduces that dimpled water in Mexico; *The Intimidators* (1974) gets Helm into the West Indies; and the current book, *The Terminators*, picks up elements from the 1960 and 1964 books, with the ubiquitous boss back in Washington, "Mac," denying Helm needed information a bit arbitrarily or paranoically. ...[1]

Of course there have been non-Helm books as well, two of them—*The Steel Mirror* and *Line of Fire*—very good indeed. Hamilton has tried his hand at shorter stories *(Murder Twice Told)* and at fairly conventional westerns *(Smoky Valley, Mad River, Man from Santa Clara, Texas Fever)*. He writes articles on outdoor subjects, especially boating (having a cruising sailboat of his own). He does a monthly column for a magazine and he has edited a collection for the Western Writers of America *(Iron Men and Silver Stars)*. There are other books but this isn't an obituary or a bibliography. All these books show the marks of the professional writer who has honed his skills across the years, while drawing upon what he knows best. Publicity materials tell us that Hamilton was born in 1916, came to the States in 1924, was the son of a doctor who was on the faculty of the Harvard Medical School, took a degree in chemistry from the University of Chicago and was stationed during World War II at the Naval Engineering Experiment Station in Annapolis (one of the books is set on the Eastern Shore). Most of this one might have guessed from the books themselves, if one believes that the book reveals the author.

Some pretty unprofessional people got into the act and made three of the

---

[1][Since this was written there have been two more books, *The Retaliators* (1976) and *The Terrorizers* (1977) the first quite good if introducing an unnecessary moment of sadism, the second much less good.]

Helm books into movies starring Dean Martin. These were fiascos which must have caused Hamilton to wince as he walked to the bank. There may be a TV series and we can hope for a better fate than Archer received at the hands of the scriptwriters. However we look at it, we're still pretty lucky, for at least 12 of those Helm books and three or four of the others are tops in their class. It takes a Buchan or Hammett or a Chandler to achieve anything like that.

P. D. JAMES

For so many years we were given a new Christie for Christmas, and for so many years Dame Agatha was called the "Queen of Detective Fiction," that we have all come to think that her reign was to be as long as that other British monarch, Victoria. Truth to tell, from *Passenger to Frankfort* onward it was apparent that Agatha Christie had (as surely so long a productive career entitled her to do) lost her touch, and the mantle was ready to be passed on. Now is the time to do so. My candidate is P. D. James, already well known in Britain if less known in the States, who when not writing about her Chief Superintendent Adam Dalgliesh is Phyllis White.

Britain has given us an unusual number of women who have chosen to write detective fiction. Of the 322 current members of the Crime Writers' Association of Great Britain, who live in the United Kingdom, 90 are women, and a goodly number of others probably are as well, having taken masculine pseudonymns. (One wonders whether men ever take women's names for this purpose—they do to write "nursing novels," after all.) Phyllis James has soared above this general company, however, and reviewers consistently compare her to Dorothy Sayers and Ngaio Marsh. Others have compared her to Margery Allingham.

Adam Dalgliesh is a more interesting person than Albert Campion, Lord Peter Wimsey or Roderick Alleyn. And on the strength of her six books to date, Phyllis James shows far more awareness of the complex nature of human beings than Dorothy Sayers did, writes with a more civilized style than Margery Allingham does, and provides plots with more realistic and puzzling turns than Dame Ngaio has done in recent years. Taken as a whole, the six novels—for such they are as well—constitute the most convincing debut of the last decade.

All of P. D. James' six books are realistic portrayals of life and death among the ill and dying. Few writers could have dealt so compassionately, so clearly, and with such a combination of civilized taste and clarity of vision, with the terminally ill. At times the books verge on the macabre and once or twice they slip into the melodramatic, but both the icicle eye and the piece of ice at the heart quickly return. For James has discovered that life is not a series of masks; it is a series of confessions. The masks are there, always in place, but they are secondary; it is in the actions, subtle, traced with a word here and a sentence there, that the confessions are made. In short, James is a writer in the classic sense, where the vital clues to the questions of Who, and, at least as important for her, Why, are slipped into place neatly, fairly, unobtrusively, sometimes as much by a turn of phrase, a sense of style, a nuance, as by overt statement. Atmosphere becomes action, the buying of the daily paper becomes the central fact, a leaning ladder becomes an obvious pointer to an unobvious conclusion.

Of the six books, four are outstanding and two are less so. This is a high average for a writer who works early in the morning, goes to a full-time job during the day, and has a lively interest in the world. On average the books have taken a bit over two years each, beginning with *Cover Her Face* in 1962. The title may or may not be consciously from John Webster's *Duchess of Malfi,* but the murdered Sally Jupp is soon found to have fulfilled the promise of the title: "Cover her face; mine eyes dazzle; she died young./ I think not so; her infelicity Seem'd to have years too many." It is (then) Detective Chief-Inspector Dalgliesh's task to play Bosola to the reader's Ferdinand. He does so with a steady, deliberating calm that carries reader, fictional household, and beautifully evoked English countryside along, always compassionately, always relentlessly, to an entirely satisfying resolution.

The second book, *A Mind to Murder,* is no less powerful. As the first focused on the need to care for an invalid husband, the second explores invalid minds, in a beautifully depicted psychiatric clinic, in which the chief administrative officer is stabbed to death. Many writers have chosen hospitals, clinics, even prison camps—the modern day equivalents of the snowed-in mountain cabins or isolated islands of the 1930s—in order to provide justifiable idiosyncracies and an artificially constricted environment for their protagonists, and many have been unable to resist cheating the reader and themselves by letting irrational behavior (against which well placed clues can count no more than well wrought urns) account for the final resolution of plot. James does not succumb to her psychiatric clinic, and in the end the solution is simple, pathetic and true.

In both these books, the character of Adam Dalgliesh is fleshed out, as much by indirection as by description. He finds "prying among the personal residue of a finished life" distasteful, for it puts the dead at a disadvantage. He writes poetry, and is happy to be recognized as a poet, but he also knows himself to be a good detective who believes in justice and retribution. He is not quite able to fall in love, for he too has a bit of the icicle at the heart, seeing himself, and his potential love, a bit too clearly to become sentimental. He is weary, but not fashionably world-weary, for he is healthily self-centered. He has deep compassion for others, but not so much as to be confused by them. As the novels progress, he becomes more decisive in his work and more indecisive about his personal life. At times he seems unnecessary to the action at all, and the books are not spoken in the first person.

Indeed, the fifth book virtually does without the carefully constructed Dalgliesh. In *An Unsuitable Job for a Woman,* Cordelia Gray becomes sole proprietor of a detective agency. She is hired to find out why the son of a famous Oxford scientist has committed suicide. In the process she learns much about the psychology of suicides, the nature of Oxford, the way in which chauvinism works its way in "civilized" society, and—with Blake— why a person would commit himself to a boundless void in order to see whether providence was there also. The writing by now is superb, with clear echoes of both Dorothy Sayers and Charles Dickens, and as chilling an empty-cottage-at-dusk scene as has ever been written. It is Cordelia who runs the risks and solves the crime, and Superintendent Dalgliesh enters only at the end to question her. Set against the hint of a possible future attraction between the two is her observation that he "sounded gentle and kind, which was cunning since she knew that he was dangerous and cruel," and also his observation to her that justice is a very dangerous concept.

Between the second and the fifth novels fall both the best and poorest. *Unnatural Causes,* published in 1967, shows Dalgliesh at his least attractive, opens with one of the two melodramatic excesses James has allowed herself, and despite much effective characterization of writers, countryhouse types, and English eccentrics, is unconvincing in its solution. Against this must be put *Shroud for a Nightingale,* set at the Nightingale Training College for nurses, beautifully constructed, with a cleverly new method for dispatching the victim, superior characterization at all levels, and an immaculate laying on of hands, clue by clue. Here mood, pace, style and atmosphere are all in perfect balance.

The most recent book by P. D. James is *The Black Tower* (1975). The setting is Dorset, described with great care. Dalgliesh has been seriously ill himself, and he reflects at length upon the changes illness brings to a person's perceptions of the world. These changed perceptions figure significantly in now-Commander Dalgliesh's ultimate resolution of the murders —as they are found to be—at Toynton Grange, a cliff-edge (both literally and financially) home for the ill. An unhappily Gothic dust jacket may infect the reader with the wrong atmosphere, for this seems the least convincing of the six books, with the black tower itself figuring a bit too obviously, both as symbol and reality, in the conclusion. The progressive diseases of the inmates of the home are not for the squeamish, yet over against the sometimes necessarily gruesome descriptions is a saving note of humor. James knows what the ill laugh about.

Indeed, James knows whereof she writes in all of her six books. She has spent her life working with disease. In describing Sally Jupp, she shows us that youth may be a kind of illness. She knows how powerful the weak can be, by using their weakness against the compassionate. She understands the strength that illness brings. From 1949 to 1968, she worked for the Hospital Service, she is a fellow of the Institute of Hospital Administrators, and she is now a senior civil servant, working in the Home Office, where she is concerned with criminal justice. Her novels are not a hobby but a second, equally real life, and she rightly sees them as serious fiction, not to be dismissed by those who think of crime writing as "mere" in any respect. Born in Oxford, educated in Cambridge, married to a doctor who returned from World War II ill and who died, unhappily and slowly, James has seen, read about and administered over death. Today she blends her two worlds, thinking in the one about the practical question of whether capital punishment is a deterrent (she believes that it probably is), writing in the other about justice and final retribution, and enjoying every moment of it. Forthright and open, her confessions are also in her books, and like the Jane Austen she and her Adam Dalgliesh admire, or like that other James in *The Aspern Papers* and *The Turn of the Screw*, her work is in the end "alone with the quiet day."

There will be more of P. D. James, for she is at work on her seventh book. She is a little worried that the moment of melodrama in *The Black Tower* may be like a writer's heart murmur, even though it won her a third Silver Dagger from the Crime Writers' Association. But she also knows that her mastery of the genre is increasing with every book and that the time is near when she will be reviewed as a serious novelist who chooses to deal with death according to the canons of a not unhonorable profession. Her publishers, Faber and Faber in England and Scribner's here, know that she is an exceptional new talent who is just subtle enough to be widely read and yet avoid pitfalls of "popularity." In the same scene of *Duchess of Malfi* from which P. D. James took her first book's title, stand the lines, "I know death hath ten thousand several doors/ For men to take their exit." May she yet explore those ten thousand several doors.[2]

WILLIAM HAGGARD

Between the amateur and the professional falls a shadow. It isn't the one Eliot had in mind nor yet Yeats; rather, it is the difference between being in control and being merely self-possessed. One is reality and one is appearance. And this is what William Haggard's books are all about: professionalism, style, nuance, the difference between what appears to happen and what

---

[2][P. D. James's *Death of an Expert Witness*, published in 1977, is well up to the standard of the best.]

does happen. Haggard remarks more than once on how easily people might be made to think as some grey eminence wishes them to think. In the fullest senses of the word, he writes of the thinking man's spy.

Haggard is by no means as well known as he should be in the United states, especially since he has written 20 books in but one fewer years, has appeared in Signet books here and in Penguins in England, and has attracted the kinds of reviews which would make many a "serious" novelist envious. Yet his publishers have not learned their lessons from their author, have not discovered how to make us think of a Haggard for Hallowe'en as Dodd, Mead has convinced us that a Christie was a sign of the Christmas season. In the late 1950s he was published here by Little, Brown, then moved to Washburne, and he has been with Walker and Company for some years. They appear to be unaware that they have a professional imbedded among the amateurs they usually publish, and if the print and paper they have given to *Yesterday's Enemy,* the latest (for 1976) Haggard, is meant to compete with the quiet elegance of print and dust jacket shown by Haggard's English publisher, Cassell, then they are simply proving my (and Haggard's) point. But professionals do not complain, and it appears that Haggard has not.

Truth to tell, Haggard has not always received good reviews. His first book, *Slow Burner,* which appeared in 1958 (from Cassell, to whom he has always been loyal), won the kind of reviews glossies call "stunning," and his second book, *The Telemann Touch,* which came crowding in soon after, added substantially to his following. One of my personal favorites (and my own moment of discovering Haggard), *Venetian Blind,* based on a fine pun, was third. Nine more top drawer thrillers followed. Then came *A Cool Day for Killing* (1968), and control seemed just a bit off. Two distinctly unsatisfactory books were next, and both rightly went little reviewed in the States. In 1971 there was *Bitter Harvest,* which shows a distinct recovery (it is a Haggard favorite) and received few reviews, after which there were two more in which the touch seemed lost, the plots unnecessarily vivid, then another fine book—*The Scorpion's Tail*—and now two curious, certainly readable, less beguiling books, one of which, *The Kinsmen,* has yet to be published in America.[3]

What has given Haggard his readership is his unwillingness to shed blood unnecessarily, his sympathy and insight into all of his figures, who are seen less in the traditional roles of villain and hero than as actors in a stylish drama in which all are motivated by a reasonable self-interest, and his subtle, ironic, detached voice. His books are not for the impatient, and while they shiver with sophisticated sexual awareness, there is never an obligatory sex scene nor an anatomical description. Some say Haggard

[3][*The Kinsmen* has been published in the United States and two more books have followed in both countries, *The Poison People* and *Visa to Limbo.*]

writes like C. P. Snow, and certainly they have in common the kind of dry prose voice that makes one think immediately of hearing T. S. Eliot read one of his poems, yet a stylish voice that can be heard above all others because it is so unhurried, so cultivated, so low-pitched that it commands attention. Snow and Haggard also have this in common: they admire, understand, and make no apologies for the Establishment.

English reviewers have not always been kind to Haggard, and clearly he can get some backs up merely by dropping an "indeed" into a sentence. *The Power House* (1966), which is about the risk that an appealing and quite recognizable Prime Minister may be brought down by a cousin who is a croupier in a gambling club, was "nauseating for the in-class know-how" that it displayed. *The Arena*, about the efforts of a failing firm of merchant bankers, Bonavias, to hold off a take-over by a group of counter jumpers from Bakerloo, is replete with the language of the City of London, language found by one reviewer to be "snobbish and silly." The same books appeal to Americans, however, who are less uptight about class connotations; the first was "even better than usual" and the second was "sophisticated...delicately cumulative."

Well, yes, there *are* moments when Haggard appears to believe that nuance is all. Civilized people do not make their points explicitly, for other civilized people can match them nuance for nuance. One puts on a decent suit when going to be grilled by the police. Indians are suspect, and so are Greeks and some Italians. Some Israelis are ignoble and some white South Africans are brave. Colonel Charles Russell, the series figure who is for several of the books the head of Security Executive (which does the kind of things that must not be discussed on the floor of Commons), and is then "lately of the Security Executive" and unable to remain graciously retired, "had a pension and a little money, hobbies like golf and some elegant fishing, the good health to enjoy a still vigorous life. Above all he had friends and not all were eminent. Some of them weren't even English." Sentences like these can make reviewers for the *New Statesman* grind their teeth. The reader is treated, says one annoyed reviewer, like a gawking poor relation.

Well, no. The reader is treated as though the reader could follow a complex plot, a subtle sentence, and a sense of place. For Haggard knows how to write. Those who are certain that the repetition of "And so it goes" makes Vonnegut a perceptive writer should avoid Haggard. And Anthony Powell. And Dickens. And Jane Austen. And Mrs. Gaskell, whose *Cranford* and Haggard have much in common, although Richard Clayton, who took William Haggard as a pen name, says he has never read any Gaskell.

Richard Clayton was educated at Lancing, the school Evelyn Waugh chopped to such fine pieces, and at Christ Church, Oxford. He went into the Indian Civil Service, was a magistrate and sessions judge, joined the Indian Army in World War II, attended Staff College at Quetta, and was seconded off to do intelligence work. Very pukka sahib. And what is the matter with that? He was obviously looking, listening, observing steadily throughout, and if his experiences have brought him to certain conclusions, is he not entitled to those conclusions? He worked in Whitehall after the war, as Controller of Enemy Property and for the Board of Trade. He comes by his knowledge of Snow's corridors of power honestly, and he knows the countries in which he places his fictions from first hand, for the most part (one may be permitted to doubt the South American republic of Candoro [innocence?] in *Closed Circuit*). He writes carefully, protects his privacy, belongs to the Travellers, and lives in Yew Tree Cottage, having given up his flat near Harley Street and his *pied-a-terre* near Venice. He is, although now 70, probably attractive to women. All too, too Bill Buckley. Or William Haggard.

And too right, mate, too. The people of whom Haggard writes do think as he suggests. They do appreciate understatement, the oblique remark, and that one doesn't put ice in a kir. If one wants to dismiss this as snob value, one will be imprecise indeed. Charles Russell—who in 1967 had turned 60, soon retired, and rather improbably leaps from a window in Switzerland in 1976, admittedly now in late middle age but still trim—strikes one as a good bit like Haggard, for they clearly think and speak as one, both are six feet tall, and they have the earmarks of their age and class. Colonel Russell admires a competent, professional enemy. He admires loyalty, even to the wrong cause. He feels that the world is not getting better and better all the time. He looks with a cool eye at all: France, although unnamed, and De Gaulle specifically are the enemies in *The High Wire* (1963), Italians in *The Hard Sell,* the Chinese in *A Cool Day for Killing,* the Americans in *The Conspirators.* He has a good ear for the language of class and age; he knows who will say "port wine" and who merely "port." In this day when publishers persistently insist that some new hawker of death has stepped into the shoes of John Buchan, Haggard has quietly set about filling them.

Haggard's titles, like his plots, are more intricate than they seem. *The Telemann Touch* is not only about a paid assassin on the Commonwealth island of St. Cree's, it is about a man's uncommon touch with people. *The Power House* shows the Security Executive itself as the dynamo of government. *The Powder Barrel* is about an oil-rich sheikdom, but in 1965. *The High Wire* is about a man stretched too tight, but it also ends in a swaying cable car high over the Alps. *The Arena* is about the City of London and also gives us a duel. *The Unquiet Sleep* is about an unsleeping government and also about drug usage. *The Doubtful Disciple* ultimately is about race-thinking and racism. None are quite what they seem although, unlike the conventional mystery, they are *almost* as they seem: plot itself is nuance.

By now Haggard has developed a set of figures who, as with any interlocking series, move in and out to serve different purposes. A minor figure in one book will return to play a major role in another. When Russell retires, Richard Laver takes over (in 1967) and does not badly *(The Doubtful Disciple)*. By 1975, in *The Scorpion's Tail*, Laver is Sir Richard and standards have begun to fall, but Russell does not begrudge his handpicked successor the knighthood he did not receive. The characters become what an earlier hint promised they would be. Yesterday's enemy returns to haunt the present in new ways.

Haggard writes about *Realpolitik*. Terrorist Japanese, resurgent Germans, cunningly neutral Swiss, Americans who put their country first, tinpot dictators from Latin America who prove capable of a "higher self-interest," "some ape in Africa," tall Frenchmen in pursuit of national glory—all are staples of his writing. It is not surprising that he offends on occasion, for these are not the standard goodies and baddies but nor are they cynical spies in from the cold. Haggard feels that *The Bitter Harvest* was ill-received in America (where it was titled *Too Many Enemies)* because of its plot. *A Doubtful Disciple* was greeted with silence, and possibly with more reason.

The Bitter Harvest is a typically complex story in which Colonel Russell plays the role of watcher. Action centers on Maurice Pater, a backbencher in the House, a person of rigid integrity who will not compromise his way to the front ranks. If he could be led to support a cause previously seen to be doubtful, he could carry many with him because of that integrity. How might the unscrupulous turn a man's integrity against himself? The original effort to make him an apologist for the cause fails, he see through it, he becomes a potential supporter of the enemy. And so he must be assassinated. All of this is unexceptional as recited here. But if the assassin is Georges Brosse, an African? If Pater has gone to South Africa, the enemy? If integrity appears to rest with the defense of *apartheid?* This plot is perhaps a little hard to bear.

And what of *The Doubtful Disciple?* Laver takes on the case because Russell points him at it. It concerns Selective Pigmentation Disease, which has been developed by the Chemical Defence Experimental Establishment in Britain. The disease attacks only those of a certain color. A scientist who worked on the disease is injured in an automobile accident and turns to religion, becoming a disciple of an evangelist. Shortly the evangelist is discredited. All seems in question and not all is worked out happily at the end. A book about racism? Or itself racist? Or about freaky religion? Or itself freaky? Might Africans turn this disease against all whites? Might an empire some felt to be racist use the disease to gain some new measure of power? This was not the kind of book likely to be taken well in 1969.

This is not ambivalence, although some think it so; Russell knows who he is and what he believes. In *The Scorpion's Tail* a group of British, Swedish, and American hippies, on pot and LSD, briefly take control of an island off Malaga. The Spanish owner and Russell exchange this conversation:

> "...And on my island they're having a last blind orgy."
> "Singing I imagine."
> "Yes. May I ask how you knew?"
> "They always sing when they're certain they've had it. It's a song called 'We Shall Not Be Moved'. When they've sung it twice they always are."
> "You're not sympathetic, then?"
> "Of course not. But nor am I exactly hostile. I'm sorry for unfortunate children."
> "All very liberal. All very British."
> "Naturally. Since that's what I am."

Or try this: Russell is thinking himself to sleep. "What was the new word? That word was *detente*. To Russell it was an arrogant sham. Why should Russia relax? She didn't need to. She too had her options but both were hard ones. One was to come West by war, when there might not be very much left worth taking, but the second was to wait in patience till the fruit dropped from the tree intact. As Russell was convinced it must. ...all communism had a very dark face, it was an unnecessarily tyrannical tyranny, but call it what you would, it worked. To Russell it was in a sense reassuring, as any discipline was reassuring. It might be needed one day in his own sad country when the Trotskyite students, the limousine liberals, had reduced it from decay to chaos."

Colonel Russell knows that the best working hypothesis is the simplest which covers all the known facts. He expects his operatives to provide him with clean, uncomplicated reasoning about highly complex matters. Yet he also knows that indirection has a cleanliness all its own. The American reader might well miss the point of an exchange such as the following, but only once: "Martin Dominy was a working operator but one day might be rather more. He was well worth sophisticating and Charles Russell began to do so. 'Quite,' he said finally. 'Perfectly logical and it covers the facts as you know them.' He was conscious this might sound pompous and pomposity he detested; he smiled, and added blandly: 'Do you mind if I play at schoolmasters?'

"'I know I've a great deal to learn, sir.'

"The tone had been mild but Martin had moved up one: He could hit back gracefully and that was important. Russell said imperturbably: 'I don't think I quite deserved that, but let's start at the beginning.'"

All of Haggard's books are worth reading, some more than others of course. Three with which to start are *The Telemann Touch*, with its admirable portrait of an assassin worth our respect; *Cool Day for Killing*, Haggard's personal favorite, with a fine opening scene of a White Rajah living in what appears to be a cross between Sarawak and Brunei waiting to be killed because he has become inconvenient to the British, who want to decolonize his tiny enclave; and my own first choice, *The Conspirators*. This last is about what appears to be a repetition of the Palomares bomb incident, when the Americans had dropped two nuclear bombs on the Spanish coast. Now they have dropped one on the shore at Devon and deny that there was a second, although someone saw a splash in the Bristol Channel at the same time. Is there another bomb? It doesn't really matter, for the question is, what can be made to seem true and by whom? The Americans who deny having dropped two, the British who obviously must have the facts, an Irish nationalist and Communist party member who has every reason to convince a nation that there are two and perhaps more? The book unfolds almost casually, yet with the reality of exceptional control, and it includes a sympathetically portrayed English Indian doctor, Anthony Shripatrao Deshmukh, who has never set foot in India, and whose wholly unnecessary death is central to the plot. In the end, there is a deft depiction of Russian racism that brings the book full circle. In between Russell makes enough outrageous statements, and makes a tape of a conversation with a good friend—being taped is "an occupational risk when you talk to the Executive"—to lose a few friends among his readership.

The professional doesn't seek friends, of course. Respect yes, friends no. A bit like the British Empire at its height. Haggard, that is.

ROBERT L. DUNCAN/JAMES HALL ROBERTS

With the publication this summer (1978) of his seventh thriller, Robert L. Duncan has placed himself front and center on one of the sub-theaters of thriller fiction: international business intrigue in a foreign setting. This seventh book, *Fire Storm*, is not, to my taste, Robert Duncan's best book, but it is a good book and it reflects all of the values, plot twists, and writing techniques that have been more disparately present in the six previous books. The three immediately previous books, published from 1970, were written as Duncan, and the three that preceded them, from 1964-67, as James Hall Roberts, a pseudonym Duncan appears to have abandoned.

The company Duncan keeps is diverse but readily identifiable. On the one hand there is Paul Erdman, who has won considerable fame and much income from *The Silver Bears, The Crash of '79*, and other all-too-convincing accounts of international skulduggery in the world of high finance. At the other extreme are Jack Higgins and Robert Ludlum, neither of whom can write, a self-evident fact that seems not to bother their readers at all, and who supply urgency, chase, improbability, sex, a paranoiac sense of conspiracy, and a world so illogical (*can* there be a sillier book than *The Matlock Papers?*) as to suspend all expectations of rational explanation. In between are such writers as Lawrence Sanders and even Joseph Wambaugh (even though he purports to write of the police). Outside this genre is (are?) Emma Lathen, despite the use of the world of banking as the excuse for most of her books.

Six of Duncan's books take place in, or relate closely to, Japan. All show a strong sense of place, an awareness of how landscape, social environment, climate influence structure. The one novel not set in Japan, James Hall Roberts's second book, *The Burning Sky*, takes place on and near the Papago Indian Reservation in Arizona. This book, which is one of the best, is as alert to social and verbal nuance as are the thrillers which set Western against Japanese culture.

Duncan is interested in the clash of cultures. His heroes, if one may call them that, are all of the West, rational, convinced that determination, planning, and logic bring victory; all are set against villains, if one can call them that, who use instinct, cunning, emotion, to achieve their ends. In each book a slow awareness comes upon the reader that the author not only knows how to do a good job of research — *Temple Dogs*, published last year, shows plenty of research into computer technology and capabilities — but that the organizing principles behind the research are those of the anthropologist, the sociologist, the professional observer of people.

This is not precisely what Robert L. Duncan is, in fact. He is a freelance, highly professional writer, who lives with his wife in Tuttle, Oklahoma, just outside Oklahoma City, and who drives over to Norman, Oklahoma, every few days to teach a course in the School of Journalism. He has lived in Los Angeles, he knows Japan, he is widely read, he confesses to having been deeply influenced by Charles Dickens (among others) as a child, and he keeps up with other thriller writers. But above all, he looks at people, studying them with a steady sense of curiosity. Like a good journalist, he has the easy skill of getting people to talk about themselves, even when they are supposed to be talking about him, a skill I have had occasion to see him exercise. This, too, is very evident in the books.

The reader's slow awareness is also the protagonist's. Western man begins with the assumption that no problem is beyond the application of knowledge and hard work. Slowly the sense of place reveals that knowledge will unravel the problem only if, by knowledge, one means the ability to respond to an emotional situation in its own terms. Both in the plot construction of the novel, and in the protagonist's ultimate sensitivity to the true nature of his problem, there occurs a moment of unreasonableness. This is generally slightly past the midpoint of each book, where a plot twist suddenly is unacceptable on the basis of the logic that has gone before. In the one book set in Arizona, an archaeologist who sets out to find a colleague lost in the desert lands west of Ajo encounters the Hohokam, a people presumed to have vanished centuries ago. All of the archaeological data provided in the book are sound, the geography well delineated, and only the moment of confrontation seems unreal—and that for a moment only, for as the unreasonable is seen to be reasonable, all else also flows with a logic of its own.

Fire Storm shows the same characteristics. There is much research convincingly and painlessly conveyed, this time on oil tankers. There is a strong sense of place, both of Japan and of the San Pedro/ Long Beach harbor area. There is a moment when a ruthless, calculating mid-echelon businessman finds that he has been betrayed by his employers, and uses his conventional weaponry to extricate himself. There is another moment when we realize that logic is not enough, for also involved in the calculus is a variable not open to fine calibration: a leader of the unpredictable Japanese Red Watch. Then comes the moment of unreasonableness, when neither hero nor villain does what would, in an ideally conceived "real world," be the next logical thing to do. Logic, if only for a moment set aside, then produces a new set of casual relationships, a new logic of its own. Man the machine, while still drawing upon his knowledge of technology, all of his awareness of likely corporate behavior, must ultimately commit himself to the path of emotion.

Duncan is fond of holocaust, of fire storm, as a metaphor for technology out of control. There are two such sudden blazes, engulfing the innocent, in his latest book; there is another in *Temple Dogs;* the desert sun in *The Burning Sky* serves the same function; *The Day the Sun Fell,* which is about Nagasaki in 1945, is the most explicit, of course. The holocaust can be understood only in terms of emotion, for to unleash it is irrational, its results are irrational, and the path of its destruction is irrational. The world of corporate business, Duncan suggests, thinks of the holocaust as simply another weapon, all life capable of being controlled toward a predicted and desired end. In *Fire Storm* our hero, Corwin, finds himself in conversation with a poised Englishman of great wealth and business acumen, Swann, and the following perhaps unnecessarily obvious interchange takes place:

> "I understand your family was involved in whaling at one time."
>
> "Indeed," Swann said.
>
> "Did the whales ever shake loose once the harpoons were imbedded?"
>
> "Rarely, I believe," Swann said. "I'm no expert. But the harpoons were designed to hold, after all."
>
> "I'm on the side of the whales," Corwin said. "Unsuspecting, suddenly barbed, hooked, trapped. No sport there, no chance."
>
> "It was never a sport," Swann said. "And there was never any mystique about it among the professionals. It was an industry, after all...."

"Our hero, Corwin": this is the moment when he shifts gears, for to this point we have seen him as at least as cold as Swann. But now Corwin is also being pursued, from directions he cannot quite fathom (although he believes he does), and there is a moment when he realizes that it is not sport and wishes it were. "Our hero, Corwin": we do not really know him otherwise, for Duncan always refers to him by his last name, and while he shows him to be resourceful, courageous, and intelligent, he does not make Corwin irredeemably attractive. For reasons perhaps known only to himself, Duncan gives his readers virtually the same figure in every book: Cooper in his first, well-received, novel *The Q Document;* Corman in the next, equally good, *The February Plan;* Cummings in *The Burning Sky;* and then, with James Hall Roberts apparently behind him, a Captain and a Christian in *The Day the Sun Fell;* Calder in *Dragons at the Gate;* Corbett in *Temple Dogs;* and now Corwin. I had dinner with Robert Duncan a few months ago, and he arrived in his Cadillac and ordered the Cordon Bleu.

If the character is consistent, so is the message. Corwin states it more bluntly than any of the other figures upon the high Cs: "Jesus, Corwin thought, they were going to make it impossible in the end, the bureaucrats on one hand who would delay and stall, seeking consensus, and this actor-revolutionary on the other who might decide to change his mind at a moment's notice." Only reason and emotion as handmaids could provide the answer. The first book, *The Q Document,* poses the safe bureaucrat against the man of emotion. The jacket copy poses the questions: Why did Red China want the Q document? Why did the Vatican send someone to buy it? Why did the Nazis believe in it even though its discoverer was a Jew? Why did a Catholic priest now contemplate murder because of it? Each question is rationally put, each is emotionally answered. Each book wrestles with conventional moralities (Catholic priests are frequently present), each explores however briefly the line between animality and love in sexual relations.

Each book also presents a genuine puzzle. Duncan confesses to having read much Ellery Queen when he was 12 or so. He feels that guilt is not capable of rational resolution but punishment may be (and he is interested in reform of our prison system, on which he also has written). He is careful of phrase, and often responds to a question with "exactly so." A bluff, big man, he likes to know exactly where his books are going, and this means that he must see to it that his readers do not. The ultimate figure of evil in *Fire Storm* may come as no great surprise, but there are surprises enough along the way to show that Duncan could imitate his childhood hero if he wished to. We are lucky that he does not wish to, for he has found a unique niche for himself. In any individual quality, Robert Duncan may not seem as strong as another writer: Tony Hillerman integrates Navaho myth and ritual into his mysteries more successfully than Duncan has done with the Papago; Erdman gives one a more acute sense of the polychrome world of international finance than Duncan does. Taking all of the ingredients together, however, Duncan is the most skillful blender I have encountered. At least three of his books are very good indeed *(Q Document, Dragons at the Gate, Fire Storm)*, and only one is less than good *(Temple Dogs)*. While one may conclude, setting the seven books back to back, that there is little growth, for the plot elements tend to replicate themselves, precisely by setting them back to back can one discover how subtly, how ably, by nuance, phrase, and observation, the steady eye of this author has seen the more clearly the world he reveals.[4]

[4][These four short essays formed part of a regular column, published originally six times a year, in *The New Republic.* I was interested to discover that while the omnibus columns, which appeared quarterly and reviewed fifteen or so books each time, attracted considerable correspondence, the articles on specific writers did not. These four writers, together with Amanda Cross—the subject of a fifth essay, not reprinted here, since it appeared too late for the compositor—represent to me the five principle trends in current detective and thriller fiction. That two essays were on British, and three on America, writers also strikes me as the correct balance. Only this essay on Robert L. Duncan gave rise to any sustained correspondence, partially because *Fire Storm* appeared to displease some corporate interests, partially because some readers imagined that I did not recognize my own double meaning in referring to his books, which are about how cultures clash, in the context of *a* or *the* Holocaust. By this correspondence I discovered (again) that nothing falls so flat as the calculated indiscretion when no one recognizes that it was calculated.]

Appendix

A number of American universities now offer courses on detection fiction. Two sample syllabuses for university courses in the field are provided here. Each was taught at Yale University, each for a single semester, both to all levels of undergraduates. The first course, taught in the Fall Term of 1977, was offered by a professor of English; the second course, taught in the Spring Term of 1979, by a major writer of detective fiction. The respective points of view are those of Thomas N. Leitch and Hillary Waugh. Both courses were called "The Detective Story."

Course One: Weekly Undergraduate Meetings

Detective stories are commonly considered a derivative, parasitical, or inferior form of literature. This course will undertake to study them seriously by placing them in three contexts: an historical context, in which the rise and decline of the detective story and its transformation into the novel of mystery or suspense will be considered; a morphological context, which will focus on the ludic structure common to all detective stories; and a critical context, in which several attempts to treat the detective story with self-conscious artistry will be analyzed and judged. The thrust of the course is designed to raise ever more persistent questions about what does and does not constitute seriousness in literary fiction by considering the detective story functionally, in terms of the human desires it satisfies. The course is therefore as much about problems of judgment and value in literature as it is about detective stories, but I assume that only people who have read a considerable number of detective stories would be interested in approaching these problems (or any other problems) by studying more detective stories.

Week I. Introductory: An examination will be given this week to test students' previous knowledge of detective stories. The exam will not be graded, but its results may cause minor additions, deletions, or transpositions in the syllabus.

I. HISTORY

Week II. Reading: POE *The Murders in the Rue Morgue* (1841), *The Mystery of Marie Roget* (1842), *The Purloined Letter* (1844); DOYLE The Adventures of Sherlock Holmes (1892), STOUT *Watson Was a Woman* (1941); WILSON *Mr. Holmes, They Were the Footprints of a Gigantic Hound!* (1944).

Optional reading: POE *The Gold Bug* (1843), *Thou Art The Man* (1844); DOYLE *The Final Problem* (1894), *The Hound of the Baskervilles* (1902), *The Adventure of the Empty House* (1905).

Early history and development of the genre. The fascination of Sherlock Holmes. A look at the Baker Street Irregulars.

Week III. Reading: CHRISTIE *The Murder of Roger Ackroyd* (1926); HAYCRAFT (ed.) *Fourteen Great Detective Stories* (1949).

Imitators of Holmes. The 1920s and 1930s in England and America. Variety of responses to the problems of construction.

Paper: An historical topic in the development of the detective story before 1940.

Week IV. Reading: VAN DINE *The Greene Murder Case* (1928); HAYCRAFT *Murder for Pleasure: The Life and Times of the Detective Story* (1941), pp. 112-222; CARR *The Grandest Game in the World* (1946).

Optional reading: BERKELEY *The Poisoned Chocolates Case* (1929).

Virtues and defects of the strict detective story. The proliferation of clichés. The rise of psychological detection.

Week V. Reading: BARZUN *Detection in Extremis* (1959); MACDONALD *The Underground Man* (1971); SYMONS *Mortal Consequences: A History from the Detective Story to the Crime Novel* (1972), pp. 151-66, 178-208.

Optional reading: FRANCIS *Nerve* (1966); LE CARRÉ *Tinker, Tailor, Soldier, Spy* (1974).

The decline of the tale of detection. Suspense stories, spy stories, Gothics. Claims for the serious novel of crime.

II. MORPHOLOGY

Week VI. Reading: FREEMAN *The Art of the Detective Story* (1924); KNOX *Detective Story Decalogue* (1928); VAN DINE *Twenty Rules for Writing Detective Stories* (1928); CARR *The Three Coffins* (1935); STOUT *And Be a Villain* (1948).

Optional reading: WELLS *The Technique of the Mystery Story* (1913); ILES *Trial and Error* (1937).

The detective story as game. Queen's "Challenge to the Reader." The rules and the revolt against rules.

Paper: A parody of one of the Golden Age detective stories.

Week VII. Reading: BENTLEY *Trent Intervenes* (1938); BRAMAH *Max Car-*

rados (1914); CARR *The Department of Queer Complaints* (1940), *The Third Bullet* (1954), *The Men Who Explained Miracles* (1964); CHRISTIE *Poirot Investigates* (1924), *The Tuesday Club Murders* (1933), *The Under Dog* (1955); FREEMAN *The Singing Bone* (1912); KEMELMAN *The Nine Mile Walk* (1967); ORCZY *The Man in the Corner* (1909); POST *Uncle Abner* (1918); QUEEN *The Adventures of Ellery Queen* (1934), *The New Adventures of Ellery Queen* (1940), *Calendar of Crime* (1951).

Each student will read one of these volumes of stories and prepare a list of characteristic elements. Discussion will move toward a structural synthesis.

Week VIII. Reading: BENTLEY *Trent's Last Case* (1912); BLAKE *The Beast Must Die* (1938); BRAND *Green for Danger* (1942); CHRISTIE *Death on the Nile* (1938); INNES *Lament for a Maker* (1938); LEROUX *The Mystery of the Yellow Room* (1907); McCLOY *Cue for Murder* (1942); MACDONALD *The Rasp* (1924); MASON *The House of the Arrow* (1924); MILNE *The Red House Mystery* (1922); QUEEN *Calamity Town* (1942); SAYERS *Strong Poison* (1930); TEY *The Daughter of Time* (1951).

Each student will read one or two of these novels. A continuation of last week's discussion, with particular emphasis on the essential structure of the detective story.

Week IX. Reading: CHESTERTON *The Innocence of Father Brown* (1911); BORGES *The Garden of Forking Paths* (1940), *Death and the Compass* (1941); BLAKE *The Detective Story—Why?* (1942); WILSON *Why Do People Read Detective Stories?* (1944), *Who Cares Who Killed Roger Ackroyd?* (1945); AUDEN *The Guilty Vicarage* (1948).

Optional reading: TODOROV *Typologie du roman policier* (1971).

Functional analysis of the detective story. Vulnerability of its conventions to satire and parody.

III. CRITICISM

Week X. Reading: SOPHOCLES *Oedipus the King* (427 B.C.); HAMMETT *The Glass Key* (1931); BOUCHER *The Ethics of the Mystery Novel* (1944); CHANDLER *The Simple Art of Murder* (1944).

Optional reading: CHANDLER *Farewell, My Lovely* (1940).

Seriousness of tone. The detective story as tragedy. The criminal and society. Guilt and the game.

Paper: A program for the serious treatment of detective elements discussed in Weeks VI to IX.

Week XI. Reading: COLLINS *The Moonstone* (1868).

Seriousness of reference. Crime as a touchstone for determining character, social relations, national consciousness.

Week XII. Reading: DICKENS *The Mystery of Edwin Drood* (1870).
Optional reading: AYLMER *The Drood Case* (1964).
Seriousness of epistemology. Detection as a way of knowing. Dickens's criticism of the detective.

Week XIII. Reading: HIGHSMITH *Strangers on a Train* (1950).
Viewing: HITCHCOCK *Strangers on a Train* (1951).
Seriousness of psychology. Hitchcock's simplification of motive and psychology. The necessity of articulated convention.
Paper: A conjectural conclusion to *The Mystery of Edwin Drood,* or an original detective story.

Week XIV. Final Examination.

[Note: The Purpose of Week XIII can also be served by reading Chandler, *The Big Sleep* (1937) and by viewing Hawter, *The Big Sleep* (1946.]

Course Two: Weekly Undergraduate Seminars

Week I. Overview of the course: Discussion of the field.

Week II. ORIGINS: Discussion of *The Mystery Story,* edited by JOHN BALL; *Murders in the Rue Morgue* and *The Mystery of Marie Roget* EDGAR ALLAN POE; *A Study in Scarlet* and *The Adventures of Sherlock Holmes* CONAN DOYLE.

Week III. THE DETECTIVE — PUZZLE: *The Innocence of Father Brown* G. K. CHESTERTON; *Trent's Last Case* E. C. BENTLEY; *The Circular Staircase* MARY ROBERTS RINEHART; *Gaudy Night* DOROTHY SAYERS; *Murder For Pleasure* HOWARD HAYCRAFT.

Week IV. THE DETECTIVE — PUZZLE (cont.): *The Chinese Orange Mystery* and *Calamity Town* ELLERY QUEEN; *Too Many Cooks* REX STOUT; *The Greene Murder Case* S. S. VAN DINE; *The Simple Art of Murder* RAYMOND CHANDLER. Assignment of fiction paper, due in Week VIII.

Week V. THE DETECTIVE — PUZZLE (cont.): *The Murder of Roger Ackroyd* and *Murder on the Orient Express* AGATHA CHRISTIE; *The Case of The Lucky Legs* EARLE STANLEY GARDNER; *Maigret Comes Home* SIMENON; *Charlie Chan Carries On* EARL DERR BIGGERS.

Week VI. THE PRIVATE EYE — HARD BOILED NOVEL: *The Thin Man* and *The Maltese Falcon* HAMMETT; *The Big Sleep* CHANDLER; *The*

Postman Always Rings Twice JAMES M. CAIN; *On Crime Writing* ROSS MACDONALD.

Week VII. THE PRIVATE EYE — HARD BOILED NOVEL (cont.): *Bright Orange for a Shroud* JOHN D. MACDONALD; *The Zebra-Striped Hearse* ROSS MACDONALD; *I, The Jury* SPILLANE; *The Counterfeit Wife* BRETT HALLIDAY. Assignment of research paper due Week XII.

Week VIII: First paper due. THE POLICE PROCEDURAL: *V As In Victim* LAWRENCE TREAT; *Last Seen Wearing...* WAUGH; *Fuzz* ED MCBAIN; *Gideon's Fire* J. J. MARRIC; *The Laughing Policeman* PER WAHLÖO and MAJ SJOWALL.

Week IX. THE SPY NOVEL: *The Great Impersonation* E. PHILLIPS OP-PENHEIM; *The Thirty-Nine Steps* JOHN BUCHAN; *A Coffin For Dimitrios* ERIC AMBLER; *Goldfinger* IAN FLEMING.

Week X. THE SPY NOVEL (cont.): *A Gun For Sale* GRAHAM GREENE; *The Spy Who Came in From the Cold* JOHN LE CARRÉ; *The Ipcress File* LEN DEIGHTON.

Week XI. VARIATIONS I: *Laura* VERA CASPERY; *Daughter of Time* TEY; *The Unsuspected* ARMSTRONG. ·

Week XII. Second paper due. VARIATIONS II: *The Young Prey* WAUGH; *The First Deadly Sin* LAWRENCE SANDERS; *In The Heat of The Night* BALL; *A Queer Kind of Death* BAXT.

Week XIII. ENDINGS: *The Final Problem* DOYLE; *Curtain* CHRISTIE; *A Family Affair* STOUT; *Après de ma Blonde* NICOLAS FREELING.

Week XIV. Final Examination Week.

Where To Obtain Current and Out-of-Print Detective Stories

Moonstone Bookcellars, Inc. 2145 Pennsylvania Avenue, N.W., Washington D.C. 20037.

Murder Ink. 271 West 87 Street, New York, N.Y. 10024.

The Mysterious Bookshop. 129 West 56 Street, New York, N.Y. 10019.

Scene of the Crime. 13636 Ventura Blvd., Sherman Oaks, Cal. 91403.

Bibliography

I

Critical and Historical Literature

There is a substantial body of descriptive, and a thin corpus of critical, literature on detective and thriller fiction. Much of the best of that literature has been drawn upon for the selections to this book, and readers may wish to read in their entirety the books from which I have taken excerpts. One journal, *The Armchair Detective* (Del Mar, California), provides quarterly bibliographies of new books and articles on the genre as well as printing scholarly and appreciative articles of an original nature. *The Journal of Popular Culture* (Bowling Green State University, Bowling Green, Ohio) frequently contains material on the subject. There is also a considerable pastiche and by-product literature, ranging from cookbooks such as Jeanine Larmoth's *Murder on the Menu: Food and Drink in the English Mystery Novel* (New York, 1972) to "biographies" of fictional heroes such as Nero Wolfe. There is even a genealogy of *The Wimsey Family* by C. W. Scott-Giles (London, 1977).

Certain books are indispensable, of course. Foremost among these are two remarkable works: Jacques Barzun and Wendell Hertig Taylor, *A Catalogue of Crime* (New York, 1971), a massive annotated bibliography which slights the post-1960 period (hence my own list of two hundred favorites which follows this section) and which is opinionated, witty, and intelligent. A unique "mystery reader's companion" filled with useful and useless information has been perpetrated by Dilys Winn as *Murder Ink* (New York, 1977). *Who Done It? A Guide to Detective, Mystery and Suspense Fiction* (New York, 1969) has a particularly valuable section on settings for crime novels and despite numerous minor errors, is a fine librarians' bibliography. In many ways it has been superseded by Allen J. Hubin, *The Bibliography of Crime Fiction, 1749-1975* (Del Mar, California, 1979). Also of value are the *Encyclopedia of Mystery & Detection,* by Chris Steinbrunner and Otto Penzler (New York, 1976), especially strong on films; *Detectionary,* edited by Penzler, Steinbrunner, and Marvin Lachman (Woodstock, N.Y., 1977), a biographical dictionary of the leading characters in mystery fiction: and two books on *The Great Detectives* (Boston, 1978), edited by Penzler, and *The Private Lives of Private Eyes and Spies, Crime Fighters, and Other Good Guys* (New York, 1979), written by Penzler. Donald McCormick, *Who's Who in Spy Fiction* (London, 1977), provides short biographies of authors. Two illustrated books, one excellent—Tage la Cour and Harald Mogensen, *The Murder Book: An Illustrated History of the Detective Story* (New York, 1971), with a fine bibliography—and one less so, Janet Pate, *The Book of Sleuths* (Chicago, 1977); and a very slight volume, *Best Detective Fiction*, by Melvyn Barnes (London, 1975), complete one's bibliographical needs.

The best history is still Howard Haycraft, *Murder for Pleasure: The Life and Times of the Detective Story* (New York, 1941). For more recent years there is the book by Symons, excerpted here; A. E. Murch, *The Development of the Detective Novel* (London, 1958), a solid work best on the nineteenth century; and from the point of view of the book as a physical object, Eric Quayle, *The Collector's Book of Detective Fiction* (London, 1972). The definitive early work is Régis Messac, *Le "Detective Novel" et l'influence de la pensée scientifique* (Paris, 1929), which begins with Voltaire and includes Dickens, Reade, Collins, and Mrs. Gaskell.

On the whole, serious critical analysis of detective fiction has been left to the Germans. Rainer Schönhoar, *Novelle und Kriminalsschema: Ein Strukturmodelldeutscher Erzählkunst zum 1800* (Bad Homburg, 1969), is strong on writers little read in English: Schiller, E. T. A. Hoffman, van Kleist, etc. Horst Conrad, *Die Literarische Angst: Das Schreckliche in Schauerromantik und Detektivgeschichte* (Düsseldorf, 1974), examines the function of terror, anxiety, horror, pity, and sex in several authors and contains a particularly fine bibliography. Also important are Paul G. Buchloh and Jens P. Becker, *Der Detektivroman* (Darmstadt, 1973), which is especially good on the differences between English and American detective fiction; and two collections of essays, Ulrich Schulz-Buschhaus, ed., *Formen und Idealogien der Kriminalroman* (Frankfurt, 1975), strong on Socialist Realism, and Viktor Zmegac, ed., *Der Wohltemperierte Mord: Zur Theorie und Geschichte des Detektivromans* (Frankfurt am Main, 1971). Bertolt Brecht's influential essay, "Über die Popularitat des Kriminalromans," is included. Jochen Vogt, *Der Kriminalroman* (Munich, 1971), 2 vols., includes Brecht and William Faulkner, while Edgar Marsch, *Die Kriminalerzählung: Theorie, Geschichte, Analyse* (Munich, 1972), is also strong on Albert Camus and Friedrich Durrenmatt. Hans Pfeiffer, *Die Mumie in Glassarg: Bemerkungen zur Kriminalliteratur* (Rudolstadt, 1960), is good on the element of criminality itself. Even so, the most influential of all works not in English must continue to be Thomas Narcejac, *Esthétique du roman policier* (Paris, 1947), and Pierre Boileau and Thomas Narcejac, *Le roman policier* (Paris, 1964).

Three collections of essays on specific authors or problems within the field are Howard Haycraft, ed., *The Art of the Mystery Story* (New York, 1946); Francis M. Nevins, Jr., *The Mystery Writer's Art* (Bowling Green, Ohio, 1970); and John Ball, ed., *The Mystery Story* (Del Mar, California, 1976). Larry N. Landrum, Pat Browne, and Ray B. Browne, eds., *Dimensions of Detective Fiction* (Bowling Green, 1976), is on the whole disappointing. More specialized works include Richard Usborne, *Clubland Heroes* (rev. ed., London, 1974), which is excellent on John Buchan, Dornfort Yates, and Sapper; Hugh Eames, *Sleuths, Inc.* (Philadelphia, 1978), weak on Hammett and Chandler but shrewd on Simenon; Colin Watson, *Snobbery with Violence: Crime Stories and Their Audience* (London, 1971), which attempts a loosely-structured class analysis; Bobbie Ann Mason, *The Girl Sleuth* (Old Westbury, N.Y., 1975), which analyzes Nancy Drew and her values; and Jean-Jacques Tourteau, *D'Arsène Lupin à San-Antonio* (Paris, 1970), excellent while solely devoted to French writers. H. R. F. Keating, *Murder Must Appetize* (London, 1975) is a slim and nontechnical inquiry into why detection fiction proves attractive. In addition to Bruce Merry, *Anatomy of the Spy Thriller* (Dublin, 1977), there is a fine study on the spy thriller by Jens-Peter Becker, *Der englische Spionageroman* (Munich, 1973), which deserves translation. William Vivian Butler, in *The Durable Desperadoes* (London, 1973), examines the gentlemen outlaws (the Saint, the Toff, Norman Conquest, Bulldog Drummond) in the context of anti-Bolshevik middle class attitudes at the end of World War I. Ellery Queen, *Queen's Quorum* (Boston, 1951), contains a history of detective short-story writing from 1845 and a list of Queen's choice of the one hundred six best short stories (often reprinted as "the 100 best"). Fereydoun Hovey-da, in *Historie du roman policier* (Paris, 1965), explores eroticism in Jean Cocteau and Mickey Spillane; Jose Antonio Portuondo, *En torno a la novela detectivesca* (Havana, 1946), looks at the field in (then) avant-garde terms. Marie F. Rodell inquires into the technique of writing in *Mystery Fiction* (New York, 1943). Robin W. Winks, *The Historian as Detective* (New York, 1969), draws parallels between mystery fiction and the use of facts as gathered as assessed by the historian.

Very little has been written on detective fiction from the point of view of philosophy. Exceptions are Routley and Harper, *The World of the Thriller* (Cleveland, 1969), Robert Champigny's tightly argued *What Will Have Happened: A Philosophical and Technical Essay on Mystery Stories* (Bloomington, Indiana, 1977), and Ereste del Buono and Umberto Eco, *The Bond Affair* (London, 1966). David I. Grossvogel, *Mystery and Its Fictions: From Oedipus to Agatha Christie* (Baltimore, 1979), is especially good on Kafka and Robbe-Grillet and fresh on Christie. The James Bond phenomenon has given rise to more than a dozen examinations of his ethos and how

Ian Fleming has contributed to the decay of western civilization, etc., etc. The best is O. F. Snelling, *Double O Seven: James Bond, A Report* (London, 1964).

Few mystery writers, other than Wilkie Collins, Poe, and Arthur Conan Doyle, have attracted individual critical studies of their work, or biographers. Graham Greene is an exception, of course, and the literature on him is extensive. David Pryce-Jones's short study, *Graham Greene* (London, 1963), despite its date, is a good place to start. *John Buchan* by Janet Adam Smith (London, 1965) is superb on the man but must be supplemented with David Daniell, *The Interpreter's House: A Critical Assessment of the Work of John Buchan* (London, 1975). The two best biographies, both the work of scholars, are Frank MacShane, *The Life of Raymond Chandler* (New York, 1976), and John McAleer, *Rex Stout: A Biography* (Boston, 1977). Jerry Speer has written an intelligent study of *Ross Macdonald* (New York, 1978). The best of several books on Agatha Christie are G. C. Ramsey, *Agatha Christie: Mistress of Mystery* (New York, 1967), Gwen Robyns, *The Mystery of Agatha Christie* (New York, 1978), and H. R. F. Keating, ed., *Agatha Christie: First Lady of Crime* (New York, 1977), but they are not good enough. Janet Hitchman has written *"Such a Strange Lady": An Introduction to Dorothy L. Sayers (1893-1957)* (London, 1975), which while interesting lacks critical judgment and is itself quite strange. Substantially better are Ralph E. Hone, *Dorothy L. Sayers: A Literary Biography* and Margaret P. Hannay, ed., *As Her Whimsey Took Her: Critical Essays on the Work of Dorothy L. Sayers* (both Kent, Ohio, 1979). John Pearson, *Alias James Bond — The Life of Ian Fleming* (New York, 1966), is overblown. Two very short efforts are little more than summaries of plots: Frank D. Campbell, Jr., *John D. MacDonald and the Colorful World of Travis McGee* (San Bernardino, California, 1977), and Robert A. Lee, *Alistair Maclean: The Key Is Fear* (the same, 1976); both are volumes in The Milford Series: Popular Writers of Today. Peter Wolfe, *Dreamers Who Live Their Dreams: The World of Ross Macdonald's Novels* (Bowling Green, 1976), is literal-minded; Francis M. Nevins, Jr., *Royal Bloodline: Ellery Queen, Author and Detective* (Bowling Green, 1974), is more useful. Because he is well versed in detective fiction, Owen Dudley Edwards throws much light on popular writing in general in his *P. G. Wodehouse* (London, 1977). There are also "definitive" bibliographies and checklists of the work of John Buchan, Raymond Chandler, Agatha Christie, John D. MacDonald, Ross Macdonald, Dorothy Sayers, and R. H. van Gulik. Some few practitioners have written autobiographies, of which the most interesting are those by Agatha Christie, Dick Francis, and Chester Himes.

Essays and scholarly journal articles on detective fiction are generally slight in nature, belletristic, such as Marjorie Nicolson's delightful "The

Professor and the Detective," which appeared in *The Atlantic Monthly* in April, 1929. A fine if dated bibliography of such articles appears in part III of Barzun and Taylor, cited above. Particularly good and lengthy introductions may be found in four older anthologies, each well worth reading: "The Detective Story," by Willard Huntington Wright, in his *The Great Detective Stories: A Chronological Anthology* (New York, 1928), pp. 3-37; E. M. Wrong's introduction to his *Crime and Detection* (Oxford, 1926), pp. ix-xxx; "'Riddle Stories',," Julian Hawthorne's introduction to the six volumes of the *Library of the World's Best Mystery and Detective Stories,* I, (New York, 1908), 9-19; and Maurice Richardson's brief introduction to *Best Mystery Stories* (London, 1968), pp. 9-13.

To these essays one should add at least six others, each of great value. In "The Detective Detected: From Sophocles to Ross MacDonald," *Yale Review*, LXIV (Autumn, 1974), 72-83, Max Byrd writes on Marlowe and others as comic heroes. Fredric Jameson, "On Raymond Chandler," *The Southern Review*, n.s., VI (July, 1970), 624-50, is perhaps the best analysis of the appeal of Chandler's work. M. E. Grenander, in "The Heritage of Cain: Crime in American Fiction," *The Annals of The American Academy of Political and Social Science*, CCCCXXIII (Jan., 1976), 47-66, asks how literature defines crime and conceives of punishment. Russell M. Brown, "In Search of Lost Causes: The Canadian Novelist as Mystery Writer," *Mosaic: A Journal for the Comparative Study of Literature and Ideas,* XI (Spring, 1978), 1-15, places the entire genre in an unusual and rewarding context. Tzvetan Todorev, "The Typology of Detective Fiction," in Richard Howard, trans., *The Poetics of Prose* (Ithaca, N.Y., 1977), is off the mark but no less stimulating for that. Martin Green, in his essay "Our Detective Heroes," in his *Transatlantic Patterns: Cultural Comparisons of England with America* (New York, 1977), is desperately wrong-headed about Dorothy Sayers, driven by his insistence on seeing all life in working class terms into misreading satire for high seriousness, but shrewd on John D. MacDonald. These six essays were to have been included in the present book until space limitations barred them.

Finally, there is a separate body of psychoanalytical literature which seeks to interpret mystery stories in terms of psychological, usually Freudian, theory. I sought at length for readable, convincing, or merely revealing examples of these studies, but ultimately was unable to find any that could compete for space as contributions to an analysis of the *literature* of detection. However, two articles are of substantial value for other reasons. One, by Charles Rycroft, on "The Analysis of a Detective Story," applies Freudian insights to Wilkie Collins. It appears in his *Imagination and Reality: Psycho-Analytical Essays, 1951-1961* (London, 1968). The other, by R. C. S. Trahair, has appeared in two versions: "A Psychological Study of the Modern Hero: The Case of James Bond," *Australian and New Zeal-*

and Journal of Psychiatry, VIII (1974), 155-65, and "A Contribution to the Psychoanalytic Study of the Modern Hero," *La Trobe Sociology Papers,* no. 28 (Bundoora, Vic., Australia, 1976), pp. 1-39.

A personal bibliography of detective and thriller fiction follows.

II

A Personal List of 200 Favorites

Those who are basically unacquainted with detective (and thriller) fiction must begin somewhere. As Edmund Wilson noted, friends tend to recommend books they have enjoyed with little regard to the reading tastes of the recipient of such advice. Among the many thousands of books into which the novice might stumble, there must nonetheless be some way of deciding where to begin. The following list of two hundred titles is provided, therefore, as a point of entry; authors are limited to no more than three titles. The editor regards all of the titles as good, although for a variety of reasons. Not all have contributed to the history of the field and not all are written with equal grace, but each has substantial merits whether for plot, well-realized setting, characterization, detection, or even trickery. For the most part, books from the early classic period (pre-1930) are omitted from the list, since so many of them have been singled out in the essays in this work. Date of publication is, on occasion, only approximate, for such information is not always clear from title or copyright pages. This list should, of course, also be read against the titles listed elsewhere, as well as against the sample course outlines in the Appendix.

Allbeury, Ted. *A Choice of Enemies.* London, 1973.

Allingham, Margery. *Dancers in Mourning.* New York, 1937.

Allingham, Margery. *The Tiger in the Smoke.* New York, 1952.

Alverson, Charles. *Goodey's Last Stand.* Boston, 1975.

Ambler, Eric. *Background to Danger.* London, 1937.

Ambler, Eric. *A Coffin for Dimitrios.* London, 1939.

Ambler, Eric. *Journey into Fear.* New York, 1940.

Anderson, James. *The Affair of the Blood-Stained Egg Cosy.* New York, 1975.

Asimov, Isaac. *Murder at the ABA.* New York, 1976.

Bagley, Desmond. *High Citadel.* London, 1965.

Bagley, Desmond. *Running Blind.* London, 1970.

Bagley, Desmond. *The Enemy.* London, 1976.

Ball, John. *In the Heat of the Night.* New York, 1965.

Barnard, Robert. *Death of an Old Goat.* New York, 1977.

Behn, Noel. *The Kremlin Letter.* New York, 1966.

Benson, Ben. *The Running Man.* New York, 1957.

Bentley, E. C. *Trent's Last Case.* London, 1912.

Bergman, Andrew. *The Big Kiss Off of 1944.* New York, 1974.

Berkeley, Anthony. *Trial and Error.* London, 1937.

Beste, R. Vernon. *Repeat the Instructions.* New York, 1967.

Blake, Nicholas. *The Abominable Snowman.* London, 1940.

Blake, Nicholas. *Minute for Murder.* London, 1947.

Block, Lawrence. *The Sins of the Fathers.* New York, 1976.

Boucher, Anthony. *The Case of the Seven of Calvary.* New York, 1937.

Box, Edgar (Gore Vidal). *Death in the Fifth Position.* New York, 1952.

Brand, Christianna. *Green for Danger.* London, 1945.

Brown, Fredric. *The Fabulous Clipjoint.* New York, 1947.

Buchan, John. *The Thirty-Nine Steps.* London, 1915.

Buchan, John. *John Macnab.* London, 1925.

Buchan, John. *Mountain Meadow.* Boston, 1941.

Buckley, William F., Jr. *Saving the Queen.* Garden City, N.Y., 1976.

Burns, Rex. *Angle of Attack.* New York, 1979.

Byrom, James. *Or Be He Dead.* London, 1958.

Cain, James M. *The Postman Always Rings Twice.* New York, 1934.

Cain, James M. *Double Indemnity.* New York, 1936.

Carr, A. H. Z. *Finding Maubee.* New York, 1971.

Carr, John Dickson. *The Case of the Constant Suicides.* New York, 1941.

Chandler, Raymond. *The Big Sleep.* New York, 1939.

Chandler, Raymond. *Farewell, My Lovely.* New York, 1940.

Chandler, Raymond. *The Lady in the Lake.* New York, 1943.

Childers, Erskine. *The Riddle of the Sands.* London, 1903.

Christie, Agatha. *The Murder of Roger Ackroyd.* London, 1926.

Christie, Agatha. *Ten Little Niggers.* London, 1939.

Christie, Agatha. *The Patriotic Murders.* London, 1940.

Clifford, Francis. *The Third Side of the Coin.* London, 1965.

Clifford, Francis. *All Men Are Lonely Now.* London, 1967.

Coles, Manning. *Drink to Yesterday.* London, 1940.

Coles, Manning. *A Toast to Tomorrow.* New York; 1941.

Constantine, K. C. *The Blank Page.* New York, 1974.

Courtier, S. H. *Murder's Burning.* New York, 1967.

Creasey, John (as J. J. Marric). *Gideon's River.* New York, 1968.

Creed, David. *The Trial of Lobo Icheka.* London, 1971.

Crofts, Freeman Wills. *Death of a Train.* London, 1946.

Cross, Amanda. *Poetic Justice.* New York, 1970.

Cunningham, E. V. *Sylvia.* Garden City, N.Y., 1960.

Davidson, Lionel. *Night of Wenceslas.* New York, 1960.

Davidson, Lionel. *The Rose of Tibet.* New York, 1962.

Deighton, Len. *The Ipcress File.* London, 1962.

Deighton, Len. *SS-GB.* London, 1978.

Dexter, Colin. *The Silent World of Nicholas Quinn.* New York, 1977.

Dodge, David. *The Long Escape.* New York, 1950.

Douglass, Donald McNutt. *Rebecca's Pride.* New York, 1957.

Duncan, Robert (as James Hall Roberts). *The Q Document.* New York, 1964.

Ellin, Stanley. *The Eighth Circle.* New York, 1958.

Eustis, Helen. *The Horizontal Man.* New York, 1946.

Fearing, Kenneth. *The Big Clock.* New York, 1946.

Fish, Robert L. *Pursuit.* New York, 1979.

Fleming, Ian. *From Russia with Love.* New York, 1957.

Follett, Ken. *Eye of the Needle.* New York, 1978.

Forester, C. S. *Payment Deferred.* London, 1926.

Forsyth, Frederick. *The Day of the Jackal.* New York, 1971.

Francis, Dick. *Dead Cert.* New York, 1962.

Francis, Dick. *Blood Sport.* New York, 1967.

Francis, Dick. *Forfeit.* New York, 1969.

Freeling, Nicolas. *Love in Amsterdam.* London, 1962.

Freeling, Nicolas. *Apres de ma blonde.* London, 1972.

Gardner, Earle Stanley. *The D. A. Draws a Circle.* New York, 1939.

Gardner, Earle Stanley. *The Case of the Crooked Candle.* New York, 1944.

Garve, Andrew. *The Cuckoo-Line Affair.* New York, 1953.

Garve, Andrew. *The Galloway Case.* New York, 1958.

Garve, Andrew. *The Ascent of D-13.* New York, 1968.

Gault, William Campbell. *The Day of the Ram.* New York, 1956.

Gilbert, Michael. *Death Has Deep Roots.* New York, 1951.

Gilbert, Michael. *The Danger Within.* London, 1952.

Gordon, R. L. *The River Gets Wider.* New York, 1974.

Greene, Graham. *Stamboul Train.* London, 1932.

Greene, Graham. *Brighton Rock.* London, 1938.

Greene, Graham. *The Ministry of Fear.* London, 1943.

Grubb, Davis. *The Night of the Hunter.* New York, 1953.

Guthrie, A. B., Jr. *Wild Pitch.* Boston, 1973.

Haggard, William. *The Telemann Touch.* London, 1958.

Haggard, William. *Venetian Blind.* London, 1959.

Haggard, William. *The Scorpion's Tail.* London, 1975.

Hall, Adam. *The Quiller Memorandum.* New York, 1965.

Hall, Adam. *The Tango Briefing.* London, 1973.

Hall, Adam. *The Mandarin Cypher.* London, 1975.

Hall, Robert Lee. *Exit Sherlock Holmes.* New York, 1977.

Hamilton, Donald. *Death of a Citizen.* Greenwich, Conn., 1960.

Hamilton, Donald. *The Ravagers.* Greenwich, Conn., 1964.

Hammett, Dashiell. *Red Harvest.* New York, 1929.

Heard, H. F. *A Taste for Honey.* New York, 1941.

Hart, Frances Noyes. *The Bellamy Trial.* Garden City, N.Y., 1927.

Herron, Shaun. *Through the Dark and Hairy Wood.* London, 1973.

Heyer, Georgette. *A Blunt Instrument.* Garden City, N.Y., 1938.

Hill, Reginald. *Ruling Passion.* London, 1973.

Hillerman, Tony. *The Blessing Way.* New York, 1970.

Himes, Chester. *Cotton Comes to Harlem.* Paris, 1964.

Hirschberg, Cornelius. *Florentine Finish.* New York, 1963.

Household, Geoffrey. *Rogue Male.* London, 1939.

Household, Geoffrey. *A Rough Shoot.* London, 1951.

Household, Geoffrey. *Dance of the Dwarfs.* London, 1968.

Hoyle, Fred. *Ossian's Ride.* New York, 1959.

Hughes, Dorothy B. *Ride the Pink Horse.* New York, 1946.

Huxley, Elspeth. *Murder on Safari.* New York, 1938.

Innes, Hammond. *The Wreck of the Mary Deare.* London, 1956.

James, P. D. *Cover Her Face.* London, 1962.

James, P. D. *Shroud for a Nightingale.* London, 1971.

Jay, Charlotte. *Beat Not the Bones.* New York, 1954.

Jay, Charlotte. *The Yellow Turban.* New York, 1955.

Keating, H. R. F. *A Rush on the Ultimate.* London, 1961.

Keating, H. R. F. *The Perfect Murder.* London, 1964.

Kelly, Mary. *The Spoilt Kill.* London, 1961.

Kemelman, Harry. *Friday the Rabbi Slept Late.* New York, 1964.

Knowlton, Robert A. *Court of Crows.* New York, 1961.

Lathen, Emma. *Death Shall Overcome.* New York, 1966.

Lathen, Emma. *Murder Against the Grain.* New York, 1967.

Leasor, James. *Passport to Oblivion*. Philadelphia, 1965.

Le Carré, John. *The Spy Who Came In from the Cold*. London, 1963.

Le Carré, John. *Tinker, Tailor, Soldier, Spy*. London, 1974.

Leonard, Elmore. *Swag*. New York, 1976.

Lewin, Michael. *Night Cover*. New York, 1976.

Lovesey, Peter. *Wobble to Death*. London, 1970.

Lustgarten, Edgar. *One More Unfortunate*. New York, 1947.

Lyall, Gavin. *The Most Dangerous Game*. London, 1964.

Lyall, Gavin. *Midnight Plus One*. London, 1965.

McBain, Ed. *Hail to the Chief*. New York, 1973.

McCarry, Charles. *The Miernik Dossier*. New York, 1973.

McClure, James. *The Steam Pig*. London, 1971.

MacDonald, John D. *Dead Low Tide*. Greenwich, Conn., 1953.

MacDonald, John D. *The Drowner*. Greenwich, Conn., 1963.

MacDonald, John D. *The Quick Red Fox*. Greenwich, Conn., 1964.

Macdonald, Philip. *The List of Adrian Messenger*. Garden City, N.Y., 1959.

Macdonald, Ross. *The Galton Case*. New York, 1959.

Macdonald, Ross. *The Far Side of the Dollar*. New York, 1964.

Macdonald, Ross. *The Goodbye Look*. New York, 1969.

McIlvanney, William. *Laidlaw*. New York, 1977.

MacInnes, Helen. *Above Suspicion*. New York, 1941.

MacLean, Alistair. *South by Java Head*. London, 1958.

MacLean, Alistair (as Ian Stuart). *The Satan Bug*. New York, 1962.

Marsh, Ngaio. *Enter a Murderer*. London, 1935.

Marshall, William. *Thin Air*. New York, 1977.

Masterman, J. C. *An Oxford Tragedy*. London, 1933.

Mather, Berkely. *The Pass Beyond Kashmir*. London, 1960.

Maugham, W. Somerset. *Ashenden: The British Agent*. London, 1927.

Meyer, Nicholas. *The Seven Per Cent Solution.* New York, 1974.

Millar, Margaret. *Beast in View.* New York, 1955.

Millar, Margaret. *The Soft Talkers.* London, 1957.

Oppenheim, E. Phillips. *The Great Impersonation.* London, 1920.

Parker, Robert B. *God Save the Child.* Boston, 1974.

Parker, Robert B. *Mortal Stakes.* Boston, 1975.

Peck, Richard. *Dreamland Lake.* New York, 1973.

Postgate, Raymond. *Verdict of Twelve.* London, 1940.

Price, Anthony. *Other Paths to Glory.* London, 1975.

Proctor, Maurice. *The Pub Crawler.* London, 1956.

Queen, Ellery. *The Roman Hat Mystery.* New York, 1929.

Queen, Ellery. *The Tragedy of X.* New York, 1932.

Rathbone, Julian. *The Euro-Killers.* New York, 1980.

Ryck, Francis. *Sacrificial Pawn.* London, 1973.

Sanders, Lawrence. *The First Deadly Sin.* New York, 1973.

Sayers, Dorothy. *Strong Poison.* London, 1930.

Sayers, Dorothy. *The Nine Tailors.* London, 1934.

Sayers, Dorothy. *Gaudy Night.* London, 1935.

Seeley, Mabel. *The Listening House.* New York, 1938.

Simenon, Georges. *The Man Who Watched the Trains Go By.* New York, 1946.

Simon, Roger L. *The Big Fix.* San Francisco, 1973.

Sjowall, Maj, and Per Wahlöo. *Roseanna.* New York, 1967.

Sjowall, Maj, and Per Wahlöo. *The Fire Engine that Disappeared.* New York, 1970.

Smith, Shelley. *The Ballad of the Running Man.* London, 1961.

Spicer, Bart. *The Day of the Dead.* New York, 1955.

Stout, Rex. *Too Many Cooks.* New York, 1938.

Stout, Rex. *And Be a Villain.* New York, 1948.

Stout, Rex. *Plot It Yourself.* New York, 1959.

Symons, Julian. *The Man Who Killed Himself.* New York, 1967.

Tey, Josephine. *A Shilling for Candles.* London, 1936.

Tey, Josephine. *The Daughter of Time.* London, 1951.

Theroux, Paul. *The Family Arsenal.* London, 1976.

Thomas, Ross. *The Cold War Swap.* New York, 1966.

Thomas, Ross. *The Seersucker Whipsaw.* New York, 1967.

Thomas, Ross (as Oliver Bleeck). *The Brass Go-Between.* New York, 1969.

Trevanian. *The Eiger Sanction.* New York, 1972.

Upfield, Arthur. *The Bachelors of Broken Hill.* London, 1958.

Van der Zee, John. *Stateline.* New York, 1976.

Van Dine, S. S. *The Benson Murder Case.* New York, 1926.

Van Gulik, Robert. *The Chinese Nail Murders.* London, 1961.

Vickers, Roy. *The Department of Dead Ends.* London, 1949.

Waugh, Hillary. *Last Seen Wearing.* Garden City, N.Y., 1952.

Waugh, Hillary. *Death and Circumstance.* Garden City, N.Y., 1963.

Williams, Charles. *The Catfish Tangle.* London, 1963.

Woodhouse, Martin. *Tree Frog.* New York, 1966.

Young, Edward. *The Fifth Passenger.* New York, 1963.